AFTER CAPITALISM

AFTER

CAPITALISM

MICHAEL SPENCE

Adonis *Press*

After Capitalism by Michael Spence was first published in Hungarian in 2012 as
A Kapitalizmus Után by Remedium, Nagykvacsi, Hungary.
The present volume is a revision of the original English.

Published by Adonis Press
321 Rodman Rd.
Hillsdale, NY 12529
adonispress.org
socialself.org

Adonis Press is a branch of the Hawthorne Valley Association.

Contents

Part 2

Introduction

This book was written, in the main, before the financial crisis unfolded in 2008. But what unfolded then, and continues still in its effects, points to the urgent necessity of radically questioning the whole basis of present economic and financial thinking. Already there are signs of the beginnings of another financial bubble which, if allowed to grow, will eventually burst with more devastating consequences than before. The only thing that seems certain today is that nobody knows with any certainty how to prevent the same thing from happening again. Was it really no more than that, in the striving to maximize profits, poor decisions were made as to the proper asset value of mortgages and other securities? Or is there some much deeper-seated flaw in the present financial structure of the markets?

In their origins, and up to comparatively recent times, banks and the related institutions that arose round them developed out of and on the firm foundation of the "real" economy, the economic activity that produced the actual commodities that people needed to live, work, and play. Behind money was the reality of actual products or products that would be produced in the future. But the financial world has moved away from what once gave it a firm foundation and into a kind of illusory realm, where values come into being and disappear again according to the way people think about them. An ever-increasing proportion of the money, or monetary value, that forms the wealth of today has no foundation in reality. Meanwhile, the world has come to see and treat money as having value in itself.

Whereas in the past, the bulk of money in circulation represented real values created through people's work, today money comes into being through the buying and selling of what are called assets but would more properly be described as *rights*: *rights* conferred today through purchase and ownership of land, houses, businesses, and the products of other people's work. I show in this book that the profits generated through the trading of these "rights" work within society in exactly the same way as does counterfeit money, except that the one is legal and the other illegal. If at some time it became apparent that a vast amount of the money in circulation was counterfeit and thus had no value, it would create a situation not very different from what we have at present. Then, too, governments could be forced to buy up the counterfeit money to avert a total collapse of the economy.

Further, I show that payments such as rents and dividends are parasitic forms of what I describe later as "compulsory gifts." These "gifts" enable some people to live off the work of others. This is demonstrated on the ground of observable economic facts, not of morality.

However this crisis may for the present be resolved, some very serious questions will remain. Capitalism by its nature creates huge quantities of what I call "capitalized debt." (I fully explore these two ideas – "compulsory gifts" and "capitalized debt" – in and following Chapter 16.) This debt builds up and must, of necessity, at some time be cleared. The present crisis shows unmistakably that this "clearing of the debt" will inevitably cause considerable personal suffering and huge disturbance to the fabric of society. Clearly the present financial system of capitalism cannot continue unchanged. Some other social form must be found.

But this crisis, the latest of many over the last two centuries, has raised in many people from all walks of life serious questions concerning our present financial, economic, and social structures. Nevertheless, it seems so far that no one has been able to reach down into the deeper underlying *causes* of the crisis, the correction and healing of which alone can prevent such crises from recurring again and again.

There is a great deal of blame put upon the "bankers" and their culture of bonuses, blame which tends to reduce the problem to a moral question. Many of us, finding ourselves in a similar situation, would act in the same way. Money has an increasingly powerful pull in our culture today, and it demands moral strength far beyond that of most of us to resist the temptation, given the opportunity to "make money" within the law. Neither is it sufficient merely to tinker with the laws in an attempt to force people to act morally. A much more radical change in the whole structure of human society is called for, one that springs from the inherent nature of humanity itself.

*

This book is based on observation of life, not on any established economic, political, or religious beliefs or theories. It starts from the perception that society, or human community, consists of an interweaving of three quite differently functioning sectors. It then goes on to show that many of today's social problems, particularly those involving money and the growing gap between the rich and the poor, the powerful and the defenseless, are consequences of a social structure founded on remnants of old theocratic forms of community on the one hand and the failure to distinguish between the three sectors of society on the other.

We are all conditioned by the ways of thinking that are the norm in the society in which we live, and it is often difficult to recognize these and free ourselves from them. Some of the ideas and observations made here may be difficult to accept. They will require a willingness to put aside the usual, established ways of thinking and an openness to new ideas that may at times seem very much at odds with normal and accepted wisdom. But to maintain openness does not necessitate an automatic acceptance of these ideas. That should arise only out of the reader's own observation and judgment.

Some ideas presented here, particularly in the sphere of economics and money, may appear to turn conventional understanding on its head and may therefore require a considerable amount of thought to follow all the way through to the end. They may make sense only when seen within the context of the whole.

So too, some of what I put forward concerning the nature of human evolution and the development of human consciousness may appear to conflict with much of modern teaching. As human consciousness evolves, each new development does not completely replace what was there before. What existed in an earlier stage continues on in a subsidiary form. What existed in the past leaves its remnants and is still perceptible today. Through careful and disciplined observation it is possible to discern within one's own inner nature, as well as in others and in society itself, particular feelings, inclinations, and traits which can be seen to be of an older nature, a carry-over from former times. Others are clearly of more recent origin.

I shall not try to put forward observations or theories for the purpose of disproving any generally accepted social or economic thinking, but will try to offer an alternative view of social life, one derived from unbiased observation. The reader may then decide for him or her self which is the truer picture in its totality, and which will provide a firmer basis for a healthy social future.

Much that will be presented may well seem impossible to realize – utopian. But everything I describe derives from an observation of actual life, of what exists in reality. It can be verified by anyone capable of observing life itself unencumbered by prior assumptions or theories. If it seems unrealistic, it is our present way of thinking, our present assumptions, that make it appear so.

What is offered will not satisfy anyone looking for any kind of "sound bite," "quick fix," or "band aid" that will offer an immediate solution to any of the many problems besetting society today.

*

The idea that human social life, or community, is actually comprised of three separate and individual sectors was put forward at the beginning of the last century by Rudolf Steiner (1861-1925), the Austrian philosopher, scientist, educator, and social thinker. Towards the end of and immediately following the First World War he wrote articles and a book, as well as giving many lectures, on the subject of what was then called "The Threefold Social Order," or "The Threefold Commonwealth," as it was first translated. His main book on the subject is now published as *Towards Social Renewal* (Rudolf Steiner Press, 1999). In 1922, he gave 14 lectures to students of economics in which he set forth an altogether new approach to money and to economic thinking. These have been published in English translation most recently as *Rethinking Economics* (SteinerBooks, 2013).

What Steiner presented at that time opened up for me a completely new approach to the social, economic, and monetary questions of today. On this foundation, and through my own studies and observations of life, I have come to the ideas presented in this book. I could not have come to what I attempt to put forward here except on the foundations of what I met in his ideas; but, though based on what Steiner gave, there is nothing here that I have not confirmed for myself through my own working experience and observation of social life, and the application of thinking and "common sense."

It is not possible in one book to give anything more than an outline of the three sectors of social life and of the nature of each. Social life is a very deep and complex subject, and to research it to its depths would take very many books, and certainly would be beyond the scope of any one person. There is much that can here be no more than indicated in outline. I do not intend to demonstrate how such ideas can be applied to any particular community, but rather to point to the reality of the threefold nature of human society itself and to much that is hidden or distorted in our present social life. It is the overall picture that is important and that I hope to convey to the reader. The detail is intended as a step towards that bigger picture, not as important in itself as an isolated fact.

At the beginning, any such radical study of social life is like trying to put together a complex jigsaw puzzle without the picture of what the completed puzzle will look like. We can assemble a few pieces here and a few more there. We then see fragments of the picture, but there is nothing to suggest how these come together within a whole; they do not indicate the totality nor how and where they might relate to each other or fit into that totality. The totality only gradually emerges as the fragments grow and begin to fit together. A further complication is that whereas a jigsaw puzzle is complete when all the pieces are assembled, this cannot be said of the puzzle of social life. Humanity is in a constant state of growth, evolution, and change, or of decline. We ourselves are part of society, we are conditioned by it, and our actions in turn affect it. But, in doing a jigsaw puzzle, we do not enter into it, nor are we changed by it. In attempting to find ways toward a more human society, we must refrain from starting with any preconceived but possibly incorrect idea of what the whole will look like.

It can be a long study before we arrive at a picture of how all the different pieces form a whole, and even then we will not necessarily have arrived at any idea of what we can actually do about it. All this will be that much more difficult, however, if we continue to hold within our thinking, even unconsciously, remnants of the picture of a unitary and hierarchical society.

Readers who look for confirmation of ideas presented here by quotes from other writers, or through references to particular events, will be disappointed. In my view, real working knowledge arises when we can verify or refute something for ourselves through our own experience and observation of life, rather than by being given references to authorities or what might be isolated events.

What we ourselves come to out of our own quest for knowledge leads to real understanding and action, not what we are told and what leaves no questions in us. If at the end of the book readers have more questions than when they started, then it will at least have been partially successful. This might seem to ask much of the reader, to make it more difficult than may appear necessary, but life also shows that little is gained by always following the easier way. If that were so, then surely many of our problems would have been understood and resolved long ago.

It will not be immediately possible to achieve practical realization of what is briefly described in this book. Some of it could take very many years, even generations, to realize. What is immediately important is that this inherent threefold nature is perceived and understood. There are actually very many people, in all walks of life, who already see something of it, but it needs now to be taken much further.

Observation of life shows that there are individuals in business and industry, the trade unions, politics, the media, and in many other spheres of social life who are looking for new ways of thinking, people who have a sense that the old ways can no longer cope with the complexities of the social conditions of our time. These are often people of great capacity who are already in positions where possibilities exist to begin transforming the social structures if provided with thought forms and concepts that are real. What is offered here is intended for such people in the hope that it can give them, at the very least, some new ideas and concepts which they will be able to take further into actual practical life.

It does not matter if the goal is not immediately achieved; *moving towards it* will bring about great changes in people's sense of social awareness and behavior.

Part 1

Chapter 1
The Need for Change

A look back at the course of human evolution will show that just in the last few centuries there have been enormous developments in technology and in the possibilities of industrial production, developments far exceeding in scope and pace anything that has taken place before. Today for the first time humanity has at its disposal the know-how and the ability to produce sufficient for every human being on this earth; enough for them to enjoy a reasonable standard of living in so far as this can be achieved through the supply of the physical necessities of life. That this is now possible can be confirmed by anyone who, putting aside all preconceived ideas and feelings and viewing the situation quite objectively, looks at the actual possibilities given by the development of modern science and technology and by our modern methods of economic production and distribution. This possibility could be realized without anyone having to labor all their working life in the dehumanizing conditions of many of our present factories and mines. It could be done in a way that would still leave individuals time and energy to partake in the activities of cultural life and so to nourish their inner life of soul. Furthermore, this could be achieved without the present high degree of waste and damage to the environment. That there is still so much poverty, homelessness, hunger, and hardship in the world is not a problem of our inability to produce and distribute what is needed. This is not an economic problem, nor is it a financial problem – *it is a social problem.*

It is not acceptable to attribute our present social failures to a lack of money. To say there is not enough money is like saying that something cannot be done because there is no way to enter it in the accounts. It is not that we do not have the means to produce what is needed – it is, more than anything else, that we do not have the right way of thinking, together with the right social structure, to bring to realization the full potential of what is now possible.

But what is a reasonable standard of living? The Earth could not sustain the world population if all lived at the level of consumption that we in the developed economies do, or expect to do. We enjoy this level of consumption just because there is a much larger part of the world population who are obliged to survive on very much less. We can see this clearly if we look at the many products we use that are produced by cheap labor, by people who are often unable to enjoy what they produce for others. We can see it when we look at the level of consumption of the Earth's oil, gas, and other resources by a population that is a small fraction of the whole. This extravagant use of resources in the developed countries does not necessarily bring greater happiness.

A reasonable standard of living for all can only be achieved if those in the economically developed countries reduce their expectations and their demands, thus making it possible for those in the less developed countries to increase theirs. But in the current situation this would be unacceptable to the people of the developed countries. In addition to this, an economy is judged healthy and sustainable only when the gross domestic product (GDP) not only increases year by year, but is experienced as doing so. More seriously, the present financial and legal structures are such that the financial system goes into crisis when there is any sustained downward movement of GDP.

What is true for the world as a whole is true for each individual country. Those who create or make money through the financial markets consume a disproportionate share of the total product while those who earn their wages through their actual work in production and services must be satisfied with much less.

Is the standard of living of any particular people to be judged solely by their economic consumption? There must be a reasonable basic level; but beyond that, does *more*, as a rule, lead to greater happiness? There is a widespread assumption that this is so, that more money, or more of what money can buy, brings greater happiness in life; that material possessions, a large expensive house and car, the possibility to travel, to spend holidays abroad, and perhaps above all to be able to have all this without having to work, are what give greatest fulfillment to life. But a close and objective observation of life, supported by an increasing amount of psychological research, shows that having more does not necessarily contribute to greater happiness. At a certain point, the inner sense of the quality of life can actually begin to diminish as many factors such as stress, fear, lack of purpose, and feelings of isolation reduce any feeling of happiness, sense of fulfillment, and peace of mind.

But human beings are not merely consumers of products, there are soul needs to consider as well: for example, the need to create, to develop latent skills and interests, to seek for a deeper understanding of life. This aspect of human life can really only be served by a healthy and vibrant *cultural life* of the community in which we live. Should not our perception of the standard of living also include the cultural and moral qualities of the community and the richness of the life of soul of its members, not just the factors included in the GDP?

Through all of history, different cultures, institutions, and social structures have come into being, served a particular people and time, and then been overcome and replaced by others; or grown decadent and faded out.

If, particularly in Europe, we go back just a few centuries, we will see social structures built on very different foundations from those existing today. Society was built on a class structure with an aristocracy as the masters over a middle class and a proletariat who, certainly in earlier times, recognized their place in society as appointed by divine order. The aristocracy held their place as leaders, lawmakers, and landowners by right of birth, that is, through heredity. But though this social order at the time seemed to be divinely ordained and unchangeable, as the nature of the human being evolved it became more and more decadent and finally, particularly around the time of the First World War, was swept away.

Then there emerged two polar opposite social orders: communism, and western capitalism based on a market economy. Each can be seen as arising out of real social evolutionary needs. But communism lost its original impulse and became destructive and decadent, and it too has to a large extent passed away, though remnants in distorted forms continue. Today capitalism and the market economy are showing clear signs of having grown far beyond their original beneficial purposes and have come to a point where they primarily serve the egoism and greed of those in a position to "play the market." If we look not just at the economic and financial spheres of human activity in isolation but at society as a whole, then it becomes apparent that, as they function within social life today, they cannot last. Capitalism and the market economy have reached a point where they are increasingly destructive of society as a whole. This is clear when one looks closely at the causes of the recurring financial crises around the globe, the widening gap between the rich and the poor, the massive environmental degradation in certain parts of the world, and the looming environmental catastrophes brought on by climate change, among other things.

What then must come after capitalism? This is a question that must be taken hold of. Or is it not possible to know this and to prepare the way for it? Must it come, as has happened too often in the past, through upheaval, revolution, and widespread suffering brought on by a final collapse of the present system?

There was a time when the church, cathedral, or temple stood at the center of the town or city, as the focus of the community. As an architectural achievement of great beauty, it stood as a House of God, a place from which moral guidance and inspiration rayed out to the people who lived and worked in its environment. This is no longer so. The great churches and cathedrals are today often little more than tourist attractions, remnants of a past age. Now it is more likely to be the tall buildings of the banks, financial offices, and trading centers that reach upwards to the heavens and stand as the great architectural achievements in our cities. It is *these buildings*, temples of a different sort, that stand as symbols of what people can strive for, of what can give direction and purpose to their lives.

In religion, people looked up with reverence to that which they felt to be infinitely greater than themselves, that which as the source of their being gave meaning and purpose to their lives. In the Divine they found their purpose and direction; in God's law they sought guidance through life, security, and hope for reward in the future. In the fruits and products of nature they saw the gifts of God. In following their leader, their king, pharaoh, or priest, they were following the representative of their God, through whom God spoke.

But now the great majority of people, at least in the developed world, act as though there is no god, no outer divine authority, and no moral law that speaks to a person from without. In so far as religion does still play a part, it is a weak affair generally limited to a person's inner private life, not determining his outer daily life and actions. Religions, including those of people in the poorer, undeveloped world, where they do still have a strong hold, teach of a god, but one that spoke to human beings in times long past. Christianity, Judaism, Islam, Buddhism as they are generally practiced today all attempt to proclaim teachings as they were given in former ages – the voices that first declared those truths are no longer heard today.

In all those areas of the world where social life is based on the particular form of capitalistic thinking that has spread from the west, from the United States of America and Europe, money has seemingly taken over from belief in God as that which actually motivates people and gives direction and purpose to their lives. Money is now an ever-present influence, it wields dominion over the way we think and live, over our sense of values and what we do. It establishes the order of human beings within society. Those who have no money must serve those who do. It has replaced the divine ordering that in former times guided a person through life, gave purpose, security, and hope of a better future in this life on earth and of reward or otherwise after death.

*

The food we eat is often not produced out of a desire or need in the producer to provide good healthy nourishment; instead the primary motive is to make money. So too with the clothes we wear, the medicines we need, the houses in which we live, and the entertainment we enjoy. There are, of course, many who do produce out of quite different motives, out of a real impulse to serve people, to provide what people need for a healthy life, but within the whole today they are a minority. Those producers who are driven by the urge to make money are often able to drive those who do wish to serve out of the market.

Must it inevitably be as it is? Is it really impossible to change the direction of the trend of our time? Are the huge financial institutions, the banks, the financial futures exchanges and the stock markets really fulfilling a socially necessary role? What is this money that has come to so dominate our lives? In itself it is useless, it has no substance. Is it real, or is it an abstraction, an illusion, or just a means of accounting of values? If so, what are the values it accounts for?

Money has been created neither by nature nor by God – it has been created by human beings. But now it has grown far beyond the control of the humanity that brought it into being. Like "The Sorcerer's Apprentice," it seems that its creator is unable to control that which he has let loose.

Money and our particular capitalistic monetary system have come into being as part of the structure of human social life as it has evolved through the ages. If we are to take control of money, to make it serve humanity rather than make humanity serve it, we must look to changing not the money itself but that which, within the evolving social structure, brought it forth in the way it has.

Though over the centuries many social forms and structures have come and gone, there is still at the foundation of most of our various structures something which has its origins in the old theocracies in which there was no thought of democracy, equality, or individual freedom. They were formed when human life was very different and much simpler than it is today. Then it was very much the group or the tribe that was the dominant societal force or unit. Today, and increasingly so, the individual person stands alone, unbeholden to the rigid inheritance of ancient custom.

Behind all present social thinking and activity is the basic perception that society is a unitary whole with a government or other leader at the head providing leadership, guidance, management, and control over the whole. Society is conceived of in the form of a pyramid, itself built up of smaller pyramids. This is the form that can be seen in virtually all social groupings, whether governmental, business, or educational, and whether democratic, religious, communist, paternalistic, or dictatorial. At the head, usually supported by a group of ministers or other such departmental heads, is the prime minister, president, chief executive officer, headmaster, or captain. Guidance, wisdom, law, and decisions affecting the whole are handed down from the single authority at the head. This is a form that comes down from the theocracies of earlier times; it is one that was proper for a time when people accepted that their leader, king, pharaoh, or priest received wisdom directly from God. But is it right for today?

*

Thorough and objective observation of society will show that it is in fact formed of three quite distinct sectors or streams, each with its own function and purpose, and each working according to its own laws. Once this threefold nature is recognized and understood, it will be possible to begin to transform society according to its own inherent nature into one more appropriate to people of today.

In the following chapters I shall attempt, first, to throw light on these three spheres or sectors and to show how, on the basis of the working together in harmony of these three independently constituted sectors, our social life can be renewed in a way that will serve the present and the immediate future needs of humanity. The perception of this threefold structure will then provide the concepts with which to examine money in a new light, particularly those aspects of our social structure which provide the foundation of our present capitalistic system. This I shall attempt in the second part of this book.

One of the greatest difficulties to be overcome is this firmly rooted picture, coming down from earlier times, of society as a single body with one central authority at the top having authority over and responsibility for all the affairs of that society. Before this can be overcome a different picture must be built up, that of one body formed of three quite separate and autonomous sectors working closely together – each sector having its own differently formed guiding or authoritative body, but the three together forming a complete whole. Most people immediately feel uncomfortable with this, they sense disorder and conflict arising out of three such bodies having no central coordinating authority. This problem will arise so long as we continue to think in terms of three similar but independent sectors, each a replica of the presently existing unitary state. But each sector is not a replica of the others, each is organically different, and in its difference complements the others.

Chapter 2

The Three Sectors –
A First Look

Human society is comprised of human beings, and its forms and functions reflect the fundamental aspects of human nature. The most immediate and obvious aspect of the human being is that which we perceive with our ordinary senses, the physical body. By this is meant everything of a person that is made up of physical substance, is subject to the laws of physics, gravity, temperature, etc. and that at death is placed in the grave and returns to nature from which it is derived.

Over against this is all that is variously referred to as soul, mind, psyche, spirit, self, etc. Whether a person believes that his "soul and spirit" are of a supersensible nature that comes from God and continues on after death, or that they are merely expressions of the working of the physical brain, is not immediately important here. What is important here is that every normal human being experiences him or herself as an "I," as having his or her own feelings, thoughts, desires, and abilities, who knows what it is to feel alone or to be loved, and who believes in one thing or another. To indicate this aspect of the human being, as distinct from that of the physical body, I shall use the term "soul," or "soul/spiritual."

Thus we all experience this twofold nature: a bodily nature which can be seen, measured, and understood through the normal physical senses, and a "soul" nature which cannot be perceived by means of these physical senses. We can only experience and know our own soul life; it cannot be directly perceived by others. These aspects of the human being that cannot be reached by our normal physical senses can therefore be called "supersensible" – they are beyond the ordinary senses. The needs that arise out of each side of this twofold nature are quite different and distinct.

If we look at a piece of handmade pottery, for example a teapot, we see on one level something that serves a practical purpose. It is made of material substances and has been given a basic form so as to enable tea to be made and poured without mess into a cup. In this respect it is made and designed to serve its practical purpose, the need of a person to drink tea, a need primarily of the physical body. But a teapot is nearly always also designed to satisfy something else – to please the eye, to nourish an inner need of the soul for beauty in form and color, the need to have and use what is a well made, harmonious, and beautiful whole. If I wish to buy a teapot, as well as looking for one that will meet my need to make and pour tea, I will also look for one that is of a color and form that pleases me, that will enhance my home.

So I look for a teapot that will fulfill two kinds of need, that of my body and that of my inner life of soul. For the purposes of making tea, everyone could have the exact same teapot; efficiency of function being the only criteria. It is the needs of the soul that lead to so many different designs and colors.

A book is somewhat different. Looked at from one aspect it could be seen as just ink on papers bound together with a cover. The ink has been put onto the paper to form certain shapes, but physically it is just ink on paper. I can trace back the whole process and all the people that were, in one way or another, connected with the actual production of the paper, from the felling of the trees to the making of the paper. Similarly I can trace the manufacture of the ink. Any person looking at it sees the ink on the paper. Physically, all people with normal vision will see the same thing.

But the perception of the meaning of the thought that the ink on the paper reveals is a very individual matter. When I see the writing, it gives me a certain concept, or idea. But this is only if I have learned to read this script. The thought or concept does not lie within the ink and paper, it is through what I have learned, the skills that I have developed in myself, that I will understand, or not understand, what the writer intended to convey. It may be that I agree with him and accept all that he has to say. Or, on the contrary, I might find the words meaningless, they may even irritate me, I may dispute their meaning with my neighbor. But all this is true regardless of how, or even whether, it is printed. The printing itself does not affect the significance of the thought.

There might be little difference in the actual *process* of printing different books, but their *content* can be widely different. One has only to consider all that is to be found in the many books printed, from novels to educational textbooks, encyclopedias, Shakespeare, biographies, nursery rhymes, and religious texts. In this can be seen something of the contrast between the utility of economic production on the one hand, and all that arises out of human aspirations, creativity, imagination, and intuition on the other – the cultural life of a community.

In this way one can come to a distinction between what is here referred to as the economic process – the production of the physical teapot and the book – and the sphere of the soul – all that the individual enjoys in the form and color of the teapot, and all that is inwardly experienced by the reader of the book. As I shall try to show later, it makes a great difference whether one's work lies within the sphere of the actual production of commodities – of the teapot or the ink and paper – or if it lies in that sphere where the needs of the soul are nurtured and the thoughts themselves are worked with.

The sphere of activity within the social life of humanity that provides for those needs that arise out of the bodily nature of the human being will be referred to as the "economic" sector or sphere, or as "economic activity." That which provides for the needs of the "soul" will be referred to as the "cultural" sphere or sector, or as "cultural life."

Human beings have a third need. Each feels the need for a "place" within human society; within the community, we recognize that we have rights and that we should be treated equally with others. Out of this need the sphere of law and the democratic state has arisen. This will be referred to as the "rights" sector or sphere, or the realm of the "State." It is the sphere of human social life that is responsible for the bringing of order into society for the equal well being of all people on the basis of justice and equity through the rule of law.

Three social ideals called forth at the time of the French revolution and widely striven for today are Freedom, Equality, and what is variously called Brotherhood, Mutuality, or Community. So long as society is seen as a single whole there will always be a conflict between these three. If all three ideals are striven for within one unitary society then each will to a certain extent nullify or cancel the other two. This has always been seen as a stumbling block by serious social thinkers. But when the three different sectors of society are recognized, and each separate sector strives towards a different ideal, then it will be seen that each has its place within the whole.

Only in the life of the soul, in cultural life, is it possible for a person to be free. In everything that belongs within the sphere of human rights, of law and order, all people will be seen and treated as equals. I hope to show later that only when the economic sphere of production is founded on mutuality and cooperation will its full potential be realized. Then it really will be possible to provide for the needs of all humanity.

It would be easy to assume that what is suggested here is that there be three different branches or sectors within government, three departments that all ultimately come under the one democratically elected leadership of the State. Due to the thought forms dominant in our social life today, it is not easy to imagine something quite different, that is, three quite separate and independent sectors of society of which the democratically elected government as we know it, but in a greatly reduced form, would be just one. This will, I hope, become clearer in the course of this book.

It is possible to identify three sectors or strands of activity within human social life. They can be briefly characterized as follows:

The Cultural Sector comprises all those activities in the community that aim to provide for the needs of the inner soul life – all that leads a person on in the search for knowledge, creativity, and understanding and that assists in the development of an individual's particular capacities and intentions. This includes all forms of education and training, religion, art, science, research and development, and also all entertainment.

A community can be socially healthy and at peace with itself only when, as a first step, within that community each individual knows himself, in his life of soul, to be free.

The Rights Sector includes all that activity which brings order into human affairs through the making of laws, regulations, and agreements and which requires people to act in a social way towards each other. It is the sphere in which, as its proper function, government will create a legal structure that is a true reflection of what arises in the community as a sense of what is right, a feeling for what is just and fair and acceptable social behavior. In this all people must be seen as equal, the opinion of each being of equal value to that of all others.

The Economic Sector: I shall use the word "economic" to indicate that area of human activity that contributes to the production, distribution, and consumption of everything we need due to the fact that we have a physical body and that is derived from the substances and forces of the mineral, plant, and animal kingdoms. This includes the food we eat, our clothing, housing, furniture, tools, transportation needs, electricity, and means of communication. Money facilitates these processes, but is not itself a component of the productive process.

In the sphere of economic life, no one person can provide all that they need. In economic life we are dependent on the working together of others in the wider human community for all that we need from the physical material world. Any thought here of self-sufficiency, of doing something on one's own, is actually an illusion. It will become clearer when we look more closely at the working of economic activity that in this realm of social life brotherhood, or mutuality, is called for by the process of economic production itself.

It is becoming increasingly the case that for many people the word "economic" calls forth the concept of "profit" in the sense of monetary profit. For the purposes of this book it is necessary that a clear distinction be made between, on the one hand, the actual activity of production and distribution of the products we use and consume – and on the other, the profit that arises out of this. It is the *products* of people's work on which we live, not the *profit* that arises out of and facilitates the process.

It will be important that this distinction, and this particular use of the word "economic," be kept in mind throughout the reading of this book.

Money

Money is not itself one of the three spheres of social life, but it plays an increasingly powerful and distinctive role in our society and reaches far beyond the economic sphere out of which it arose. It has, in a certain sense, taken on a life of its own and become of far greater influence and power in our lives than is generally realized or acknowledged. It permeates all three spheres of social life, often in a way that brings great suffering and harm, but it does also bring the possibility of freeing humanity from the necessity of long hours of labor. Our succumbing to its temptations has spawned capitalism through firstly treating certain aspects of both human rights and cultural life as economic products and creating markets in which these are bought and sold. Particularly through the markets in "rights" it has been able to generate huge sums of capital "out of thin air." Money as such and its role beyond the true economy will be looked at beginning in Chapter Fourteen.

Threefold Society as an Expression of the Evolving Human Being

In earliest times, human beings gathered the food that nature itself provided. With the birth of agriculture came the purposeful transformation of nature, and, at a further stage, the substances of the earth, and of the plant and animal kingdoms, were transformed into useful products. The making of clothes, weapons, and utensils, the building of homes, and gathering of wood for fire – all this activity, this labor, formed the foundation, the core of the economic sector of that community.

In order to make their labor more fruitful, people have, throughout the ages, come to shine the light of their thinking and creative imagination on to the labor of their limbs. They have divided the work among each other, each becoming expert or skilled in one particular operation of the process of production. They have searched out and found new substances, and new properties and uses of the substances. Through the imaginative and thinking powers of their souls they have used these substances to make tools with which to work at the productive process. All that thus arose in cultural life fructified economic activity, which thereby became many times more productive.

When human creativity fructifies economic production there is an increasing need to work together cooperatively. In today's economic production an individual can achieve nothing alone. No one truly makes anything for him or herself; what each needs is obtained from the work of others. In economic activity it will come to be seen that brotherhood, or mutuality, is called for out of the very nature of the activity itself.

The economic life of the community will be considered more deeply starting in the next chapter.

*

There was a time when the behavior of the individual human being within the community was closely held in check by what was experienced as divine commandment expressed through the particular religious teachings of the social group. What came from the leader, in his role as the mouthpiece of God, gave form and structure to the community.

At a later stage, this outer structure and the discipline maintained by the church lost its power. The individual came to experience an inner voice – conscience – that spoke of what was morally right or wrong. But this voice was often weak, unable to move the individual to act in the appropriate way. An outer law had to be established. The vacuum created by the falling away of that which earlier spoke to human beings as divine commandment from above came to be filled by law created by human beings themselves. The "State" came into being and society was given a structure, a framework, based on law. This law was a poor substitute for the moral law out of which it arose and which it endeavored to bring to expression. But when the voice of God came to be heard no longer, it was all that humanity had. The law of the State, human law, came to replace Divine commandment.

The role of the State, of law and human rights, will be looked at in greater depth starting in Chapter Five.

*

If we look out at the world, we see, as the foundation of all life, the inorganic world, that of earth, water, air, heat, and light, and the earthly forces such as gravity, electricity, and nuclear energy. Above this we see the plant world in all its myriad, complex, and beautiful forms growing out of and covering the earth. Then we see beyond these the animal kingdom in all its multitudes of species from the simple amoeba to the most evolved apes. At the peak of perceptible earthly creation is the human being.

In the mineral world we do not perceive life. We find life first in the plant, but there we find it in a kind of sleep. The plant takes in nourishment from the earth and the air and grows and brings forth its flower and its seed according to its nature. In itself, it is perfect – imperfections and disease all come to it from without.

In the animals we find a waking life. We find also temperaments, emotions, and impulses, but not an awake thinking consciousness.

In the human being we find a consciousness that has developed far beyond just that of being awake to one that looks out at nature and questions what it sees there, a consciousness, too, that has an inner impulse to create, not just to create out of necessity but to create for its own sake, a consciousness that strives to achieve the impossible, to climb the mountain "because it is there." In the human being there arises also the consciousness of good and evil, of right moral action.

Human beings are not satisfied just to be. Nor do they find it enough to be active only in the satisfying of physical needs, as is apparently the case with the plant and the animal. They see the stars and the moving planets, the sun and moon in their courses, and the changes in the seasons. Questions arise and the human being begins to perceive, or imagine, connections and meaning in it all.

Through the ages these questions grow. We look out at nature spread around us and within which we live and of which we, in our bodily nature, are a part. We strive to "know" it, to understand what it is, how it grows. We look within and strive to know from whence we came and to where we go. *Is there a deeper purpose and meaning to life, or is it all an accident of physical substances and forces? Is there a god? Is there some world or spiritual place beyond what is accessible to the ordinary senses, some spirit land to which I go when I die, or is death final?* Human thinking and imagination have striven with such questions since earliest times.

Feelings, emotions, and impulses rise within us. We hanker for that which brings pleasure and entertainment. We aspire to beauty, harmony, justice, and knowledge. We try to bring to expression in art what we feel within our own being, and to improve our knowledge and abilities through education. We strive after the impossible, the unattainable, the unachievable. We go, and keep going, that little bit further, faster, higher than has been gone before.

All that comes into being as the cultural sector of society has its start, its beginning, in the individual, in the egoism of the individual soul. But what has its beginning in egoism can rise to service for the whole community. The teacher teaches because, in the first place, the need or impulse to teach rises within the depths of his or her own being. But in the teaching the teacher can rise beyond this egoism and truly work out of the needs of the children. But to so come to one's true work out of such an inner impulse there must be freedom. In all cultural life freedom must prevail.

The nature of this cultural sector of social or community life, and the question of freedom, will be looked at in greater depth starting in Chapter Eight.

Polarities

In their characteristics, the cultural and economic spheres are polar opposites. In observing cultural activity, we are constantly led to the single human being. We can only know something when we experience and know it ourselves. We cannot, for example, experience beauty *for* another person. In economic life we are led in the opposite direction, away from the individual to humanity as a whole. Here the individual person cannot provide for him or herself, but must rely on the work of others.

In cultural life egoism has its rightful place. All creativity, art, imagination, and invention arise in the first place out of the egoistic soul needs of the individual. In economic life a person works to produce what is needed by others – there is in economic activity something that is, or should be, inherently altruistic. The person working in a factory making parts for a computer does so because people need computers, not because he finds in his work that which fulfills the needs of his own soul. That he works "for money" conceals this deeper reality.

Rights life comes in between. It arises within groups of people who live or work in some form of community – whether that is a small local community, a country, or world humanity. Each group will come to its own particular laws. An individual living alone on an island will not develop any sense of rights or need any laws.

*

The idea that society has a threefold nature is not new or unique. In certain communities of former times it was symbolized by the "Book," the "Sword," and the "Plough," or as the "Priest," the "Soldier," and the "Peasant."

Today also there are people who see something of this threefold nature. But of those who do, many do not see the wider picture, so there is a tendency to distort it. It is often characterized in a way that does not conform to its true nature, for example in terms such as "business," "government," and "civil society." This might be thought of as using different terminology for what is described in this book. On the surface it may certainly seem so, but if studied more deeply it will be seen that the three sectors described here cannot be designated in this way, as to do so can only lead to confusion. For example in education, according to this categorization, a school run as a business would be in a different sector than that of a state school, or again different from that of a charitable, or not-for-profit school. But it is the nature of the activity – education – not the structure of the school that determines its place.

Chapter 3

The Economic Sector – Basic Concepts

As indicated earlier, I shall use the term "economic" to mean *all human activity involved in the production, distribution, and consumption of the goods and services that fulfill those human needs and wants that arise out of people's physical bodily nature.* The term "economic" then should not here be confused with the earning or accumulation of money. Money arises out of the process of economic production; it facilitates and makes much of this activity possible, but it is not part of the actual economic process. In order to arrive at a working knowledge of economic activity proper it is necessary, at the beginning, to put aside the money and look solely at the activity itself. I will take up the question of money as such in later chapters, particularly in and following Chapter Fourteen.

I shall use the word "labor" only in its meaning of manual or physical work. For reasons that will become apparent I shall not use it for "manual workers" collectively.

In any study of economics it is first necessary to know the place or perspective from which it is being viewed. It can be observed from the place at which each person or organization stands – that is, from the point of view of what is of greatest benefit to the individual person or organization (microeconomics). Or it can be observed from the periphery – that is, from the place from which one sees it in its relation to the interests of the community as a whole (macroeconomics). By this I mean that we can consider the economy subjectively from the point of view of what is most advantageous to ourselves, or objectively from the presumption that the task of the whole is to work as a unity in order to provide for the needs of the whole community so that each person is able to acquire what he or she needs as his or her share of the total product.

In this study I shall look at economic life from the point of view of the needs of the community as a whole, not from that of the individual. By "individual" I mean the individual person or individual organization. I take as a starting point the view that the task of the economic sphere of social life is to organize itself in such a way that it can produce what is needed by the community as a whole and distribute to each member that which is needed by each. Ultimately, the community can only be the world community. The problems of the poor, the hungry, and the homeless will never be solved on the basis of each person, organization, or country looking after only themselves. Life has shown this to be true with a vengeance, despite all theories to the contrary.

As a foundation for what will be built on later, much can be learned from a very simple imaginative picture. This will help to form some of the basic concepts and the way of thinking that is put forward here as necessary for a realistic understanding of the economic sector of human society.

The Blackberry Picker

Imagine a simple village community whose members often have occasion to walk along a road, perhaps to their places of work. On the edge of a wood near the village there are many blackberries growing wild. They do not "belong" to anyone, so may be taken by whoever cares to pick them. But there is the problem that they are on the other side of a river and can only be reached by a long walk via a bridge further down river.

If, on the way home, a person makes a detour to the woods and picks some blackberries, this cannot be thought of as included within the village economy. These berries do not enter into the general circulation of goods; they are not part of the local economy, the cooperative or shared work of the community. The activity here is done only for the person doing the picking, or his or her own family.

The labor, if it can even be called labor at this point, is not part of the communal economic activity.

But one man, while picking berries for himself, decides that he will pick extra to sell in the village market. The moment he ceases to pick for himself and starts to pick for the community, his activity changes; his work becomes "economic labor." The harvest of blackberries, the product of his labor, enters into the general circulation and exchange of goods, that is, into the economic life of the community. He supplies blackberries for others in the community, and he will obtain in exchange something he needs that others have produced.

Now suppose that he decides to make a business of picking and selling blackberries. He sets up a stall on the roadside at a particular location, "X", from which to sell them. He has to make several journeys between his stall and the woods to pick and transport enough to make it worthwhile. He then has a stall with pint size baskets of blackberries for sale.

Someone coming along the road buys a pint of blackberries. *What is he actually paying for?* This is an essential question of economics. If we are really to understand the economy in such a way as to organize it to serve the community as a whole in the most efficient and productive way, then we must begin by perceiving the real nature of such an exchange.

The blackberries where they are found growing wild have no "economic value," that is they have no value arising out of the communal economic activity. No work has been done to plant, look after, or in anyway nurture them. There might be other values that can be placed on them, but there is no value arising out of any actual work of production, that is, no "economic value."

It is, of course, usual practice to give natural resources a monetary value, but this should not be confused with the economic value described here. This value given to a natural resource is in reality a monetary value given to a "right" or "permission." For example, in this situation there might be other people living in the woods who claim to "own" the blackberries and who refuse to allow our picker to take any unless he pays them a share of his takings. Here, clearly, we are dealing with something that is not part of the economic process of production itself, but something of quite a different nature even though it may well have an effect on the price. It is something based on force or ownership, not on the productive process, and as such will be considered in detail later.

Or it might be a "potential" economic value, that is, one given it due to its potential to make a profit. But here again, this is not a value arising out of the actual productive activity. It is important to distinguish between economic value – created through the economic productive process itself – and other kinds of value.

On the bush, as nature grew them, the blackberries have no true economic value. But at the roadside they do have an economic value. What is it that gives rise to this economic value? The substance of the berries has not changed; it is the same now as it was while on the bush. The economic value cannot lie in the substance. Nor can it be the value or cost of the actual labor that is expended in picking and transporting them. If the blackberry picker carried a large stone from the roadside to the woods and then back to the road, no value would have been created – any value in the stone would be the same as it was before. No one would want to pay him "for his labor." The labor itself is not what matters to the person who wants blackberries. It is the blackberries that the buyer will eat, and it is therefore the blackberries, or, to be more exact, the economic value of the blackberries resulting from the labor, that he pays for, not the labor itself nor the time. Labor as such can have no economic value, only the product of labor can have it. The economic value is attained by the labor but is not the labor itself. It really does not make economic sense to think in terms of it being the labor that is paid for. Nor can it be the time that the buyer saves. It is always the result, the *product* of labor that is of economic value and is therefore what is properly paid for.

The economic value must lie in the change in the blackberries that has resulted from the labor, in this case the change that has resulted in their being at "X" instead of on the blackberry bush in the woods.

It might sometimes be easier and more convenient to act as though the labor itself has a value and that it is this labor that is purchased. In practice this might in certain circumstances appear to be the only reasonable way to act. But if we think that economically we are purchasing labor and we act on the basis of this being a reality, then we bring into social life something that is not only untrue but that also divides people in that one person experiences himself as purchased by another. This does and always will bring disharmony and conflict into social life.

*

Imagine now a further development of the situation. A person walking along the riverbank notices that a tree has been blown across the river by a recent storm. Then she observes what the blackberry picker is doing. She shows the picker how, with a little skill, he could both shorten his journeys and at the same time sell his blackberries nearer to the village. The fallen tree could easily be used as a bridge providing an easy way to cross the river. The blackberry picker follows this advice and sets up his stall at "Y." The walker continues on her walk and plays no further part.

Although the walker does nothing of the picking, transporting, or selling of the berries, her perceptive and imaginative capacity transforms the process, creating a different economic value. The labor becomes more effective, more productive, in that the same work will make more blackberries available to the community, and they will be nearer to where they are wanted. They will be cheaper, but this cheapening process is itself of value to the community. We must not only see value in terms of the monetary price. There is a value to the community in something becoming cheaper – the cheaper it becomes, the greater the value.

Here it can be seen that a value created by labor has been modified by human intelligence. These matters are by no means simple, they cannot be understood solely by applying logical thinking and seeking definitions. Rather it is necessary to imagine concrete situations.

The question of what is "economic value" can be taken further with another picture.

The Conveyer Belt
Imagine the production of car engines in the old conveyor belt method of manufacture. A person stands at a certain place at the belt. A partially completed engine comes before him and stops.

The worker then attaches a new pipe to it with two bolts, which he tightens. The engine then moves on to the next person.

For what is the worker paid? What is it the owners or management want from him? Is it the movements he makes, the actual time he takes or the energy he uses up? Or is it something else? If he makes all the necessary movements but nothing results, the management is not going to want to pay him. They will not have what they want. What they actually want is the pipe put in its place and bolted down and the engine, as a result of his work, coming one step nearer to being complete and functional.

That change is the true economic value that management pays for. That is the sole purpose of their employing the worker. If we look more exactly at what actually happens in this situation and at the real nature of the payment, we cannot come to any other conclusion than that the management purchases from the worker the change that takes place as a result of his work. Labor itself is of no economic value. The engine, which provides the power for the car into which it will be put, is the sum total of the results of many people's work. It is not the actual work itself, nor the time, which will power the car forward.

As will be seen when we look into this question from other perspectives later, it makes an enormous difference to the individual worker, and thus to the social life of the community, whether we think in terms of the purchase of the products of labor, or of the purchase of labor itself.

If we are to understand economics, we have to develop flexibility in our thinking – we must cultivate an imaginative way of thinking. Concepts such as economic value cannot be grasped with hard and fast definitions. They have to be seen, to be grasped in their ever changing form within the actual economic process. It is also important to distinguish economic value from other values. It is this economic value that we are concerned with here when we refer to value.

The Two Value-Creating Activities

All economic values come into being through the interweaving of two value-creating factors: human labor and human imagination or creativity. These two can be seen as the creative factors in every productive activity.

First human labor takes hold of a product of nature and modifies it. This may be by extracting it from the ground, growing it, moving it, changing its shape, or in any other way transforming it. In doing so, it creates a value, an economic value. This is one value creating movement – human labor working on nature or the products of nature.

The other value creating movement is when human thinking, creative imagination, or ingenuity organizes or divides the work to be done in such a way that it makes the work itself more productive. A simple example of this can be seen in a group of people washing dishes after a meal. They will not each separately take their own plate, wash it, dry it, and then put it away. That is clearly a very inefficient and cumbersome way of working. No, they will divide the work between them, one or more would wash all the plates, others would dry them and yet others put them away. At this level people hardly think about it, it is obvious. But it is through observation and thinking that the work comes to be divided out and that each does only a part of the whole. This is what is properly called "division-of-labor."

Today, within an economy based on division-of-labor, not even washing up is simple. It might appear so, but much is usually not seen. We can ask: who is actually involved in the washing up, is it only the people who are there round the sink, washing, drying up and putting away? Did they also go down to the river and fetch the water, or cut the wood for a fire to heat it? No, they did not. Others did that, only on a rather larger scale. Very many others fetched the water, and if one takes into consideration all the people who made the pipes which carried the water, and those that made the pumps, then we see that a great number of people were involved. Of course they were also involved in many other activities in the community requiring water. In the same way we can say that there were also many others who contributed to the generating of the power used to heat the water.

Though unseen, and themselves not knowing it, all these many other people are also there helping to wash up. If one asks how many people are involved in the washing up, the answer would be very many thousands, or even millions, some perhaps in far-off countries. It is human creative imagination and invention that has brought about the situation that the water is collected centrally and pumped through pipes for everyone that needs it, instead of each one going down to the river and collecting it; so also for the heat and power.

Every economic productive process is founded on the working of these two value-creating activities. This can be seen in every article we have or use. The raw materials from which each is made can be traced back to their origins in nature. The chair on which I sit was once part of a tree, or more probably, parts of several trees, growing in the forest. They were cut down by human labor, transported to the sawmills where they were cut up, and again transported to where people worked further on the wood to make out of it this chair. Then follows the work of distribution so that it reaches me at the place where I can sit on it at my desk. In all this we see people laboring. But also there is human thinking, ingenuity, creating the tools – the saws, the planing-machines, the means of transport – and organizing the work so that it is most efficient. I have this chair, in the first place, because these two activities have taken place. This also means that many thousands of people have been active in order that I can have it without having to make it myself.

The Value-Creating Tension

There is a third value-creating factor, but one of a quite different nature. We see this if we again look at the example of the blackberry picker. He stands there with his blackberries for sale, the result of the two activities: his labor of picking and carrying them, and the creative imagination that resulted in the labor being made more productive.

A person coming along the road may be eating an apple. Some way behind him is another who does not have an apple, and is hungry. As these two come in turn to the stand of the blackberry seller they will each feel a different need for the blackberries. The seller, if he is crafty, will drop the price when the first person comes and then increase it again for the second. There is always a tension between the buyer and the seller depending on how strongly each wants what the other brings to the transaction. This can be called a "value-creating tension." It plays no part in the actual activity of producing the product. It is something of quite a different nature from the two value-creating movements already discussed, but it does play a large part in the economic sphere, it is always there affecting the price.

It is important that a clear distinction is maintained between, on the one side, the two value-creating movements, or activities, and on the other the value-creating tension. This tension is something that is unpredictable; it arises out of people's different feelings, sentiments, and needs. These are in a constant state of flux; they change from person to person and over time.

Chapter 4

The Economic Process — Division-of-Labor

The Basic Economic Process

We can trace everything we use, wear, or eat, our means of transport, our housing, electrical appliances, and all the many other economic products we have or consume to their origin in nature. The economic productive process starts at the point where human physical work or labor first takes hold of what nature provides and begins to transform it. This can be by working on the substance and changing it, as when wood is made into a table, or by merely moving it to the place where it is to be used, as when the finished table is moved from the factory to the shop, or coal from in the earth to the fire place.

Human intelligence or ingenuity can make this work more efficient or productive. It does this through a process I shall call "division-of-labor." This process can take two forms but is usually a combination of both. Either the work to be done is divided between a number of people so that each concentrates on one part of the productive process; or it enables some people to make "tools" which in themselves are not needed, but which enable others to work more productively in producing what is actually used or consumed. These tools in their more complex form are what are now generally referred to as technology.

Division-of-labor can be shown, in its very simplest form, through an imaginative picture. Because the sphere of economic activity is so complex and difficult to observe, it is helpful to consider it in its simplest state where the many other factors usually at play are excluded or reduced to a minimum. In this way we can begin to see what is also at work in the most complex economic productive processes.

Imagine a very simple community where everyone makes everything they need for themselves. There is no division-of-labor, no sharing of the work.

"A" decides to make himself a shirt. He also needs a pot and will have to make that as well. With a little reflection it will be clear that the making of each of these will involve a considerable amount of time and work. He will have to grow or otherwise gather up all the materials needed and make all the tools he will use before he can even begin to actually make the shirt. He will then have to do the same in order to make the pot.

Quite separately another person, "B," also decides to make for himself a shirt and a pot. He also will have to do the same considerable amount of work. But the situation for each will be radically changed if one of them comes to the idea that they divide the work between them. "A" will make two shirts and "B" two pots. So "A," in making a shirt for himself, instead of then also making a pot for himself, makes a second shirt for "B." In the same way "B," instead of making a shirt for himself, will make a second pot for "A."

Now the whole situation is changed. "A" makes a shirt for himself. At the same time he makes a second shirt for "B." The first shirt that he makes for himself will still take the same amount of activity as before, but the second will take considerably less; he will already have the tools, and to procure twice the materials is not twice the work. So for "A" to make a second shirt there is a kind of bonus, it will take much less time and effort than it would have taken if "B" had made it for himself as well as making his pot. By dividing the work between them, their work becomes more productive. The same applies to the making of the second pot by "B" for "A."

What is apparent here is the principle that when the work is divided, when a person concentrates on the making of one product, or even just one part of a product, making what others want rather than only what he himself wants, the work becomes more productive, or the product becomes cheaper. This principle is at the foundation of all economic production, from the simple situation of people sharing the washing up to the most complex industrial processes such as the manufacture of motor cars or computers. It is what makes it possible for each of us to acquire products that it would be impossible to have if we had to make them all for ourselves.

We can see this clearly, for example, in the electric light bulb. If a person had to make one on his own, including the making of all the tools needed as well as the gathering up of the raw materials, it would take him very many years. But because of division-of-labor it is possible for him to buy one with the money that it takes the average person in any industrially developed country a matter of minutes to earn – he can "make" a bulb in just a few minutes.

Division-of-labor starts when human thinking and imagination begin to divide up the different activities in the process of production. As will be shown later, it continues with the invention of tools, machines, and technology. It is here especially that the human power of creativity makes economic labor more efficient and productive.

Purchase and Sale

"A" and "B" now exchange the second shirt for the second pot, and "A" gets the pot that he originally wanted. He has done this not by making it himself with all that entails, but by the much simpler means of making a second shirt and exchanging this for the pot made by "B." The exchange, or purchase, brings back together that which was first separated, or divided out, through division-of-labor. In making something, not for himself but for the other, each gets what he wants with less effort, and so each is better off; each profits.

The exchange is the completion of the process, or a stage in a process, not something in itself. The economic process starts with organizing and dividing the work, so everyone is involved in making part of what others want. Through the sale and purchase the process is completed by distributing to each the item he wanted and would otherwise have had to make for himself, or go without.

With the complexity of economic life today when money comes into the transaction it is almost impossible to see this, but the fact is that sale and purchase are always the *completion* of a process. That which is divided through division-of-labor is reinstated in sale and purchase so that each then receives what he needs.

What has just been said is true of the economic productive process. We must not get confused by the fact that there are many transactions that are treated as economic exchanges but in fact are something quite different. As already pointed out, they are often in reality the purchase or sale of "rights." We will look at these pseudo-economic exchanges or purchases later.

Profit

In the example above, both "A" and "B" gain in the transaction. In the exchange of products each received something that was of more value to him than what he gave: each made a profit. If this were not so, the exchange would not take place. In all exchanges, wherever there is sale and purchase and where there are no other factors from outside the realm of economics bearing down on and distorting the proper balancing within sale and purchase, both sides make a profit. We tend always to think of profit in terms of money, and that it is the one who receives money who makes the profit. But if I buy a pair of shoes, it is because the shoes have more value to me than the money. I can wear the shoes, not the money. I gain on the exchange, I make a profit. For the shopkeeper it is the other way round. He can do more with the money than he can with the shoes. It is the profit each makes that is the motive behind the exchange. If I did not make a profit, if the shoes were not of more value to me than the money, I would not buy them, I would keep the money.

Thus profit is the impelling force in the economic sphere that keeps the whole in movement. This force is at work both in the productive activity and in the sphere of sale and purchase. Just as it is division-of-labor which gives to economic activity its bounteous nature, so it is profit which is the impelling force that keeps the whole in movement.

To avoid confusion, there are two elements in the economic process of production that will need some clarification here: "economic value" and "price."

Economic Value

As discussed in the last chapter, "economic value" is created when, through the process of division-of-labor, a product is produced. We saw that the economic value lies in the product, but is not the product itself nor is it to be found in the actual substance as it exists in nature. The value is the result of the shared work of the division-of-labor; for the maker of the shirt in the previous example, it is the value in the shirt of the pot that was gained by making the shirt. The economic value is the increase brought about by the two streams of activity, physical labor on the one side and human creativity on the other, each working to fructify the other. We have to come to perceive or sense this value, it cannot be rigidly defined.

When "A" made the shirt for himself there was no economic value created in the sense that it did not enter into the economy of the community. He made it for himself, no one else was involved. This might have a value in his personal economy, but here we are concerned with the economy of the community, not that of the individual. In division-of-labor, the economic value of the shirt that a person makes is not the work that he put into the making of it, but the value to him of the pot that he can obtain by means of the shirt.

Price

When "A" and "B" agree to exchange the shirt for the pot there will eventually come the question as to the relative values of each. Are the "prices" of one pot for one shirt, and one shirt for one pot, fair? It could be that much more work has to go into the making of shirts than is needed for making pots. If so, the value of the pot received in the exchange by "A" will not be as great to him as the shirt is to "B." "A" will not have profited as much as "B" in the sharing of the work. "A" will then demand that he receive more than just the one pot for his shirt. All other factors being equal, there will always be a tendency to exchange products of equal economic value. A fair price, that is x number of pots for one shirt, will be achieved when in the exchange the economic values on either side of the exchange are in balance.

But this is seldom achieved. While it is the two value-creating activities working together that form economic value, in the forming of price the third factor also comes into play – the value-creating tension introduced in the last chapter. This arises not out of the productive process itself but, firstly, out of the human factor, out of the feelings, desires, and needs of human nature and, secondly, out of the state of the market and the many other factors effecting price, some of which will be looked at later. They can affect the price in either direction. In an economic sector that sets out to provide for the needs of the community as a whole there will always be a striving towards bringing price into line with economic value.

If in a community a balance comes about between the number of shoemakers able to make just the right number of shoes for all who need them, and all the other people making all the other products, the price will settle at a certain mean figure – a fair price. If then something happens, another shoemaker comes into the area, or some of the population move elsewhere, or it becomes fashionable to go barefoot, fewer shoes will be needed than are being produced. If nothing else happens, the price will drop. This means that the shoemakers, in selling their shoes, are not able to obtain in exchange something of equal economic value – the money they receive for the shoes buys less economic value than that of the shoes sold; they receive in exchange less than they give.

The price could be fixed by some means such as by law, by subsidies, or by some other way of affecting price. But this would not alter the fact that there were now too many shoemakers making shoes. The drop in price is an indication of a change in the social situation. The oversupply will not be solved by artificially increasing the price; that will only hide the real problem. The cause of the change of price is not in the price itself, so the cure will not be found in the artificial fixing of the price.

Price is an indicator. It works just as a thermometer does in indicating the temperature of a room. If the room is too cold we do not warm it up by artificially forcing the thermometer to register a higher temperature; we put more wood on the fire, or turn up the heater. So in economic life the price indicates the "temperature" in the social life of the community in the sphere of the production and consumption of commodities. We must leave the price alone and look for the cause elsewhere. In this case it is that too many people in the community are making shoes. Adjustments must be made within the community to bring the number of people making shoes and the number of shoes wanted into balance so that the price once again returns to the mean point. This can only be done by people who are able to rise above the immediate interests of the individual to the interests of the community as a whole. As I shall explain later, this can be achieved through what I call "economic associations."

Instead of a conscious appreciation of the problem followed by necessary action, at present it is largely left to the tension factor in the market place to determine what is produced. We can see all around us that this does not result in a socially healthy balance. We must find a way in which human intelligence and creative imagination can take the place of the tensions of the market. It is not that the market has no place, it does fulfill an important role. It is through the price arising freely in the market place that the true "temperature" of the economic situation is revealed and can be read. It must come about that, having "read the temperature," conscious human intelligence and creative imagination can take the necessary action.

No individual can by himself grasp the wider working of economic life. Each can know it only from his own particular place in it and in so far as it is his own interests that concern him. But the totality can be grasped when individuals, each viewing the whole from his particular place, are able to come together to form a whole. Then the group can rise above the narrow perspectives of the individuals as individuals. When those involved in economic life come together out of their separate activities it will be possible to take hold of the whole. This way of working will be looked at later in Chapter Thirteen under "Economic Associations."

The Mean Price

How do we arrive at an idea of what we might call the "mean price," one that equates as nearly as possible with "economic value?"

Imagine again a simple closed village community where everyone worked in the economic life of the community. If everyone worked to produce the different products needed by the whole, and assuming everyone did the same amount of work within the village economy based on division-of-labor, then the economic values each produced would be equal and reciprocal. We would, of course, also have to assume that everyone had similar capacities in their work. Assuming also that no other factors affected the values, then what one person produced in a day would be exchangeable for what any other produced in a day; each would have the same economic value and the same price.

In this case, each person can earn what they need, that is, each can obtain an equal and fair share of the total product of the community activity by doing one day's work. In this we see the starting point, the foundation, of the economic life of the community. If nothing else came in to complicate and pull it out of balance, all people would labor equally at economic production and all would have the same standard of living. Of course in actual life very many things do come in to distort this in one direction or another, but this reciprocity, this balance, should be seen as a reference point or starting line for any study of the economic sector. Economic and social science is really the attempt to understand all that affects and distorts this, and to strive, so far as it is possible, to bring it back into balance.

An "Ideal" or "True" Price

Taking this balancing of economic values as the foundation or starting point, can we imagine how we might move from this to an "ideal" price within a more complex community; one based on the needs of consumption rather than on production, and allowing for the different abilities and needs of all members of the community? It would also have to take into account the fact that with modern technology at work in what has become a world economy, it is no longer possible to know who or how many people have been involved in the production of any particular item. It would also allow for the fact that this world economy could, if it was so willed, produce enough for all humanity. We might then come to an ideal concept of price as something like this:

> A 'true price' results when individuals receive, as counter-value for the product they have made, sufficient recompense to enable them to satisfy the whole of their needs, including of course the needs of their dependents, until they will again have completed a like product.
>
> (Steiner, *Rethinking Economics*, p. 67.)

There is much in this statement that will be taken up and discussed in the further course of this book. To our present way of thinking it will immediately appear as nonsense that a) the price should depend on what a person needs rather than the value of what he gives, and b) the price refers to the cost of future production, and c) the price could be seen as true for one person but not so for another, each producing the same product.

This may not be something that can be applied at the present time, but the thought of an ideal or true price can be very helpful as an imagination towards which we can strive, something that is actually more within the realm of possibility than we might think.

Consumption

To continue the story of the shirt and the pot, "A" uses the pot that "B" made, and "B" uses the shirt that "A" made. Both items are eventually used up, the shirt wears out, the pot gets broken, or starts to leak. In both cases they, or more correctly the substances out of which they are formed, are discarded and returned to nature. So the cycle is completed, the economic values created through division-of-labor and exchanged through purchase and sale, revert back to nothing in consumption – the whole is truly an organic process.

This cycle is the essence of everything that can rightfully be included in the economic sector of social life. Anything that is not part of this cycle cannot truly be called "economic" but must have its proper place in one of the other two spheres of social life.

Here we see it in its very simplest form. But it is there also in the most complex of industrial manufacture, distribution, and consumption – the creation of values through division-of-labor and ingenuity, followed by sale-and-purchase, and leading to the using up of those values through consumption.

The Origin of Money

In the economic sphere people make things, or parts of things, that are wanted by other people. What is made is then exchanged for things made by others. As soon as this process of dividing the work progresses beyond a very small community, money comes into being. It must of necessity do so. In the economic sphere this is the foundation, the starting point of money.

Money first arises at the level of exchange, in sale and purchase. The tailor who has made shirts will not want to have to exchange each one for something he needs; the people who want his shirts may not have produced the things that he needs, and they do not want to have to do so. There has to be something that can represent the shirt, or more exactly, the "economic value" in the shirt. It can be a token, a promise to pay, or something that itself has value that will be excepted by others as standing for the same "economic value" as the shirt.

If there were no money already present, then certain commodities would themselves become money as has often happened in history. The precious metals, gold, silver, bronze, and copper have all been used as money. But there have been times when other products of nature have been used, such as when tobacco was used as money in Maryland and Virginia in North America in the 17th and 18th centuries, and cigarettes in much of Europe immediately after the Second World War. It is not possible to "get rid of money" as some would suggest. It would of itself reappear.

Factory, Crafts, and Agriculture

It is in the factory that division-of-labor is at its most developed. So it is in the products of the factories that we see prices at their lowest when we take an overview of all prices.

Where division-of-labor is not able to play so large a role, prices will not be reduced to the same extent. For example, where human labor remains a substantial part of the production process as in the craft industries, the products will always remain comparatively more expensive. In crafts something of the cultural life combines with the economic productive process – skill and artistry have to be involved in the activity if the result is to be both artistic and functional. By their nature, crafts will always be labor intensive. They are "crafts" to the extent that they are individually crafted by human hands. The more labor intensive the craft – the less division-of-labor is able to play its part – the more expensive the product will be.

In agriculture, economic activity works directly with nature, with living plants and animals. Earth, sun, air, and rain all play an essential part in the production process. Today it is slowly and painfully coming to be recognized that when this role of nature is not properly recognized and division-of-labor is allowed to enter too far into the process, such as in factory farming or monoculture, then the health giving nutritional qualities provided by nature are reduced. To the extent that division-of-labor cannot fully enter into agriculture, which therefore remains comparatively labor intensive, its products will always be more expensive when compared to the products of a factory. For this reason organic and bio-dynamic agricultural products tend to be more expensive than those of conventional agriculture as they allow nature itself to play a greater part in the production of the foodstuffs.

There is still another important contributing factor to this tendency for the products of agriculture to be expensive.

Agriculture is a joint working together between nature and human activity. The economic price of the product of this combined work can rightly relate only to that value resulting from the human activity. The work of nature, which is outside human economic activity, cannot properly be included within the forming of price. But there is always a tendency in human nature not to differentiate between these two, and to include in the price something of the value created by nature. In prices of agricultural products there is nearly always something of the nature of rent.

There are, of course, many other factors that will affect the price of a product beyond the actual process of production. Some are built into our present social structure. As we will see when we discuss rent in Chapter Seventeen, there is a kind of "compulsory gift" element that has to be added to the prices of all products subject to any form of rent.

The Limits of Economic Activity

In any study of social life as a whole, the proper boundaries of economic activities must be recognized and established. There are, in the main, three boundaries to the process of economic production and distribution within which the economic sector must be confined. Something of this could be seen in the examples just given and should become clearer in the further course of these studies.

The process of economic production starts at the point where human labor first extracts the raw materials from where they are found in nature and begins the process of transforming them into commodities, thus creating economic value. The raw materials as they exist in the land, and the land itself are given by nature. They are not produced by human economic activity and so cannot be said to have that which results from such activity: economic value. We may buy and sell land and treat it in the same way as a product of economic activity, but it is not such a product. As we shall see later, if we buy land we are giving it an economic value, as though the land were produced by economic activity.

Labor itself, too, cannot be included within the sphere of economic production. We speak of the "cost of labor" and treat it in just the same way as we speak of raw materials or commodities, but, as illustrated above, the labor itself does not enter into the economic process. It is always the result or product of labor which becomes the commodity that is sold and consumed.

In the same way, the imaginative, creative, and inventive genius of human beings has a very great effect on the economic process, but has its origin in the cultural sphere and is not a product of the economic process.

Thus, in brief outline, we have three basic limits or boundaries of the actual productive process. One boundary lies between economic activity itself and the land or nature from which it draws its raw materials, that which is "God given." A second boundary comes between it and the human beings who work at the process of production – neither they nor their labor are a part of the economic process. A third boundary lies between economic life and all that streams towards it from the cultural sphere of social life. All these "inputs" have their effects on the economic process but are not part of it. The nature and importance of these three boundaries will, hopefully, become clearer as we proceed.

The Study of Economics

Modern economic science is, in the main, based on the assumption that the methods of study appropriate to, for example, physics or chemistry are also appropriate to economics. But people cannot simply be looked at as little different from the chemicals in chemistry, or the molecules and forces in physics. These substances follow certain laws, which can be studied; their nature and behavior can be known and relied upon as consistent and predictable. We observe them from outside, we are not ourselves part of the chemical reaction that we observe. But in a study of economic activity we are dealing with something that we ourselves are part of. We observe it not from outside but from within; and here our observing and thinking about it can itself change that which we are studying. What we observe also has its effect on us, it works on our feelings and so also affects our wants and needs. Human behavior is ever changing and unpredictable. Our impulses, needs, and values cannot always be foreseen. We are beings who think and feel, and we act according to the thoughts and feelings that arise within us. In economics there can never be the same kind of scientific certainty that there can be in the physical sciences.

Anyone who has studied the various theories that have been used to explain recent economic and financial situations will perceive that time and again these theories have been evolved by people with real insight and good intentions. But there have always been others who, also with real insight and good intentions, have come to very different theories. But no matter which theories have been taken up by political and economic leaders – theories which have at the time enabled them to take hold of and bring the economy back into some sort of order – they have been unable to achieve any lasting improvement.

The economic sphere is probably by far the most complex and difficult of the three to take hold of. By its nature it cannot be grasped through logical thinking alone, nor is it possible to arrive at any meaningful definitions. It can only be perceived through active imaginative participation. It is in constant flow and movement – what is true in one place and moment ceases to be completely so the next. To understand economic activity sufficiently to effectively work with and influence its course, we must come to perceive and understand it in its movement, in its constantly changing state, not in any hypothetical state of rest.

The study of the economic sphere of human activity requires powers of observation and imaginative thinking beyond what people are used to. Here we can only try to grasp something of its basic nature. What is important is not that one fully understands the economic sphere – that actually is not possible for the single individual – but that one develops a sense for it, a feeling for its nature. Then we will begin to see and know how economic life can be taken hold of and made to serve humanity.

Before looking further into the economic sector and into money and finance, it might be helpful at this point to look next at the nature and character of the Rights and the Cultural sectors.

Chapter 5
Evolution, Human Consciousness, and the Origins of Law

The laws, rules, agreements, conventions, and customs of a society give structure and form to that society. They give, or should give, to the community a framework within which people can live, work, and play in an ordered, just, and secure social environment. This structure or framework forms the skeleton on which the community is built. A community without laws is formless, chaotic, and anarchic.

From birth until death we live within, and are held by, a structure of laws, rules, regulations, customs, agreements, etiquette, and standards of recognized right or acceptable behavior. For much of the time we are not even conscious of this, certainly not of the full extent of it. When, for example, we do no more than walk along a pavement or footpath, our rights to do so are given and hedged in by an invisible structure of laws and restraints created and put there over a long period of time by custom and by the State.

The Evolution of Law

In the West we do not have to go further back than the Greek and Roman civilizations to come to the beginnings of government as we know it today. Before that time leadership was generally founded on some form of "divine commandment." In those earlier times, that which gave order and structure to society was seen as handed down by God through the various religious disciplines and teachings. Coming from God, divine commandments had a quite different moral power over people than do the laws of today. While the rightness of divine law can never be questioned by those who see God as omnipotent and as their Creator, it is always possible to question the human-created laws of the State.

There are, of course, very many peoples of the world who are still ruled to a greater or lesser extent by some form of religious law or Divine commandment. But, in the main, this is law given in the past, of which only the written records remain, not a living and present divine guidance. Written law always opens the way for disputes to arise as to its interpretation, its meaning, and its appropriateness for our time.

Today it is widely recognized that, in a just society, laws will arise through a democratic process. But democracy is a very recent development. Our social structure has evolved over a long period of time, much of it formed in earlier periods when people felt very differently towards one another, when their sense for what was right and just was not necessarily the same as it is for people of today. Religion once held a powerful controlling influence over outer everyday behavior, but this is no longer the case. Although over the ages people have changed, certain aspects of our legal and social structures have *not* changed, but have continued on from earlier times into the present in forms that are no longer appropriate and often anti-social.

The legal possibility of "owning" something, for example, which gives basic form to our modern society and way of living, has its origins in the distant past. So too the social thinking that has given form and structure to our present employment laws and system of "remuneration" for work. Though itself of comparatively recent origin, corporate law itself has arisen out of social structures that have their origins in ancient theocratic societies. In the second part of this book I shall go more deeply into these aspects of the rights sphere. I shall attempt to demonstrate how they form the foundation on which our present capitalistic economy is built, and will show that without changing these undemocratically arrived at aspects of our rights life there will be no possibility of understanding and overcoming the power of global corporations, nor of healing socials ills such as the increasing divide between the rich and the poor and all that arises out of this.

Before discussing the rights sector as it exists today, I will briefly outline in broad strokes some of the changes that have occurred in human consciousness from earliest times, particularly those that have played a major part in transforming the relationship between the individual and society.

Three particular developments or changes in human consciousness effecting social thinking are important here:

- the development from "divine commandment" to the "law of the State"
- the evolution from "membership in a group" to the "single individual"
- the awakening of a consciousness of "universal humanity" and of equal rights for all people.

The discussion of these developments will also throw light on important aspects of the cultural sphere that I shall attempt to describe beginning in Chapter Eight.

From Divine Commandment to the Law of the State

In earlier communities the social structure and the law were experienced as given by God through divinely appointed leaders. These leaders, the prophets, pharaohs, and kings, held their place in the community by the perceived direct and present will of God.

Later there came a time when the voice of God was no longer heard with the same clarity. That which God had given came to be written down, and increasingly it was this that was studied in order to come to an understanding of God's will. Later still, the consciousness of any present will of God was lost altogether and the leaders led through God's will as given in the past.

At the next step, the leading classes of society were not seen as directly appointed by God, but as appointed through heredity, through the bloodline. People of all classes held their place in the community through inheritance, an inheritance that stretched back to an appointment by God in a distant past.

Later this belief in an appointment by God faded, but the structure of society with its basic legal concepts established during those earlier stages continued on. The leading classes held on to their position through their control of the instruments of power and their ability to bring into being laws establishing a secular legal structure to society that mirrored the former god-given one. This ensured a continuance of the existing hierarchical structure with themselves at the top and in control.

In our day, leadership and position in society through inheritance is no longer acceptable. Leadership can, or should, only be determined by the will of the people themselves – those that are to govern must be democratically elected by a system in which every person has an equal vote. Where originally it was the will of God that held sway, now it must be the will of the people.

These stages, of course, flow into and overlap one another; nowhere is there a clear step from one stage to the next. At any one stage much that belonged to the past is still active, and something of that which is to come in the future already makes its appearance. Aspects of all these developmental stages can still be found in certain areas of human social life today.

Alongside this evolution of a social structure formed by divine commandment to one based on human-created law, and interweaving with it, was a change of human consciousness from feeling oneself primarily as a member of a group to experiencing oneself as an individual separate from the group.

The Group and the Individual

There are, in all of us, two aspects of our inner being that tend to pull in opposite directions. One is that which marks each of us as an individual with our own personal opinions, feelings, values, and judgements. The other is that in us which derives from, or finds comfort in, being a member of a group.

All that we experience as our own inner being: our thoughts and feelings, yearnings, opinions, and values, what we refer to when we say "I," we can call our soul. But much of this is not, to begin with, our own – it comes to us from the group of which we are a member. We can each ask ourselves the question: How much does what I feel and think, my values in life, my judgments and decisions, my sympathies and antipathies, arise out of, or become conditioned by, the group of which I am a member, and how much of it is truly mine alone?

When I first asked this question of myself many years ago in my late twenties I was deeply shocked at what I found. I had always thought of myself as an individual with my own thoughts and opinions; and I thought that I made my decisions based on my own values and judgments. But I came to see that far more of me than I liked to acknowledge arose from the fact that I was a Spence, male, white, born into a Christian, upper-middle class British colonial family. I came to, what was for me, the disturbing conclusion that very little of what I thought or believed, the moral values I held, and the decisions I made, were due to myself as an independent human being; by far the largest part was a sort of conditioning from my wider family and the social environment into which I was born. In this I was not a free human being.

Over against this was a deep need to be myself, to find my own values, to make my own decisions, to work my life out for myself, to be me.

Just as every individual human being has a soul, that which can be called the "individual soul," so also every group has a kind of group consciousness or "group soul." This is particularly strong in groups based on a blood relationship. Both of these "souls" are present in every human being, one stronger in some and the other in others.

*

The further back we look into human evolution, the more we will find the domination of the group over the individual. In very ancient times ordinary people were little more than components of a family or tribal group with little personality of their own. They found their being, their role and place in life, as a member of the group, not as a separate individual. Because of this, their life could be sacrificed in battle for the benefit of the group in a way that would never be acceptable today. The death of a soldier was experienced more as a loss to the group than as an individual tragedy. A person was born into a certain place within the group and lived, worked, married, raised children, and acted at all times according to that place and within the will and ordering of the group. Marriage, for instance, ensured the continuation of the group based on the blood, so there could be no marriage outside the group. The sanctity and continuity of the bloodline had to be maintained. This is still the way of life for many people, often with a strong religious element.

Outside of this family or tribal group, the ordinary person was lost, cut off from his or her true identity. Only in the leaders could there be found something resembling individuality and the ability to develop new thoughts and ideas within the single human being.

Each group – family, tribe, or people – had its head, its leader or leaders. They were the advanced or gifted individuals through whom the Gods were felt to speak and who led the people. In the holy sanctuaries, in the mystery centers and in the temples, guidance and wisdom were given to these leaders – the prophets, kings, and priests – and from them it was passed down to the ordinary people. In those earlier times people had a very different consciousness than we have today. Much of the knowledge given to the leaders could be dimly known, as in a kind of dreaming clairvoyance, by all members of the group. That it was received into the tribe and thus into the group soul meant that it was dimly experienced by all.

Gradually, over time, this has changed. Today, though it does still have a hold on the individual, in most industrially developed nations the group soul no longer dominates as it did in earlier times. But we can still find instances of how in people's souls there is a yearning for an old group-soul form of life.

In the early nineteen-seventies, for example, an elderly woman turned up at the college in the English countryside where I then worked. Fifty years before she had worked as a 'second under-kitchen-maid' in the old country house that had become the main administrative building of the college. It had then been a private home, occupied by a family with four sons. She was eighteen years old when she started and she had worked for this family for two years. That was just after the First World War. To serve this family, there were sometimes up to fourteen servants, many living in the house, and an equal number of gardeners. She herself had lived in the village and walked each morning across the fields and entered the house through the back servant's entrance.

In all the time she worked there she had never been to the front of the house. When I took her there I sensed that she still, after all these years, had a feeling of not belonging in that part of the house; her "place" was in the kitchen. This feeling must have played a very strong part in her life to have lasted so long. The way she talked about it all deeply impressed me. She still looked back to that time with great warmth and a certain nostalgia. She had been the lowest of the servants, but she had still felt herself as one of the "family."

After leaving she continued to follow the lives of the family, particularly of the four sons. Now, fifty years on, she could still tell me what they were all doing. I sensed that she looked back to that part of her life as a time of fullness, a time when she belonged, when she was part of a big family. She had her place according to the rightful order of things, and the family members had theirs. She did not see them as owners but more as the head of the wider family or community of life; the eldest son would follow the father as family head, and if she had stayed, her own children would follow her and be their servants; that was the rightful order of things, the divine ordering. There was no question of "equality," but of each in their rightful place, each with their responsibilities and work contributing to the whole, the "family."

She told me, but with a tinge of regret in her voice, that she now lived on a pension, and that she was "alright." But there was no human contact – just an organization that sent her a check. It was safe and secure, but she did not belong, there was no one who cared, no wider family of which she was a part as there once had been then.

This was a very clear, if increasingly rare, instance of what was in earlier times a widespread, perhaps almost universal, sense of a person having a place according to the rightful ordering of society – that one's place, whether as servant or master, was given through hereditary.

Less than a century later, the very idea of being a servant in that older sense is generally no longer acceptable. One might employ someone to do the cleaning of one's house, but as an employee, not as a servant.

Out of the group consciousness of the old communities based on bloodlines there is emerging the individual consciousness of each human being as a distinct individual, each with a personality separate from the group, and the right to be seen and treated as such.

And now something else has come to the fore with a certain evolutionary power.

The Consciousness of One Humanity

Alongside, and as a polarity to the emerging recognition of each person as an individual, is the dawning recognition by humanity as a whole, of the equality of all people in the world, of universal human rights.

The feeling for "human rights" as something to which all people are equally entitled irrespective of race, creed, or color, is relatively new in human evolution, and still has a long way to go. Though there have been individuals and small groups of people who felt something of this in earlier times, it did not become the force it is today until after the middle of the twentieth century.

One illustration of this is the way people felt about, and reacted to, apartheid in South Africa, beginning especially in the 1960s. In nearly all parts of the world, people strongly opposed the institutionalized segregation and oppression of apartheid. White South Africans were ostracized and excluded from international sporting events such as the Olympic Games and from other cultural exchanges. There was a widespread movement to ban all trade with South Africa, which became, for decades, a kind of world-pariah.

Considered in the light of the entire world situation of the time (apartheid was enforced by legislation from 1948 to 1994), South Africa was certainly far from being the only place where killing, torture, and conditions of subservience and degradation were in existence, but the international condemnation of South Africa in particular was exceptional. What was the difference?

The difference had to do with the particular nature of apartheid, together with the changing consciousness of humanity. What lay behind other tragic and violent events of the time (the United States' involvement in Indochina, the Indonesian occupation of East Timor, for example) was *primarily* of a political, economic, or even religious nature. These events came about where a people wished to enforce their particular interests, or the need for land or resources. But the *essential humanity* of the other was not directly denied as it was with apartheid. (The struggle for Civil Rights in the United States is of course an exception.)

Apartheid existed at a time when, among young people in many parts of the world, there was an awakening consciousness of something inherently divine within each human being. This was something transcending color, sex, religious belief, nationality, or ability – all that by which people are differentiated; it was a recognition of something in which all people are equal. In South Africa, the denial of just this was backed by law. Apartheid was founded on the belief that black people were a lower form of humanity.

An increasing number of people perceived this as a denial of "that which is of the substance of the Divine in each human being" – that which is beyond, and more sacred than, the outer physical, bodily nature of a person. This is the innermost core of every human being, the sacred essence of their being. It is what is also sometimes referred to as "Spirit," as distinct from "Soul." In our time, there is a growing awareness that this "Divine Spark" is equally present in every human being, irrespective of all that makes them individual and different.

*

The gradual awakening of the feeling in human souls that all people are equal, out of which the idea of democracy has arisen, is still at its early stages. Even in those countries that have led the way towards democracy, reality has lagged far behind the original or professed ideal. The history of the United States includes a long and far from resolved relationship between race and inequality, from the institution of slavery, to the Jim Crow laws and other forms of institutionalized segregation and discrimination, to the present incarceration rates of minorities and all that it entails, and much more besides. In England, at the beginning of the nineteenth century, only those men who already stood in certain positions in society, such as landowners, were recognized as sufficiently mature to be given the responsibility of the vote. The others, including all women, were seen as immature and needing to be led by these few. Eventually, recognition of equality was extended to all men, but the recognition of the equality of women came much more recently.

The legal structure of society must come to be formed in a quite different way from that of earlier times. Though still in its beginning stages, the demand for democracy is increasingly entering into people's souls.

Chapter 6

Equality and the Role of Government

As I hope to show in later chapters, the cultural sphere of social life concerns itself with everything that is individual and particular to the single human being. The rights sphere, on the other hand, concerns itself with bringing order and agreed arrangements into that which lies between people. It arises out of, and must always be guided by, what is to be found equally in all people, what we may term the "universally human," as opposed to that which is single and individual in each one.

There are people who would never act anti-socially towards members of their own family or close community, stealing from or harming them in some other way, but who would readily do so to others with whom they have no such connection. Whatever it is in their feelings that prevents them from acting in this way towards their family and friends is absent in their relating to other people. Most, if not all of us have something of this failure in our social feelings.

In addition to this there is something within us, stronger in some than in others, that leads us to think that what suits or benefits oneself is good, or at least not as anti-social as others might think. A person who enjoys the thrill of fast driving in a high performance car will seldom have the same feeling as to what is a reasonable and safe speed as will the hesitant driver. People can have quite genuine but different opinions as to what is right or moral behavior. A person who owns land may feel fully justified in excluding others from it, while a non-landowner may well feel that it is an individual's right to be allowed to walk over God's Earth.

If one person physically harms another, the injured one might feel that he has a moral right to avenge the harm done. But the community may well feel otherwise: that if such a thing were allowed only the strong would have vengeance, while others more weak would suffer; that the community itself must therefore deal with such anti-social actions.

So there is the necessity that in certain circumstances the control or constraint which cannot be provided by a person's own conscience, self-discipline, or social judgment must, for the well-being of the community and all its members, be provided by an outer authority.

So too, whenever people come together for some purpose, they will find that they need to come to agreements as to how they are to conduct their affairs in order to reach their goals.

It is the creation of the necessary laws, rules, regulations, administrative arrangements, and agreements to ensure reasonable social behavior of individuals, and the building of the necessary structures for the ordered running and protection of society, that is the proper function and sphere of activity of the rights sector.

Equality – The Basis of Law

The guiding factor in the rights sphere of social life is the equality of all people. When considering this aspect of social life, all members of the community must be perceived, not as unique and individual, but as equal. Courts of Law around the world feature statues of the figure of "Justice" – a woman, blindfolded, holding the scales of justice in one hand and a sword in the other. She is blindfolded to show that she does not judge, or even see, what is individual but treats all who come before her without partiality.

It is helpful, in defining the sphere of rights, to distinguish between two sets of criteria by which value may be placed on a person's opinion. On the one side are all those matters where value or weight is given on the basis of the expertise, experience, or individual capacity and insights of the person giving the opinion or judgment. For example, one would place much greater value on the opinion of a teacher concerning the educational needs of a child than on that of a farmer. But, on a question of the right soil conditions in which to grow wheat, preference would be given to the opinion of the farmer. In matters of expertise we cannot say that everyone's opinion is equally valid.

Opposite to this are those instances where the particular capacity or expertise of the individual is irrelevant, where each person's opinion is equally valid and where only by listening to all opinions can one arrive at a sense of how the community as a whole feels about something.

This second area is the proper domain of the rights life and of all that establishes law and order in a community. The foundation of the rights life of a community, its laws and regulations, must come to be an expression of the majority, or common opinion. This is of course not so simple, nor should it be: minority opinions and feelings are also real and cannot just be overruled.

As a basis for rights life, feelings cannot be said to be right or wrong. It is the way that people of a particular country or community actually feel that must be the foundation on which the law is built if it is to be truly democratic, not the way they ought to feel. If the majority of people feel that it is right to take each other's property, then the law of that community must reflect that. Today it is increasingly true that people will not accept any teaching of what is moral or good behavior from any outer authority unless they themselves also feel it to be so.

The term "common opinion," as used in this book, has a wider meaning than just the majority opinion. While the opinion of the majority must of necessity be given greatest weight, nevertheless this must be softened by, or must give some ground to, all other differing opinions. The fact that in a democracy it is the majority opinion that dominates is itself an indication of the inadequacy of any democratic form of law making, but this is all we have at present. Only a going back to divine commandment, if such a thing were possible, could give us something of a higher and greater moral structure. But that would allow for no individual freedom.

*

"Equality" as a demand of the rights sector is not easy to define. How does one see two very different people as equal without denying their individuality? How can people be different but equal? Every human being, whatever his or her individual characteristics, is a member of humanity and participates in that which is universally human – each one is equally human. As was indicated in the last chapter, the feeling for this is something that has only comparatively recently begun to enter widely into people's consciousness.

Though this growing consciousness of equality is present in more and more people, it is still very difficult for most people to say clearly what it actually is that is equal in people. Many mistake equality for sameness and so become confused, as it is clear that in many respects people can be very different. The ability to see what is equally present in every human being, while also recognizing everything that makes them individual and different, is a very important step and leads to insight into the nature of the human being and of humanity. It is a crucial factor in the social changes taking place today. Those in whom this perception has not yet emerged strive to hold on to the old forms of social structure, those who do see it demand something quite new in human relationships.

It was out of the earlier stages of this growing feeling for the equality of people – though then the equality of only some people – that the original impulse of democracy was born.

Democratic Government

Laws and regulations are established, in the first place, by the State. Within organizations, institutions, and smaller communities other forms of "law" are arrived at such as rules, customs, conventions, traditions, standards of social behavior, and mutual agreements.

The State has to bring order into social life where that order cannot be arrived at through people's normal individual moral behavior, self-discipline, or religious beliefs. It has to counter the egoism of the individual where that egoism would be detrimental to the rights and interests of others. For example, in questions such as health and hygiene in the work place, or the commercial handling of food, the interests of the public must be protected from the egoism of the producer. The necessary laws must be enacted to ensure the agreed-upon standards are maintained.

Laws must apply to all people equally. If there are exceptions, such as the police or fire engine going through the red traffic light, it is because everyone recognizes and accepts that this is necessary and for the benefit of the community, not the individual driver.

At present a country calls itself democratic if its government is chosen through a free and fair election, in which anyone wishing to stand for election is able do so. In such an election it is recognized that each adult member of the community has an equal right to a vote. Each vote carries equal weight in determining which candidate has received the greatest number of votes and is elected. The government so elected is considered to be democratic, and it then governs on the basis of the promises upon which it was elected.

At this point the important question arises: in its legislative capacity, is the government elected to make the laws it thinks are best for the country, or those that it senses are what the people themselves feel to be right? Do we elect those people amongst us who, because of their greater wisdom, we choose to rule over us, to decide what is good for us, and what is right behavior, or should we elect those who can sense the feelings and the will of the people as to what is moral, right, and just, and who formulate the laws accordingly?

Increasingly today and into the future, the only justifiable basis for any law will be that it is grounded in what people generally feel to be right and just. In a community of free people, the people themselves can be the only authority as to the laws that will form the structure of their social living in community. The task of the government must be to listen to what the community itself feels is right and, where necessary, to form the laws accordingly. Laws created on this basis will receive respect and support even by a minority who do not feel the same.

There are, of course, serious and distorting factors that too often play into the forming of law, usually in the form of the influence coming from the many and varied interest groups within the community. These range from powerful business and financial interests, pressure groups such as trade unions, manufacturer's organizations, and churches, to the political and financial interests of the politicians themselves. The usurping of the power to affect the making of law by such interests is greatly facilitated where members of government are seen, or see themselves, as appointed to rule rather than to enact into law what the people themselves feel to be right. When this happens, the idea that the work of government is an expression of the will of the people becomes a charade and cannot be considered truly democratic.

*

Let me give a simple illustration of the working of law from my experience as a member of a village Parish Council. On one occasion a question came before the council as to whether to recommend that a license, that is permission, be given to the new owners of a shop that would allow them to sell alcoholic drinks. This shop was just outside the local elementary school. After some discussion, the basic question was considered to be: "What sort of community environment does the local population want for their children? Do they want the sort of community where alcohol is sold just outside the elementary school, or do they want their children protected from the kind of environment that accompanies the sale of alcohol?"

It was not expressed directly, but there was the feeling that the council's responsibility was to come to a decision based on what was sensed as the will, the common feeling, of the local community. Of course there would probably be people who felt otherwise, but the council had to go by what the majority of people felt, though always taking into account the feelings or opinions of those others. In this, the opinion of every person in the community was equally valid. Extra weight was not to be given to individuals on the basis of their wealth, professional expertise, religion, or intellectual ability. If expert opinion was sought, such as that of the teachers of the school, this was only because it was sensed that the community itself would consider it necessary to do so.

It was interesting that when someone raised the point that giving the license would affect another shop already selling alcoholic drinks, this was put aside as not being the concern of the parish council, rather it was something that had to be worked out in the course of trade. Both these decisions showed an interesting and healthy understanding of the true task of the rights sector.

The common or majority opinion will not always arrive at the best or wisest decision, and to follow it will not always be in the best ultimate interests of the community itself. There are occasions when what people generally feel about something has to be tempered by wise thinking. That can only be done by individuals with the necessary background knowledge and the ability to think it through. While what is felt in the common opinion to be right must always be the foundation of law, those elected to govern, to legislate, must be elected not only for their sensitivity to this common opinion but also for their capacities to bring informed thinking to it. But they must always do this within the acceptable range of what the public feels to be right. This can only happen in a healthy way when those responsible for such decisions are not at the same time also responsible for, or in a position to influence, matters belonging properly to either the cultural or economic sectors.

The Creation of Boundaries to Economic Activity

If social life is, according to its own nature, to be separated into its three sectors then certain boundaries between them must be established. The rights sector will have an important role to play in the setting and maintaining of these boundaries.

Let us look at a simple but illustrative example. Imagine a simple village community in an area where there are many trees. The people need wood for their fires, and there are a number of woodcutters whose work it is to supply the wood. Economically, the most efficient way to produce the wood is to cut the trees nearest to where the wood is wanted. To do anything else would increase the work of production and so make the wood more expensive for those who need it. But this will have the effect of denuding the environment of the village of trees, something we will assume the village community does not want. This is not a problem the woodcutters themselves can solve. Even if some of them have the moral strength to leave the trees in the vicinity of the village, there will be others who will take the economic advantage of cutting just these down. That is a fact of human nature.

Clearly the village community must have a say as to what trees are cut down. In their need for wood they have to find a balance between what they will have to pay for it and their wish to preserve the environment. Here, the rights organization of the village, after consultations with the woodcutters as to the effect of any prohibitions, must lay down rules as to what trees may be cut. In this, their decision must be a reflection of what is felt and wanted by the community. The woodcutters, within the bounds set for them by the community, can then do their work freely and efficiently.

This is a simple but effective illustration of the divide between the economic and rights realms, and of the different tasks of each. What will also be clear is that if the woodcutters are in a position to influence those who make the rules, or if those in the rights life whose work it is to make the rules, have any personal interest in the economic life of the community, then the community will suffer the consequences. The whole will work effectively as a unity and to the advantage of the community as a whole only so long as the parts are kept quite separate and are able to work independently.

At the level of the village it is easy to see the need to separate the economic from the rights spheres of activity, and it is not too difficult to imagine this being achieved. But we must be able to expand our imaginative faculty so that what we see as true for a village community we also see as true for the wider society of the country as a whole, or even of the world. But it is not so easy to see this at the level of government, which at present we tend to think of as carrying responsibility for all aspects of social life, not just the legal and rights element.

The organs of the rights sector must be given the task of establishing the necessary constraints on the economic sector by placing limits to its activities beyond which it must not go. These constraints should include:

- strict control of access to, and use of, natural resources
- the disposal of waste and emissions into the environment, including noise
- any other such matters adversely affecting the community

Government as we know it cannot do this while it is also responsible for the economic welfare of the community, particularly when it expects to be re-elected based on its economic performance.

Similarly, the rights sector must provide the necessary safeguards for the freedom of the individual within cultural life. The right of each and all to follow the religion of their choice, to come to their own beliefs, and to hold their own opinions must be established and protected. This must extend to the right of all parents to the education of their choice for their children free from any influence or manipulation from economic or political interests.

*

There is already a widespread understanding of the need to prevent outside personal interests, whether economic, financial, or cultural, from interfering with political decisions. But while those in government are given responsibilities for the whole of social life, including economic and cultural matters, such interests will always find ways to influence decisions. Decisions will be based on what the leaders think is culturally or economically right and good for the people. In such conditions, law will not be founded solely as an outcome of the will of the people. This can only be achieved when the three sectors of society are separated out and work within their own spheres as independent bodies.

The Separated Rights Sector

It is not easy to put aside the present almost universally held concept of government as it exists and imagine three quite separate and distinct spheres of activity, *one* of which carries responsibility for all that which I have pointed to as coming properly under the term of "rights life," and for that alone. Government as we know it would cease to exist.

If the cultural and economic sectors, with all that they include, are to be fully separated off and government is to have no involvement in them except in providing the boundaries and safeguards as described above, then a very large part of what government deals with at present will have to be removed from its control. It will have as its central task no more than the creation of the legal and regulatory structure of society according to the expressed will of that society. That suggests a fundamentally different idea of government than the one we are used to, one with a much more narrow function. In fact, the word "government" would no longer be appropriate.

What remained as an elected democratic body would have no responsibility for, or direct involvement in, any of the other spheres of activity that at present come within the presumed mission of government, except in so far as they have to be supported, circumscribed, or enforced by law. These spheres include, for example, education, science, health, the economy, and finance.

For many people this may seem far too radical and therefore impossible to accept. But it is the nature of social life itself and the needs of present day humanity that call for this separation of the three sectors. It is a natural continuation of the evolution of humanity and human society as I tried to portray it, very briefly, in Chapter Five.

None of this, of course, could happen overnight. But without first building an imaginative picture of the social structure towards which all the facts of social life and our present human nature point us, and towards which we can strive, we will never get even close to creating a healthy, free, and just society.

At present, we expect our elected leaders not only to have expertise in matters of law, in those areas where everyone's opinion is of equal value, but also in areas where very different specialized knowledge is required such as in finance and economics, education, science, health, and nutrition.

Can we really be surprised if such elected people make decisions, for example, in educational matters, on the basis of what is good for the economy, or if they see children as all needing the same education? Again, will they not sometimes confuse what is needed for the production of healthy food with what is best for the economy?

In order to do their work properly, those responsible for the making of law based on a sensing of what lives in the community as common opinion need to cultivate the necessary capacities within themselves to perceive all people as being equal, taking no account of all that differentiates them as individuals. But these capacities are just those that must be excluded from any decision making in the sphere of the human soul, that is, in cultural life, which must work from the basis that all people are different, unique, and individual. Competence in the one, by its nature, excludes competence in the other.

In the same way, those with the necessary abilities to make competent decisions concerning the economic process of production and distribution will not, because of those abilities, be similarly competent to establish laws and regulations according to the will of the people.

Surely, if we come to see all this, the idea of separating out the three areas of social activity will begin to make sense. The time when it may have been right for a single supreme authority, divinely appointed or not, to be expected to have competence in all these different areas has passed. Something quite new must come about; the structure of human society needs to find forms that are appropriate for today and into the future, not ones suited to the theocratic societies of the past.

*

It will not be easy to let go of the idea of a safe and entrenched existing form, of a central government that plays the role of a sort of paternalistic figure who dispenses wise control, authority, and security, and to think of replacing this with something lacking any central authority.

But what is put forward here is not something thought up as a possible solution to present social problems. It is what arises out of an observation of social life itself. It is what anyone will come to see who is able to take a completely fresh objective look at social life in its totality, having first put aside all preconceptions and existing assumptions.

Chapter 7
Rights, Morality, and Law

In its essence, law arises, or should arise, out of the sense or feeling in people for what is moral, fair, and right. In the depths of every human soul there is an inborn tendency, a predisposition to live and act out of what is morally good. Passions such as greed, envy, pride, egoism, and all that lead towards the anti-social and base impulses and emotions in the human being, if allowed free reign, will overlay and repress that which is the true and inherent nature of the soul. It is, or should rightfully be, out of this common feeling in people for the moral, for what is right and just, that law is founded. But since people and organizations who have particular interests are too often in positions to influence the making of the law for their own benefit, the law comes to be distorted. If, as put forward in this book, a strict separation of the rights sphere from those of cultural life and economic production were established, it would be much harder for such individual interests to manipulate the law for their own benefit.

The law that prohibits criminal or anti-social activities can rightly be none other than that which is found within the depths of human souls as moral feeling transformed into an outer framework, thus imposing moral behavior from without and overriding the weaknesses and passions that are also there in every human being, but particularly in those who have not overcome them through their own self-discipline.

The strength of democracy is that, within its proper sphere of activity, and on the principle that every person's opinion is of equal value, it can arrive at an ordering of society that is a reflection of the moral impulses of the members themselves. It is important for the future that democracy be given full responsibility for those areas of social life concerned with the making of laws, regulations, and administration; that is, those areas where every person's opinion is of equal value. It must be excluded from all those areas where individual judgment and expertise must be the deciding factors.

What are Rights?

In recent times "rights" have come to play an increasingly important role in the life of each of us and in society. In Chapter Five, I tried to give some idea of how this feeling for human rights arose alongside and as a consequence of the emerging of the consciousness of the individual human being out of that of the group, family, or people based on blood ties. But what is a "right" and who gives it? Is it God, the state, or an individual's conscience?

In very early times there was no, or only minimal, recognition or consciousness of individual rights. The interests of the single person were subordinate to the needs and continuity of the family or group. This can, perhaps, be seen most clearly in the soldier who did not have a separate right to life as an individual. His life was valued only in so far as he was a member of the group; it could be, and often was, sacrificed in the defense or interests of the group. The same applies in such matters as marriage and place of work; these were to a large extent determined according to the needs of the group. There were no individual human rights. Today, all people are seen to have rights, even soldiers.

Take, for example, a phrase we hear in relation to children in underdeveloped countries: "every child has a right to education." It is, of course, a sentiment that almost any person would agree with. But at this stage is it anything more than a feeling or sentiment? We might think and say that a child has such a right, but if there is no school or teacher, what does it mean to say the child has a right to education? If the child has such a right, then who gives him or her this right that cannot be fulfilled? Whose responsibility is it to provide what the child has a right to? These are all valid questions, but still we feel that we cannot deny the right of the child to education.

This helps to illustrate the nature of "rights." The feeling for what is a right is something that wells up within a person, it has its roots in conscience, and arises when a person comes to a recognition of the innermost nature of the other human being, of the universally-human in every individual, of that which is equal in all people irrespective of all that is different in or separates them. That which in earliest humanity was experienced as coming from above, from God, and brought down through the prophets or high priests as divine commandment, is now experienced as coming from within human beings themselves.

Now, instead of the divine commandment from God above, we have the voice from within each person and the democratic State. Ideally, this State attempts to build a structure of laws and regulations that are an outer reflection of what is experienced within as a sense of "right." But this can only ever be an inadequate imitation.

There is much today that is increasingly felt as "right," but which has not yet come to expression in law. In later chapters I will come to a number of questions relating to "ownership" and "wages" where I will try to show that important parts of our legal structure still have much in them that are a continuation of what was right for the ancient theocratic societies, but which today do not reflect what is felt by people as right. I will show much that would be very different if our structure of laws were truly a reflection of what people today feel, and will increasingly feel in the future, to be morally right and just.

The Written Law

However law is arrived at, it finally comes to be written down, and it is as it is written that it must be observed. But in its written form it takes on certain properties that can be used to give it an interpretation that was never intended by its original drafters.

Any small group of people working or living together will establish some kind of guidelines or rules to ensure the smooth running of their community and to give form to the social relationships within it. It might well be that these are agreed on at a meeting of all those involved. If the group is small and closely knit, it might also be felt unnecessary to write these down.

Later, as the group becomes established, and particularly if and when new people join, such agreed upon rules will come to be written down, but at this stage that which is written will be treated as a record or memorandum of the discussion and the decisions made.

It is important to see that the written notes or minutes of the meeting are, at this early stage, felt to be not the rule itself but a memorandum of an agreement establishing the rule. The way the members of the community enforce the rule and relate to each other within the community will to a great extent be determined by the way they experience this written form of the rule. In the sphere of rights, of law, and human relationships, people are, in the main, guided by their feelings rather than their thinking.

When, at this earlier stage in the life of the community, there is a dispute, what is written will often be felt to be a guideline, not an absolute that must be obeyed. The group will base the resolution of the dispute not on the written rule, but in taking what was written as a reminder of the factors that led to the agreement of the rule, and they will see how these factors pertain to the present situation. They will apply all of this within the present circumstances and to the personalities involved and so come to a decision based on these present factors. At this level, however the dispute is resolved, it remains at a human level, even if this expresses itself as bad feelings between people.

As the group expands and becomes more established, as it becomes "institutionalized," it will come to be more difficult for it to work in this way, though it will seldom be impossible. When it gets to the size where the members of the community cannot all know each other, or where they do not find it possible for each to hold a picture of the whole in their consciousness, it will have reached a stage when it becomes necessary for rules to be decided by a smaller group, perhaps elected by and acting as representatives of the whole. These rules, decided by this smaller committee, will have to be written down. What is written will now come to be seen as itself the rule, not a memorandum of an agreement.

This is a very crucial threshold. It is now that the written word itself becomes the law, and the law becomes rigid and insensitive. When there is a dispute sometime in the future, it is the written law that must be studied to determine the offense. The law then lies there in the particular words used and in the meanings of those words, not in the intentions of those who drafted the law.

In human encounters it should always be possible to find some sort of understanding, compromise, or flexibility, even if it is only a recognition of the inability of a particular person to understand the situation and be flexible. That is human. But between people and the law as the written word there can be no human understanding or flexibility. What is written is absolute. One can only try to find ways of interpreting the words in a different way, or find some meaning in the words that was perhaps not intended by those who formed the law. In this way one gets around the law.

In the human soul the written law is experienced in sharp contrast to what was, in ancient times, experienced as the divine commandment emanating from an all-caring creator.

*

Let me illustrate this with a very simple picture. Imagine that a group arranges each month for a visiting lecturer to talk to them on some aspect of common interest. The timing of the lecture means that it follows immediately after the coffee break. As a result, many members bring their coffee mugs with them into the lecture. This disturbs others, and many complain.

The problem is discussed within the community and it is agreed that coffee mugs should not be brought into the lecture room. If, subsequently, someone does bring a mug into the room, that person would then be reminded of the previous agreement. It would be an unusually difficult person who would quarrel about this and continue to act in an anti-social way. If, instead of coffee, the mug wrongfully carried into the lecture room contained tea, a person would not typically argue the point, as it was the bringing of drinks into the lecture hall that was clearly the source of the problem and the subsequent agreement, not only coffee.

But when such a problem arises in a larger or more established community or institution, it can work out rather differently. The rule will be established by a committee who will put it into written form, and as such it will be posted according to the usual procedure for such rules. We will assume that they do this quite simply by wording the rule as "coffee mugs must not be brought into the lecture room while a lecture is being given."

The rule as written has a very exact meaning. A person breaks the rule only when he brings a "coffee mug" into the "lecture room" "while a lecture is being given." He can argue that he is not breaking the rule if he brings a tea cup with coffee in it, or brings the mug of coffee in before the lecture starts, or if for some reason the lecture is given not in the lecture room but in the hall.

In any community or organization there is always the inclination to write rules down. Indeed, this must be done at a certain point. But it follows that the *written word* itself becomes the rule, or law, not the *original agreement* that was present and understood by those for whom the written word was merely a memorandum or reminder. For the individual who feels estranged from the process through which the rule came about, the intention or moral objective behind the rule will not be compelling. The rule, or law, exists then only within the possible meanings of the words in which it is framed. Because of this, it is to some degree inevitable that people will be inclined to interpret the law in a way that furthers their own interests.

In a small community it may never come to this, but in a wider community such as that of a large business or institution, and more particularly within the legal system of a country, this can be a normal attitude toward the law.

In such a written law, a person can come to feel that he is caught up in something from which all human intention, understanding, or compassion has been removed, something that has become dead, mechanical, and inhuman.

What is this inhuman character of the law?

The Inhuman Nature of Law

In every human being, often hidden in the innermost depths of their soul, there is a desire to know and conduct life on moral principles. Whether it is discernible in their actions and behavior or whether it is submerged by the passions, problems, worries, and obstacles that too often outweigh the good, it is nevertheless there in every human soul. It rises out of that which is the essentially human in a person, that wherein all people are equal. Though not the same, it is deeply connected to, and is a foundation for, "conscience."

Although this living impulse toward the good touches upon what is highest in each human being, that which is created as an outer structure of laws by the State becomes a dead, inhuman image of the same.

In acknowledging and treating people as equal, as we must do in the rights sphere of social life, we also, by that deed, deny their individuality. This denial can be experienced as an attack on one's own separate identity, on one's individuality.

The policeman, the tax inspector, and the immigration officer are all servants of the State. If they are to fulfill their role properly in society they have to apply the law equally to all people. To do this, they must be able to put aside all that identifies each individual as different from others. They must make themselves blind to the color, gender, or different virtues and abilities of people, to their ethnic origins and religious beliefs. They must not, for example, apply the law in one way to people to whom they feel sympathy, and in another way to those to whom they feel antipathy, or who are different from themselves.

This is not always easy; it can be experienced as dehumanizing, both by the one who has to apply the law and by the one to whom it must be applied. Anyone who has been caught up on the wrong side of the law will know this out of direct experience. This feeling of the inhumanity of the law is dimly experienced by very many people and explains much of the antipathy felt towards the State or the government.

It is only the individual human being administering the law who can give it a human touch, a human face; the law itself has no "human face." But to do this, a person must decide when to apply the law and when not to, and even be prepared to go beyond the law. But this, for obvious reasons, can be a dangerous practice and is not normally acceptable.

*

Here again we can see the importance of separating those aspects of social life belonging to the rights sector from those belonging to the cultural and economic sectors. This is just as important in organizations or smaller communities as it is in society as a whole. Individualism and people's different abilities can contribute to division in the community, can lead to feelings of isolation and dejection. While some are clever, skilled, or clear thinkers and so can do important work, others do not have those abilities and can feel unimportant or of less consequence. Only where there is, alongside that which divides people from each other, something else that reunites them in the essential equality of all people, that recognizes each as a full member of the community, can that which is divided be brought together again into a unity.

So too, that which is dehumanizing in the legal process and which denies what is individual and unique in a person, can be overcome when there is, alongside the rights sector, a strong and active cultural life in which what is unique and individual in each person is recognized and acknowledged by the community.

Conscience and Law

There are times when opposition arises between, on the one side, the law and those whose task it is to uphold it, and on the other, those who are prompted to act in opposition to the law by the voice of their conscience.

A government does at times have to make controversial decisions. It might, for example, have to make a decision that will have consequences for the environment and which, though supported by the great majority of the population, is strongly opposed by a minority. This opposition may come from a deep moral sense of what is right. It may be so deeply felt that individuals are prepared to endure considerable hardship and suffering in order to stand up for what they see as right, good, and moral. Can we really say that they are wrong and must conform to the will of the majority?

In such situations it is often not possible to be sure that one side is right and the other wrong. In a certain sense both can be right – two opposing opinions. It raises the question as to the validity of law based on the majority opinion. Who is to say what is moral and what is not? Is one person to be bound by that which others decide is moral or immoral just because they are the majority?

But can the minority, however strongly they feel the moral rightness of their opinion, but who have no other way of convincing others, ever be justified in turning to violence to achieve their aims?

In earlier times when it was accepted that the law emanated from God there could be no questioning of it. But today we do not hear the voice of God; we each only hear, more or less strongly, the voice of our own individual conscience, our own feeling for what is right.

Outside, there is the law, rigid and inflexible, established, in the best of circumstances, by the government on the basis of the opinion of the majority. Against this, there is a person's own inner sense for what is right and just, a conscience that impels him or her to act accordingly.

By its nature, the law cannot be flexible. To make exceptions and to judge who should be excepted would require an authority from outside the rights sector. Such an authority would need to utilize capacities of discernment that have no place in rights life, where one must deal solely with what is equal in all people.

Nevertheless, there is sometimes a feeling in the community that a person is right to stand up for what he or she believes, to oppose the will of the majority, that one must not always give way to the judgment of equals. There must be occasions when it is right for people to act on the basis of their conscience when this speaks strongly within them. Many people do sense that the moral and social development of the community is strengthened when there are people who, out of the courage of their convictions, stand up against authority. A community in which everyone conformed to the law without question, where there were no rebels, would be one without life and without development.

*

When we see the contrast between the implacable and dehumanizing nature of the written law and the human and adaptable moral law, the law of our soul and spiritual nature, something of the character of rights life becomes apparent. We no longer hear the voice of God nor that of any other universal authority that proclaims a moral law from outside the individual – certainly not one recognized and accepted by all people. So now we have no alternative to the "law of the State," however inadequate that is, except chaos.

Chapter 8

Cultural Life –
The Needs of the Soul

Is the human being there to serve the economy, or is the economy there to provide for the needs of the human being? In the social thinking of today, much seems to presuppose that people are there to serve the economy, both as workers and as consumers. There is a strong assumption that the economy is a given reality with a life of its own, and human beings have to find their place in it if they are to live and have what they need. If asked, most people would agree that *human beings* are primary and that the economy should be serving *them,* not the other way around. But, despite what we may come to when we do think about it, at present we tend to act as though the opposite is the reality.

*

In every human soul, often buried deep, there are questions concerning life. I became aware of this many years ago in discussions with people I regularly met through my work in the motor trade. These were mainly people in their late twenties or thirties. I came to see that most of them, when they were younger, had questions concerning the meaning and purpose of life. But they had found no answers to their questions, not in their education, not through science, nor in what religion had to offer: no answers that spoke truly to the questions arising out of their own inner depths. So they had come to forget their questions, and they took from life what they could. Deep down in the slumbering depths of their souls, however, it was apparent that these unanswered questions were still present. They kept a sense, however dim and neglected, that there must be some larger purpose to life beyond just working for money and enjoying what it buys.

The youth of today are on the same path, but with even deeper and more urgent questions. The ongoing failure to resolve or even to address these questions, together with the inability to fulfill the impulses welling up from within their souls, comes to expression in many different ways; from the intense striving for personal wealth and power characteristic of today, to the various forms of vandalism and delinquency that are often the result of an authentic but distorted aspiration towards creativity, self-discovery, and artistic expression.

In the fifties and early sixties of the last century, just after the Second World War, one could experience in some men who had been involved in the fighting, an unexpected nostalgia for their time in the armed services. I met a number of men who had been engaged behind enemy lines in North Africa and in other dangerous activities. It was not the violence of war that they fondly recalled, quite the contrary, but that during the war they had striven, and often suffered, for something greater. Rightly or wrongly, they had a feeling that there was an ideal behind what they had then been doing, behind the risks and dangers they faced. That ideal – country, family, justice, Christian values – whatever it was, was something greater than themselves and something worth fighting for.

Are there ideals worth striving for today? Where can a young person find them?

*

Religion today seems to have lost its way, and ever greater numbers of people in the modern world have ceased to find any real inspiration in it. Yet it is still possible and not uncommon, if we are able to look out at the majesty of nature, beholding the immense power and beauty and mysterious complexity that is on display there, to stand before it in a state not unlike wonder and holy awe.

If we place over against this the concepts and ideas taught by the established church of the nature of God the Creator and of Jesus Christ, then we feel a great chasm; it is not possible to reconcile the one with the other. It is almost impossible for a thinking human being to unite the mental picture of the Creator given by the church with that of the creation that we see all around us. Today, if one is to embrace what is taught in almost any religion, one must put aside all that can be directly known of the experienced world and accept, by way of a kind of blind belief, what has come over from the past. Objective observation of life and the power of thought must be set aside. But what we are expected to believe gives little, if any, inner spiritual nourishment to the human soul which must thereby feel deprived of truth and reason.

In contrast to this, the idea that the human being is something not very different from a supercomputer in need of programming is now taking an increasing hold in life. Where religions have been unable to move out of the past, out of old teachings that were given when the human being had a very different consciousness and social environment, scientific thinking has been unable to reach beyond an image of the human being that may provide great factual knowledge as to our physical make-up, but is quite unable to give any convincing answer to the deeper questions arising within our souls regarding the true nature of our being.

*

We are unceasingly bombarded with the thought that there is nothing more to a human being than what arises out of our bodily nature; that we are the product of, and determined solely by, a random mix of inherited DNA. This picture is constantly impressed upon us by the media, by commercial advertising, and in the science, nature, and educational programs on television. One senses it behind much of government thinking, particularly in the forming of policies for health, medicine, and agriculture. It can even be found as the basis for some of today's religious thinking.

This perception of the human being increasingly forms the foundation of much of the teaching in our educational institutions

– our schools, colleges, and universities. Though individual teachers may sense or believe – and there are many who do – that there is something more to the human being than this, too often they are unable to work out of what they sense as the true reality. Teachers are often overshadowed, and imposed upon, by the beliefs inherent in the educational system in which they work, including its concept of the human being. Often this is a result of government and political interference in education.

Today's prevalent explanation of the human being is a cold and lifeless one that does little or nothing to inspire us to strive for greater things, or to improve ourselves. It does not touch our deeper questions and inner impulses. It does not fit into our own experience of life, nor ring true to our sense of ourselves as living, feeling, and thinking beings.

*

In life today, particularly in the developed countries, great emphasis is placed on the economic and financial aspects of life. For many people, the essence and purpose of life comes down to not much more than working for money and hoping to enjoy what it can buy. There is an assumption that in order to live a full and successful life it is enough for a person to earn or acquire sufficient money, not only to obtain all that we need and want, but to also give us, in our own and other people's eyes, confirmation of our standing and importance as successful human beings.

In earlier ages, and even into comparatively recent times, much greater resources were put into serving the life of soul. Religion and the ideals of courage, truthfulness, goodness, and humility were dominant factors and penetrated into all aspects of a person's life. Today the pendulum has swung far to the opposite side. A person's soul life is seen as of little importance outside of himself.

Working for a more affluent lifestyle, owning a bigger and better house and car, and perhaps even something like a yacht, is seen by the great majority as being what life is about, the ultimate mark of achievement. Giving children the ability to earn money once they have grown up is seen as the principal purpose of education today. Having the qualifications and skills to fetch a high price in the job market is a widely aspired-to goal in education and in life.

The pressures influencing the human soul from outside are enormous today. The need of all the many and diverse organizations, interests, and businesses to "do business," to "sell" their products or services, exerts great pressure on people to want something other than what they would out of their own inner nature. The soul is bombarded with advertisements of great ingenuity, persuading and conditioning it to desire or value what the commercial world wants it to buy. But there is little or no concern with the wider effects on the soul of those so influenced. From all sides, the human soul is attacked for purposes other than its own, but where is the concern for the development of the soul for its own sake?

We are taught to fear the future by the insurance and pension companies: the qualities of courage and confidence are undermined by their need to do business.

Is our society so empty of that which serves the needs of the soul that very many people can find little more in life than the fulfillment of their sexual urges, and are content with a life largely spent in front of a television watching sports, sitcoms, and game shows?

*

Because science appears to explain everything about the human being through extensive, painstaking, and detailed research into the human body and particularly into the mechanism and function of the DNA, many have come to believe that this proves there is no non-physical aspect of a living human being. But it does not in any way prove this. It shows no more than that we are coming ever closer to knowing the intricacies of how the human physical body works in its physical function and make-up. To say that this indicates that there is nothing more than this physical body is no more valid than to maintain that, because one can find in the mechanism of the automobile everything to explain the intricacies of its controls and its movement from one place to another, there is therefore no human being whose will to go to that particular place is what actually moves and steers it and whose needs brought the car into existence in the first place. The car presupposes the human being, but this reality cannot be found in even the most exhaustive study of the mechanics of the car itself.

A person has an existence that is separate and independent of the car, but when we are in the car our movements are restricted by what the car can actually do. An engineer can alter the car so that it can go faster or he can put a limit to the possible speed. This will mechanically condition the driver's existence while in the car, but it will not change who or what the driver is, nor make the driver one with the car.

Might not the physical body be a sort of vehicle for the human "ego" or "soul" – a soul that is not subject to the laws of this physical world but that needs the physical body in order to be and act in the physical world?

Whatever we may think is the actual reality, the *experience* felt by almost all people is that the "soul" is a reality. Even if this soul experience is thought of as emanating from the physical body, it is experienced as distinct from it. A simple expression of this is when a person says "I" or "my body." In our soul, we reach beyond the confines and restrictions of the body. We can feel for another, sense the pain, joy, or interest of another within our own soul. We can be disabled or develop illness in our physical body but remain strong and healthy in soul, just as we can become sick in soul but remain healthy in body.

It is in our soul that we carry our longings, intentions, and impulses, as well as our feelings, thoughts, and imaginations. It is from the unconscious depths of our soul that our individual needs, our particular impulses and longings arise. It is there that each human being is different, unique, and individual. Each person strives for the freedom to bring to expression that which arises out of his or her own soul, that which makes each of us utterly unique. The artist, actor, teacher, scientist, explorer, politician, architect, doctor, and entrepreneur all find fulfillment in their lives to the extent that in their work they can bring to expression what they experience as a need of their own soul. Even an athlete or football player does so because, in the striving for perfection of the physical bodily performance, he or she finds the soul satisfaction of achievement and individual identity. Ultimately, it is only in realizing the deeper impulses of one's own soul that one is able to go beyond immediate pleasures to achieve that inner sense of fulfillment that brings an inner and lasting joy to life.

There is, in fact, much in life which can only be explained by something *other* than the laws of natural science, by something which appears to be of a supersensible nature: that is, a nature that cannot be explained through what can be perceived through the ordinary senses. This should not be confused with what today frequently goes under the name of religion or "spirit," and which is so often in conflict with clear and objective observation of life and which at best can claim to be nothing other than a belief.

*

It is not intended here to go deeply into the argument as to whether or not there is a God, or some other kind of supersensible existence, will, or intelligence, other than to point out that it cannot be stated as a fact that there is no God, no supersensible or spiritual reality. Nobody has ever proved that there is no God. It might be genuinely held that there is no God, but that is a belief, it is not a known fact.

To anyone able to objectively view their own experiences, and also those of others, there is much in everyday life that will admit to no other explanation than one of a supersensible nature. But for a person to come to this view requires a mind that is open to the *possibility* of the existence of a life other than the one we all know: bounded by birth and death, confined to physical space and time, and only perceptible to the ordinary senses. Anyone who can maintain an unbiased observation of life and an openness to consider new thoughts and ideas in the light of what is observed will come to real questions as to the possibility of a reality beyond the purely material world.

This possibility is given added weight when we look into a phenomenon that has grown quite recently out of human sensitivities, particularly during the last century. This is the idea or feeling of the equality of all people. I have already looked at this from the aspect of law and democracy, but there is another aspect of this phenomenon which can throw light on the question discussed here.

The sense of the equality of all people has taken powerful hold of large sections of humanity. But what is it that arouses this feeling that human beings are equal? We can look at two people who are clearly very different. We can look at everything that is different in them: the difference of sex, color, physique, intelligence, abilities, moral qualities, beliefs, and cultural background. In all this we cannot say they are equal, to do so just does not make sense. In their bodily build and make up they are different, and in their soul qualities they are each unique and different. So in what way are they equal? It cannot be in their physical body, nor in their soul – in both they are clearly different, not equal. If this feeling or perception that human beings are equal has reality behind it, then there must be something else in the human being that is perceived, or sensed, other than body and soul. It can only be something that is universally present in every human being, part of each person's make-up but beyond that which differentiates them. Could it be that people are actually coming to a perception of *spirit*, or of a divine nature, that is equally present in every human being?

*

These questions are experienced, in different ways, by most people. It is not my purpose here to attempt answers, but to point to the fact that the questions do exist and that there is a real need to strive towards finding answers. This is central to the task of all those whose work lies in the cultural sector of human social life, most particularly those involved in the education of the younger generation. It will not be possible to develop the insights, the imaginative and conceptual faculties, and the moral strength needed for the future of humanity until the cultural sphere of society becomes truly healthy and strong. But so long as the cultural sphere of society continues to be dominated, influenced, or controlled by either economic interests or those whose work lies in the sphere of the State, it will fail to meet the soul needs of humanity.

Deep in the soul of each human being there is something that strives to come to expression, something that is of the essence of our own being, something that cannot be explained as simply arising out of the physical body. If people were to bring to an active observation of life an objectivity free from any preconceptions and personal inclinations, they would see this. But there seems often to be a fear of finding something that cannot be explained through the ordinary laws of the material world. It is a constant source of amazement to observe how people, even those claiming scientific objectivity, will ignore certain obvious facts in life, pass them by as though they did not exist, convincing themselves that there must be some ordinary material scientific explanation. Is this because they see in them a threat to their particular field of knowledge?

From the depths of the soul comes a certain wisdom, an inherent knowledge of one's own life's path and work. This unconscious wisdom, if listened to, will guide us through our life's tasks, often leading us to our next step and revealing the nature of that which has to be dealt with or overcome. It gives to each of us a certain authority in the performance of our work so long as it is work according to our own individual soul destiny.

Something of this can be seen quite clearly if we pay objective and careful attention to the biographies of people. It is more easily seen in the life stories of those who have, in one sphere or another, made their mark in life, but it is there in the life of every human being.

Listen to or read with deep and tender interest the biographies of people who have striven to achieve success in their field, particularly those who have had to struggle through opposition, poverty, prejudice, or other hindrances. Follow the story of their hopes, intentions and ambitions, their trials, sufferings and successes, and particularly what led them into their work or profession and drove them on. Whether one approves or not of what they did, is, for this exercise, unimportant and should be put aside. It is the striving individuals and what led them to do what they did that is important.

If one is able to do this quite objectively and with many different biographies, then it will become apparent that their lives were not a haphazard series of events, but that there was something like a particular driving force or intention that led them to do just what they did, some impulse deep in their souls that impelled them to follow a certain path and way of life. There are many instances where people have gone through considerable hardships and apparent sacrifice, even from early childhood, in their struggle to fulfill the urge they felt within themselves. This urge, like a driving force, led them on through life as they constantly sought to achieve their goal. In the lives of some people this is revealed very clearly, in others it is not so obvious. But when, out of real heartfelt interest, we take the time to talk and listen to people about their lives, we will come to know that something of this wise ordering of life that often seems to begin even at birth, is there in every human being.

We come to see a particularly clear expression of this if we look into our own biography, and are able to remember or develop a sense for what it was that led us to do what we did, or to take up the precise work that we chose. Or was there a yearning to do something other than what life forced on us? Is it not possible to observe something like a guiding thread that leads one on through life's journey?

What is this that steers one person into a particular way of life or profession and another into something quite different? What directs one to the practice of law, another to playing the violin, and still another to charity work caring for the homeless? What is it that conducts each, not only into that work, but into the way of life that their choice brings? The musician lives in the world of sound, spending hours each day playing the piano, violin, or guitar. The lawyer lives in another world, a world of law, of litigation, of argument, and logic; the charity worker in yet another. If we listen to two musicians talking to each other about their work, and then two lawyers, and then again two charity workers, we will become aware of three quite different ways and qualities of life, three different worlds of experience. We may also come to see that only through doing their best in their chosen fields can each find real fulfillment in their lives.

Many people are unable to find a place or profession in life where they can bring to expression what lives in them as a life impulse. But that does not mean such inner yearnings do not exist. For some, these yearnings may not be apparent, but they are there, buried deep. And because they are there, unfulfilled, there arises frustration, discontent, and even resentment and anger with life and the community. Too often, the education a person received as a child has failed to bring to life, or has even actually suppressed, what would have later ripened into a life's work.

People will achieve a fulfilling and satisfactory life only when they are able to find a place in the community through which to bring to expression, or work out of, the impulses arising from the depths of their own soul. Only a person in whom there exists the impulse and the need to work with music will have the possibility of growing into a truly creative musician. Only such a one can have the inborn talent to achieve real mastery of the art. And when such individuals are enabled by the society in which they live to create out of their own genius, then many in that society will find nourishment for their souls in the music thus created.

What is true of the musician will, in its own particular way, be true of all whose work is based on the creative capacities of the soul.

*

If we look at some of the leading thinkers, writers, politicians, and commentators of our time, we will very often see individualities who are unique in their personalities, in what they bring out of themselves, and in their aptitude for their particular work; so also the leaders of business, industry, and finance. There we can see clearly how those with a "sense for the market" or an "instinct for business" will be much in demand. Similarly, leading journalists and reporters "have a nose for the news" as well as, often, great courage and persistence in ferreting it out. Their education, so far as it fulfilled its proper purpose, enabled them to awaken to themselves, gave them the tools of their craft, even influenced their opinions and colored their thoughts. But behind all this it is always possible to find what is at the foundation of their being, that which gave purpose and direction to their thoughts and impulses, something uniquely of themselves that was there even before their education. This "something" will be seen as absolutely real, as a manifestation of what is sometimes called a person's "destiny."

When we come to observe this, then we will see something more. Not only does there exist in each human soul that which leads towards some particular goal, task, or interest, but alongside this there are also faculties, capacities, and talents, perhaps still undeveloped and latent, that can enable the fulfillment of that task. There are always those who, whether as writers, scientists, entrepreneurs, inventors, or doctors, are able to go further than others, to see that which has not yet been seen, even to perceive that which is not yet perceivable, to imagine that which is not yet imaginable. What actually are we referring to when we say that a person has a "sense for the market," an "instinct for business," or a "nose for the news"? What is genius? Behind these expressions lies the recognition of a particular intuitive capacity that is there but more or less dormant in most people, and active and perceptible in others.

All people have at least some such intuitive capacity, though perhaps what is intuited is not so clear and vivid. Very often we pay little attention to it or take no notice of it at all: we brush it aside as an aberration, perhaps fearful of the unexplainable or the derision of our friends.

If we look at all that can be produced by manufacture and industry, at all the inventions of machines and technology, the knowledge of substances with their particular properties, if we look at all that has been discovered, researched, and perfected in the fields of engineering, medicine, psychology, art, literature, and in all the other fields of human activity; if we then also take into our observations all that has been discovered through the courage and determination of explorers, whether into the far reaches of the

Earth or into space, we will see that all this and much more has been achieved by human genius. Money itself produced none of it; money cannot create genius – genius cannot be bought. Nothing beyond a shadow or pale copy of it can be achieved by employing and paying people for it. Only when money is used, not to buy, but to *free* that which is already there as impulse and talent in the human soul does anything worthwhile come into being.

It is not enough for people just to have work where they can earn their wages or salary. There is a purpose in life other than this. Strong in the human soul is the need to develop itself and its own powers; to develop courage, creativity, compassion, and love, and to accomplish the work that it feels as an impulse arising out of the depths of its own inner being. Only the attainment of what we aspire to from out of the depths of our soul, if we can uncover it, can make life something to be thankful for. To satisfy only the surface or transitory needs of the soul, such as those that arise out of our bodily nature, does not give anything of that deep and abiding sense of fulfillment that comes from working out of one's deeper life impulses.

*

If the cultural life of the community is truly to serve the human soul, it must be built on three pillars, the three pillars that can be referred to as science, art, and philosophy or religion. While the three sectors of social life have become hopelessly entangled and need to be separated out, these three pillars of cultural life have become estranged from one another and have grown into three quite independent branches of learning. They each tend to act in isolation, as though each is the only sure way to an understanding of life – of the human being and the world in which we live. But science, art, and religion or philosophy are all three striving after the same truths, and only the three working in harmony, each providing a view from a different direction, can hope to reach a true understanding of life and of what it is to be human.

Chapter 9
Cultural Life –
Its Work and Nature

As indicated earlier, by cultural life I mean that whole area of activity within society that serves, or arises out of, the "soul life" of people. At the core of cultural life are all forms of education, religion, art, and science. This includes organizations such as museums, art galleries, churches, theaters, and concert halls. Popular entertainment of all kinds, though often or largely driven by economic interests, does at times aim to fulfill certain soul needs as well, and to that extent falls within the sphere of cultural life. Activities such as research, architecture, and engineering also come within its orbit, but they too can serve other, usually economic, purposes.

The nature of the cultural sector, and of the work of all those active in it, is very different from that of either the economic or rights sectors. While in the economic sector people participate in what is, in reality, an activity of the outer world, and in rights life are involved in what is active between people within a community or group, the work of the cultural sector is concerned with that which is individual and unique in each human being.

In economic work, a person serves an outside purpose, joining with others to produce a product that will be used by other people. The work of the rights life fulfills a role determined by the community. Only in the work of the cultural sector can people fully and truly work out of the impulses and needs of their own soul.

Of the three, the cultural sphere of activity is today by far the least recognized and valued. The working of the economy, whether it is healthy and productive or weak and failing, is experienced by everyone very directly; for many it is seen as the very foundation of life. Countries are judged by the strength of their economy and their annual growth. When a person talks of a "developed," "developing," or "undeveloped" country, it is understood that they are referring to the state of its economy, not to any moral quality, educational achievements, or quality of social life that may have been developed.

People are also very conscious of the sphere of the State, of the establishment of laws, rules, and regulations and the extent to which these are reasonable, fair, and just. The government is seen as the central and ultimate authority on all matters of social life; as such, it is important to and affects everyone within the community. Even the important parts of what should be a separate and independent cultural life, such as education, are perceived as lying within the orbit of governmental responsibility.

Cultural life as a distinct and separate sector is hardly recognized.

Cultural Work

People have an inner need to work, to be active. The vast majority find no satisfaction in doing nothing. A person who is not active becomes a vegetable, dehumanized. Even if we have no need to earn money, we will still need to occupy ourselves with "work" of some kind, we cannot just do nothing; the soul demands creative activity of some kind.

For most people, however, there is also the need to earn money. This fact has a growing tendency to dominate people's thinking and has to a great extent masked the fact that they actually have an inner need to work. In many cases, particularly in the cultural sector, people would, out of their own inner necessity, do just the work they now think they are doing "for money." It is a sign of the weakness of our cultural life, and particularly of the inadequacy of our education, that so many people are not awake to their own inner needs. They do not know that, if only they had the imagination to see it and the strength to adapt themselves to the possibilities within the work, what they are doing "to earn money" could often be transformed into an activity that gives them great inner fulfillment and sense of achievement.

If, as an example of cultural activity, we again consider the work or profession of a teacher, we will come to see that most, particularly those that are good teachers, do actually teach out of an inner necessity that lies within themselves. Still, many tend to think in terms of teaching "to earn money," so they value their work according to what they are paid.

Teachers, too often, are given little freedom today – in most schools they are obliged to teach according to the methods and content laid down from on high. They are neither able nor motivated to awaken to what led them to teach in the first place, and to call on the wisdom, impulses, and capacities that they may find within themselves. The very things that would improve a teacher are not brought to life. They teach according to the methods they have been shown and often no more than that. Children do not then receive from their teacher, alongside the knowledge content of the lessons, the moral life impulses that are so sadly lacking today.

Freedom requires courage, both in those who grant it and in those who are given the freedom. Today in our social life there is too little courage. If teachers were given greater freedom and encouragement to teach out of what they awaken to within their own souls and to call on the wisdom and talents that come with this, the education of the coming generations would indeed be brought to life. Then teachers would know that they are teaching because it is their life's work, and would find in this work a love and sense of responsibility for the children and a deep satisfaction and fulfillment in life.

Something similar to this could be said about all those whose work lies in the cultural sector of society.

*

If cultural workers do not produce marketable products in the way that economic workers do, and so have no such products to sell, what are they paid for or how do they earn a salary? What is the nature of this salary? These questions will lead to a clearer perception of the different nature of each.

Motives and Payment for Work

Consider first, by way of example, the work of a poet and place this against what a person does in a factory working at a machine making some part of an electric light bulb. These are two extremes, but as such they accentuate certain differences.

The poet is someone who belongs essentially to cultural life. More than almost any other cultural worker, the poet can create poetry without any assistance from economic activity. The musician must first have an instrument, the painter needs canvas and paints before setting to work, but the poet can wander into the fields or the inner city and there bring to birth the poem solely from within. It may help to write it down, but even that is not essential to the process of creation. The poem does not exist within material substance as does, for example, a painting. Because of this it is not easily subjected to sale and purchase.

The poem is essentially an expression of an inner experience, feeling, or revelation. In any of us there can arise a strong need to give outer expression to something that we experience inwardly. The poet achieves this through poetry, the painter through color, and the musician through sound. We sometimes hear it said of a person that they are, for example, "a born poet," "a born teacher," or "a born architect." This implies that the individual spoken of is endowed with talents, capacities, or knowledge of a strength and quality that could only have come through birth. Here, in a common expression of our language, is the suggestion that there are people who do indeed bring something of their life's work through birth.

In the example of the poet we can see the basic nature of the work of anyone active in the cultural sector, whether they are artists, teachers, scientists, priests, or entertainers, though it is not always so obvious in some as it is in others.

The situation of a person in the economic sector who works at a machine making one part of an electric light bulb is quite different. The light bulb is purely utilitarian – there is nothing about it to nourish the soul of either the one who is involved in its production or in the one who uses or looks at it. It is something produced through the cooperative working of very many people; no single person can say that they made the bulb. Clearly, people make light bulbs because others need them, not because any individual has a need to make them. It is the opposite of the poet creating the poem. Work in the sphere of economic production is in nearly every way opposite to that in the cultural life.

*

In economic activity, purchase and sale have a proper place. A producer sells his product and receives money in exchange. Is this also true in cultural life? To answer this question it will help to make another simple comparison.

Imagine that a person needs some money. He decides to cook twelve pies and sell them at a market stall. We can imagine the process; he must first acquire all the materials, then prepare, mix, and bake them. This involves a certain amount of work. When finished, he takes the products of his work to market. There he has the twelve pies, which he hopes to sell for $15 each. Someone comes along and buys one. The baker gives the customer the pie and receives $15 in exchange. There is an actual exchange – a pie for $15. The baker then has only eleven pies left, but now he has $15 in his tin. And so it continues until he has sold them all and there are no pies left. Instead of the pies, the baker now has $180. When others arrive hoping to buy a pie they must go away hungry.

Here we see sale and purchase within economic life at its simplest. There is an actual exchange of the product of a person's work with money, the token of a similar value. Each party hands something over, each parts with ownership but gains ownership of something else, something that is of more value to him than the thing which he gave over.

Imagine now that a person is going to give a lecture. There is a charge of $15 for entry to the lecture. We will assume this is the amount that goes to the lecturer, ignoring any charge there might be for maintaining the hall, etc.

What is the nature of this charge? Is it a purchase in the same sense as the charge for the pies, or is it something different?

Is there an exchange? The listener will hand over the $15, but does he actually receive anything back *in exchange*? It cannot be said that he receives the knowledge "in exchange" in the same way as the pies are exchanged for money. The speaker does not hand over the lecture, or a part of it. Nor does she hand over the knowledge. She does not part with either; she does not have less knowledge at the end of the lecture than she did at the beginning. On the contrary, most speakers find that they actually gain in the speaking. Nor will there come a time when what she has to say has all been bought and there is nothing left for the next person. In fact the opposite can be true in that it is often difficult to lecture to a very small audience. Up to a point, the lecture itself will improve and everyone will benefit when more listeners come in. We cannot say that there is a given amount of knowledge that has to be shared and the larger the audience the less each receives.

The speaker, if she is acting in accordance with those impulses that she carries within herself, like the artist, will actually need an audience. She finds a fulfillment and a confirmation of her work, her creativity, in the interest and satisfaction of the people listening to her. One could even imagine, in a far-fetched way, the lecturer paying the audience; she needs them to listen to her just as much as they need her. So too, the teacher needs the children; teaching is the fulfillment of a life impulse. In the same way, the architect needs the person who wants a new building, and the actor needs an audience.

But there does have to be some form of payment to the lecturer; she needs money in order to live. If it is not an exchange, then what is the nature of the payment that she receives? Almost everything that applies in the case of the pies is the opposite in the case of the lecture. If there is no exchange, we cannot truthfully speak of a "purchase." To call it so merely leads to a false understanding of the real nature of the transfer of the money. Neither can we say it is a purchase of time.

It would be more correct to call it a contribution or gift. The money she is given frees her from having to earn what she needs by working in an economic productive process. It is a contribution in that it frees the lecturer to do something that, in truth, she wills to do anyway and from which those who thus free her also benefit. This "contribution" or "gift" nature of payment within the cultural sector will be discussed more fully in and following Chapter Twelve.

Of course the baker in the example above might also derive some enjoyment or fulfillment from his work. But that can hardly be the case for someone, for example, working in a factory at making electric light bulbs, or parts for motor cars. The baker brings an element of craft to his work, and he meets his customers, but that is not the case in the bulk of economic productive work. This polarity between the economic and cultural spheres of activity will be taken further in later chapters.

*

It is vitally important that we see clearly the difference between the two situations illustrated in the above examples. We have to look behind the money, which too often obscures the true reality. There is, on the one side, the work a person does out of a motivation that arises from within. Over against this is the work that has to be done, not because any person has a particular need to do it, or finds benefit in doing it, but because others need the products of the work. Almost everything in the customary thinking of our time tends towards casting a veil over this difference.

These are the two fundamental motives that lie behind all work. They are two poles of social life, just as there are two poles of a magnet. Though in almost all work something of each is to be found, one or the other is always the primary impulse or motive.

One arises, in the first place, out of egoism, out of the need each person has to give meaning and purpose to their own life, to fulfill their own destiny. At this pole is the work and activity that makes up the cultural life of the community.

The other pole is where the work comes about through the needs, not of the one doing the work but of others, of humanity. It is not an untrue picture to say that a person is called to work in a factory making motor cars or electric light bulbs because we, the people of today, need these products. If we did not need them, they would not be made. In the factory a person joins with others in the work of producing and distributing what is needed by the community. Humanity needs such products, products where the motive for the work does not lie in inner personal needs as it does in cultural activity. This is the basis of economic activity where altruism or mutuality is a primary demand that arises out of the nature of the work itself.

What is essentially important here is that those who work in cultural life come to recognize that they are doing what lies in their own interest, out of their own soul impulses. To approach their work as though they are doing it for money is a denial of this; it will actually affect the work in a detrimental way, it will mechanize it. So long as money is seen as the motivating factor of their work, the work itself can never be truly creative. Deep down in the unconscious depths of their being, many people actually know this, but those thought forms that properly belong to the economic sector of activity have come to pervade our lives. We absorb these ways of thinking from our social environment from an early age and they overlay and suppress this knowledge, but seldom do they actually extinguish it.

*

All the creative, entrepreneurial, and management skills and the inventive genius of those who initiate, manage, and develop the economic activity of social life are initially born out of the cultural sphere. But though these capacities arise and are nurtured in cultural life, they enter into the economic life, and there they must follow and obey the laws and mutuality of the realm of economic productive activity. Even the individuals who bring the creativity of cultural life into economic production cannot be as free there as those whose works lies in cultural life; they must submit to the mutual or altruistic nature of the economic productive process.

In the same way, the awakening of the feeling for the equality of all people, for what is just and right and the ability to sense what lives as common opinion in the community, can only arise within a healthy and strong cultural life.

Authority within the Cultural Sphere

People can "know" something to be true, good, or beautiful only when they have perceived it to be so. A person can never learn or know something "for" another, each must do it for him or herself. But here the question immediately arises – "can we not know something to be true, good, or beautiful because it is generally accepted to be so by our culture, or taught to be so by the religion into which we were born?" This leads to the further question "are we bound by birth and the culture in which we live, or is it possible to be a free individual?"

If we are to follow a particular religion, we can only do this as free human beings when we ourselves have come to recognize it as true and choose to follow it. So long as we accept the teachings of any particular religion as true because it is the religion into which we were born, or because it is an integral part of the culture in which we live, we are no more than a member of the group, not free individuals.

A free individual can accept from another person something to be true, good, or beautiful only when he or she recognizes the experience, capacity, and integrity of that other person and consciously and knowingly decides that, within a specific sphere of knowledge, they can accept as true what that other person claims to be true. But even then, we might hesitate to say "I know..." Free individuals can, in the first place, only accept themselves as authorities for their decisions and judgments, and secondly accept another person as an authority only in so far as they recognize in that other person something which gives him or her authority.

If individuals are compelled to accept something as true, good, or beautiful, not on their own, but based on an outside authority, they may act outwardly as though it is so, but inwardly they may come to question it, and to feel that they are acting out of an untruth. If people are forced to live what they feel to be a lie, they will suffer the consequences through all areas of their life. Or they may allow their inner questions to go to sleep; they may forget them, and so come to act on the basis of outer authority in the way of a robot. That too will have its social consequences.

In earlier times what was perceived as God, or Divine revelation, spoke through the leaders of the people and gave them knowledge of what was true, good, and right behavior. All ancient communities and religions were based on this pattern.

But this is no longer acceptable to an ever increasing number of people. Today God, by whatever name used, is no longer experienced as speaking to humanity from outside, from heaven above. Any authority that now speaks from outside or from above is experienced as one speaking from out of the past, or one that is an earthly authority.

What is now heard, increasingly, is the voice that each person experiences as coming from within, through one's own inner strivings, and through the impulses and tasks that each soul brings with it from birth. We have to learn to listen to our own inner voice.

Before we can be free from outer authority within cultural life, and in order to have firm ground on which to stand, we must awaken our own inner self. We must develop the ears to hear that which speaks to us from within, and come to know the inner wisdom that each of us has in relation to our own particular path through life.

When we can truly develop and speak out of this wisdom, we will, within our own particular field, speak with a certain authority. We have to learn to recognize when a person in this way "speaks with authority."

*

As discussed earlier, when we look back on our own or on another person's life and work, it is possible to see something of a direction, a meaningful thread running through it – life is not all a haphazard series of events. The difficulty is to develop the sensitivity to know something of this early in life and to work with it consciously, instead of coming to know it only later when we look back.

Such ideas are not always easy to accept. So many of the existing thought forms that dominate cultural life today deny anything other than chance or mere coincidence. That there might be something else, something not explainable through ordinary physical science, can engender in people a sense of insecurity, of being on unstable ground. Nevertheless, a careful study of people's biographies will reveal evidence of something other than chance.

Once we do come to recognize that our path through life is not just a matter of chance but that there is something like destiny giving form and direction to it, then we will be able to bring a new interest, motivation, and fulfillment to our lives. This must not be a matter of mere "belief," but must be an outcome of clear thinking or of common sense brought to bear on careful, objective, and exact observation.

In our time, and increasingly in the future, in everything that concerns the life of soul, all forms of outer authority will of necessity fall away. We see this already in the fact that the younger generation tend more and more to find their own way in life; they do not follow what they see as the old ways and habits of their parents. Social forms such as marriage are seen by many as not appropriate for them. Students want teachers who speak out of their own experience and do not merely pass on what they learned at university or from books. This trend can even be seen in the armed services. Soldiers are today treated as individuals who can and should think for themselves to a far greater degree than in the past. This is not only due to the greater technological nature of modern warfare, but to the nature of evolving humanity.

Unique *versus* Equal

If each human being is to be inwardly free, then cultural life must be founded on the recognition of that which is individual and unique. As was discussed earlier, true rights life is founded on the recognition of what is equal in all people. But that which must be excluded from rights life – all that is different and unique in people – is an essential aspect of cultural life.

The establishment of the principal of equality in rights life provides the firm foundation for individuals to experience freedom in the sense that each one can be a full and individual member of the community irrespective of who or what they are. But equality carried over into cultural life becomes a tyranny of the ordinary or common element over all that is unique and individual. Similarly, freedom, a central demand of the cultural sphere, of the life of soul, when carried over into rights life, will lead to the tyranny of the talented and shrewd individual over the many.

Any social group or organization, if it is to fulfill the needs of its members in a socially healthy way, must contain within it these two principles: equality and freedom, the freedom, that is, for a person to be different and to bring to expression their own individual qualities. But these two will be in conflict with each other and destructive to the community so long as they are not each confined within their own rightful domains. So, for example, a healthy society will ensure that every child has an equal right to education, but an equal right not to the same education, but to the education best suited to the child as an individual.

There will, of course, be difficulty with this thought if the child is seen to be entering life as an empty vessel that has to be filled with knowledge. So long as the child is seen in this light, then there is indeed a good argument for giving every child the same education; but then, too, we could expect each to become a replica of the other. But clearly this is not so; each child is unique, has his or her own particular impulses, feelings, and capacities.

Responsibilities of Those in Cultural Life

If what has just been said is true, and objective observation will confirm that it is, then what does this mean for the people actually involved? Cultural life can exist, and those who work in it are free to do so, only because there are other people who work in economic production providing the material goods and services that the cultural workers need for their life and work. But in contrast to cultural work, those who must work within division-of-labor at a machine in a factory, at the check-out of a supermarket, or inputting data into a computer, will receive little or nothing that nourishes their soul from the actual work they do. These workers have to let part of their inner soul life go to sleep, to give up something of their own soul needs.

Because those who work in cultural life receive from the economic sphere the material products and services they need, they in their turn have a responsibility to provide the nourishment of soul the workers in economic activity need but cannot find in their work. They have a responsibility to do so because cultural life cannot exist unless there are those who first labor at economic production. Something is owed by cultural life to those who labor in economic production. The payment of money alone does not, and cannot, discharge this debt.

The cultural sphere of social life must speak to all of humanity. In all our cultural institutions and organizations there needs to be awakened a sense of responsibility, not just to their immediate circle – to their audiences, students, and customers – but to the whole of the community. In educational establishments, museums, art galleries, theaters, concert halls, and opera houses, there needs to grow a consciousness of, and a will to serve, the soul needs of the community as a whole – so also in the places of scientific research, and in the studios and offices of architects, engineers, town planners, and designers. The design of the environment, the buildings, furniture, machines, and tools should all speak to the human soul of its true nature, while at the same time properly fulfilling their utilitarian functions.

To accept that the paying of money absolves this responsibility is to look only on the surface of life. We have to learn to look beyond the money and penetrate to the deeper personal relationships of life.

*

This awakening of, and listening to, that which speaks from the depths of human souls through their individual capacities and destinies, and through their tasks and impulses, is what gives to the work of the cultural realm its life, purpose, and orientation. The artist strives to bring to artistic expression something that wells up from within. A true work of art arises when something is revealed through it that is real and true in the realms that a person comes to know by entering the deep veiled depths of the life of soul and spirit. Only then can such a work of art truly nourish the soul of the one who gazes on or listens to it. Then it can reveal what is truly moral because what is expressed is in harmony with the life of soul, it arises out of the same sources from which the soul is born.

A pressing task of cultural life is to awaken to the nature, life, and inner needs of the human soul in its present state and as it will continue to evolve into the future, and out of this to focus on what each person bears within them as capacity, resolve, wisdom, and destiny.

When a person over a long period, particularly through childhood, is seriously deprived of proper nourishment for the body, this will show up in stunted growth, ill health, and an emaciated body. Deprivation of proper nourishment for the soul will also result in stunted and emaciated growth, but of the soul. To objective observation of the soul life of people today, the poverty of the soul is all too obvious.

There is a growing concern as to what is and what is not healthy for the body, and as to how people can be protected from what is harmful. But there is little serious concern for and study of what is or is not healthy for the life of the soul. Is it not also possible that there too, some things that give short-term immediate pleasure may have deeper long-term harmful consequences on, for example, moral life?

In all that works on the life of soul in the culture of our time – music, art, dance, films, theater and entertainment, all that comes through television and the internet – is the same concern given to what is healthy and what is harmful to the life of soul as is given today to what is healthy or harmful to the physical body?

The need to provide, for all the community, this soul nourishment must become the ground and aim of all those who work in the cultural sphere of humanity. Only in the fulfilling of this task can there be justification for the cultural worker benefiting from the products of those who must labor within the dehumanizing economic process of production.

Then there will arise the understanding and capacities that alone will be capable of resolving the deep and widespread social problems of our time.

The Leadership of Cultural Life

Because of the nature of cultural life, there can be no central leadership, no appointed body having authority over all. Within each area of cultural life those working in it will come to recognize certain individuals who, through their experience, commitment, inner impulse, and wisdom are leaders in their particular fields of work. They will be the people to whom others naturally turn for guidance or advice because they are seen to speak with inner authority. In this way, their leadership will come through recognition, not through appointment. Through this recognition, and therefore with the support of their colleagues in their fields of work, these individuals will, each from their particular areas of work, come together as necessary to form a leadership, or representative group, for the whole. This will be particularly necessary when a group of people from cultural life have to meet with representatives from the rights and economic sectors of the community to discuss the cross-sector matters and the well-being of the community as a whole.

Chapter 10

Work, Payment, and Human Freedom

If we observe people quite objectively but with real compassionate interest, we will see that there is a subtle difference between when they work wholly out of the need to earn money and when they work out of a real interest in the work itself. When they work solely for the money, it is always possible to experience a kind of inner barrier behind which they withdraw something of their own self, something of their soul. There is some part which does not become involved in the work, but is held back, undefiled, and only comes to life when the work is finished. But when a person works out of an interest in the work itself, it is as though something of his or her inner soul can shine forth and become involved.

As was shown in the last chapter, the possibility of working out of interest in the work itself is particularly strong for those whose work lies in or close to cultural life. The nature of the work there will always make it possible for people to find inner satisfaction in their work – to do it for its own sake – provided they connect inwardly with what they are doing. The very reason for the work of cultural life lies in the nurturing of the life of the soul.

This is to a large extent also possible for those whose work lies in the rights sector. In certain respects, rights life lies between the cultural and economic spheres. A person who works in the rights sphere of social life fulfills a role set by the community. This is work that arises out of the needs of society itself, not those of the individual who does the work. The role of the police officer, for example, arises out of the needs of the community, not of the individual. The individual chooses to do the particular work, but the community determines it. Still, this work might well provide inner fulfillment for the one performing the role or function that the community requires.

For those whose work lies wholly or mainly in the economic realm, that is in the actual work of production and distribution of products – "on the factory floor" – it is again somewhat more complicated. There it is not easy for a person to find inner fulfillment in the work itself. Before that can happen a transformation must first take place in society from thinking in terms of "payment for work" to thinking in terms of "payment for the product of the work." Only then will it be possible for a person to find interest and inner satisfaction, not necessarily in the work itself, but in the product and in the people who will use the product.

*

Whatever we may think of it, for the vast majority of people today, the money they receive as wage or salary is one of the most important factors in their lives. What they will be paid is a major consideration in deciding whether they take up one work or another. The wage they receive largely sets their standard of living, influences how and where they live, puts limits on the possibilities of their leisure hours, and shapes the circle of their friends.

For most people, money touches their life of feeling and so is a very personal matter. What they are paid is the standard by which they judge themselves; it gives them a sense of personal worth, of success or failure, of importance or inadequacy.

Feelings that arise in people are real, and they affect the life of society. They need to be listened to and understood. In this sense, it is not a question of feelings being right or wrong, but that they exist. Feelings cannot be changed at will. Change can only be brought about over a long period of time through study and observation of the actual realities of life. A community that does not take into account the feelings of its members, irrespective of the nature of those feelings, will find antisocial forces entering into the community. This is particularly true where it concerns money. Money always has the tendency to awaken feelings that are antisocial and destructive.

The thinking behind the way wages and salaries are determined, and how they are calculated and paid, works deeply, though often unconsciously, into the feelings of the recipient and so has deep social consequences. If social life is to be developed truly out of the needs of all its members and is to provide a harmonious and supportive environment, then the way wages and salaries are calculated and paid will need to be looked at afresh.

Is Labor Purchased?

Almost all current thinking and social arrangements are founded on the assumption that it is the labor or work itself that is purchased – that workers sell their labor. Such terms as "cost of labor" and "labor market" are in common use in economic life and are an outcome of current social thinking while also reinforcing it. At one time it was only the labor of those paid "wages," as opposed to those paid a "salary," that was treated as a purchase. People who followed a professional calling or vocation were given a salary. There was a clear sense that such people followed their profession as a life's work, not selling their labor, nor even doing it "for the money." But as economic life has developed and come to dominate social life, so the thinking based on the concept of purchase has penetrated into all aspects of work. Even such professional people as teachers, actors, and police officers are now coming to see their life's task as labor and their salary as the purchase price of their labor and skills.

Our present practice of treating labor as a commodity that can be bought and sold has its origins in the earlier practice of slavery, which allowed for human beings themselves to be bought and sold. This will be discussed in greater depth in Chapter Eighteen. Here we can point to the fact that as human consciousness evolved from the domination of the group over the individual to where the individual has become dominant, so the older relationship between owner and slave has evolved through, for example, landowner and serf, master and servant, to employer and employee; in other words, from a relationship in which the whole human being was owned by another to one, as now, where it is the labor of a person that is owned by another.

The old master and servant relationship continues on in a transformed way in the employer/employee relationship. But here the sense of being part of a family group is no longer there to sustain the individual. Many organizations try to develop some form of "family" culture, but the reality is not there; it does not belong to the present time. People increasingly demand their independence and freedom to be themselves. To be part of a group or family is also a commitment to that group. This commitment can lead to a feeling of being unfree.

Into this evolving relationship between one human being and another has entered, in comparatively recent times, something new – the machine. If, for example, a ditch is to be dug, we can employ a human being, a laborer, or we can use a machine. From this comes the image of the human being as a machine that can be employed. Just as we can hire a machine, we can, in the same way, hire a person. But the machine is not a living being, it has no purpose in itself. It is made specifically to do certain economic work. For the human soul to feel itself treated as a machine can be a terrible and dehumanizing experience, even if unconsciously so.

*

I tried to show earlier in Chapter Three, in the examples of the blackberry picker and the person working at the conveyor belt making engines that, viewed from the perspective of the economic process of production itself, it is simply not true to say that it is the labor that is purchased. In economic activity, it is always the product of the work that is wanted and which is paid for, not the work itself.

Consider what actually happens when a laborer is employed to do a particular job for a certain number of hours each day. If "employment" means that his labor has been purchased for a time, that it is now owned by the employer who has bought it, then the laborer is not a free human being. He might not be owned as was a slave, but part of him still is; he does not have free use or control over his own limbs. It will probably not be stated or even consciously thought of in these terms, but the assumption at the base of the relationship between the two is one in which, for the hours of employment, the employee's labor, the actual activity of his limbs, belongs to the employer, who can direct it according to his own purposes.

Let us imagine that the employer, or his manager, wants a ditch dug. He instructs the laborer to dig it as marked on the ground and to a certain depth. It could be either a machine or a man who does the digging. The employee, the individual human being, becomes machine-like and does what he is ordered to do. All that is individual, that thinks and feels and is alive within him, separates itself off from the work that is carried on by his bodily limb system at the behest of the employer.

This was not such a problem when people did not feel themselves as distinct individuals, when their consciousness was embedded, as it were, within a group, a family, or people connected through a blood relationship, through a line of descent. But now that connection is very much weaker, often dissolved altogether, and people experience within themselves the awakening need to be free and individual human beings. To have to give something of this free individuality up, to have to sell something of oneself and become subservient to another in order to earn money with which to obtain what is needed to live will become less and less acceptable as humanity moves into the future.

When we experience our work as purchased, as owned by someone else, it conflicts with our own, if unconscious, need for individual recognition and freedom. Because of this, we create artificial barriers between our self and our work, which gives rise to the tendency to take no responsibility for the work; we sleep through it, or rebel against the system. Or it can be that something of our individual humanity dies, and we become a sort of machine-like clone of the organization for which we work. We see this often today in the life of certain institutions, businesses, and corporations.

I was given a clear illustration of this many years ago when we had contracted with a builder to put up a building at the college where I worked. Part of my responsibility was to keep an eye on the building work. Pre-insulated central heating pipes to carry hot water between buildings had to be put in a trench and buried. After many had already been covered up, it was discovered that some were faulty. This meant that they all had to be dug up again and examined.

I had got to know the young man, the plumber, who had been putting the pipes into the trench and connecting them up; we often had a talk about many things; he was what one would take as an ordinary, open, basically honest, and responsible young man. I asked him if he had not seen that the pipes were faulty when he put them into the trench. Yes, he said, he saw they were faulty, but he was paid to put them into the trench and join them up. That for him was quite simple, he was not responsible for the success of the project, he merely did what he was paid to do. He had sold his labor, and it was up to those who bought it to direct it properly.

Though it was his arms and legs that did the work, he was not responsible for them, they were hired out. For so many hours in the day he was divided in two: part of him belonged to the company that employed him and the other part was still himself; but this part that was himself was separated off and not involved in the other, it went into a kind of sleep. This is not an unusual or extreme example, but quite ordinary.

Something of the above example is always present when people are paid to do certain work – when their labor is bought and used by someone else. It lay behind much of the industrial unrest of the last half of the twentieth century, and it expressed itself outwardly in the form of workers demanding an increase in the price paid for their labor. But in the unconscious depths of their souls there was a demand for a separation of the payment of wages from the actual labor.

This was expressed very directly at the height of the strikes in the 1970s by a shop steward when his union went on strike demanding what, by any criteria, was an unreasonably high wage increase. It was quite clear that if the strikers' demands were met, the firm they worked for would be bankrupted. When asked if he did not see this, he gave a remarkably revealing reply. He said something to the effect of: "Yes I know that if our demand is met, the firm will be put out of business. But so long as our wages are calculated on the same basis as the other inputs to the factory, we have to strike." I may not have his exact words – the newspaper report that I kept has been lost – but they struck me very forcibly at the time, particularly the last phrase, "we have to strike." It was as though they sensed some evolutionary force working in the depths of their souls just below the level of consciousness, an impulse that demanded that human beings be freed, that they be no longer subjected to purchase and sale as are the other inputs to the factory.

When people who are otherwise reasonable human beings act in an unreasonable way, we have to look below the surface of things to find the deeper causes.

As human beings, we live in our movements and activity – these are part of our being. When society artificially separates the labor (movements and activity) of human beings from the human beings themselves, instead of separating human labor from the products of that labor, then we include in the sale of the product an integral part of the human beings who made it: their labor. Just as there has grown up over the ages an increasing revulsion against slavery, against one person owning another, so there will in the future increasingly develop a revolt against one person owning the labor of another.

Or is it the Product of Labor that is Purchased?

People are employed because the employer needs what they will produce, the product of the labor that has some value. The labor itself has no economic value. Economically speaking, it is always what results from the labor that is purchased, not the labor itself. That is the economic reality.

If someone makes jam at home and sells it at the local market, he is clearly selling the jam, not his labor. In calculating the price, he may well take into consideration the time and work involved, but he and the buyer will think in terms of it being the product that is bought and paid for, not the labor.

To think this way is comparatively easy where a person works independently and there is a distinct product. It becomes more difficult where the person is employed, for example, to clean floors. Clearly it is the clean floor, the product of the work, that is wanted, not the labor as such nor the time. Even if someone still considers it simpler to calculate the "price" of the cleaned floor by the time it takes to clean it and so pays the cleaner an amount per hour, it is the product and not the labor that should be considered 'bought.'

The difficulty is to remain conscious of the fact that it is the clean floor that is being paid for, not the labor or time it takes to clean it. This might appear to be splitting hairs and to be giving the matter more significance than is justified, but it is not so much the outer administrative arrangements as the way people *experience* these arrangements that affects their life of feeling. If either the employer or the employee think in terms of the wage being payment for the labor, it will have very different implications for their relationship and social interaction than if they both think in terms of it being a payment for the cleaned floors. One might also think of it as a purchase of the change in the condition of the floor that resulted from the work. The relationship then comes to be one between two free human beings, not one between an employer and employee, or a superior and an inferior.

The work in a factory is even more complex. Each person makes only a small, often undefined, part of a whole. But the wage, though still today calculated by the hour, can even now be thought of and treated as a purchase of the product of the work, or as the worker's share of the sale price of the final product.

When people are obliged to sell their labor in order to live, they are robbed of something vitally human; the moral impulse to do a good job will be more or less suppressed. It is natural in this situation to focus more on raising the selling price of one's own labor than on the quality of whatever it is that is being produced. But when it is the product of labor that is bought and not the labor itself, there will be more of an inclination to attend to the quality of the product, to provide something of equal value in exchange for a wage – the focus will tend to move towards the product of the work.

An important element of the fabric of society is what can be called the "thought forms" that live in society and affect the way we think and act. These cannot be easily changed, some are very deep-seated. The thought that it is the labor or time that is purchased lies very firmly in the habitual thinking of our society. To change this to the recognition that it is the product of labor that is purchased will take a long time and very much effort.

This also applies to those who work in both the cultural and rights sectors. But here we cannot even say that we purchase the product of their work. As I pointed to earlier and will take up again later, in the work of cultural life we must come to think in terms of freeing individuals to do *their* work, the work they have the will to do. In the work of the rights sector, the wage frees people to fulfill a role they have chosen, but one determined and needed by society.

*

What is the next step that must be taken? Humanity has progressed in a way that can be characterized as evolving from "owner and slave" through "landowner and serf," "master and servant," to "employer and employee." All these stages can still be found in different parts of humanity today, but the overall trajectory is to move from the earlier stages to the later. In none of these stages is the individual worker free; in all of them there is still an aspect of slavery. How can we come to a social form where the individual is finally freed? This is one of the most important social questions of our time, one that is already coming to expression. Within the unconscious depths of people's souls there is an ever-growing demand that no part of the human being be owned by another, that the dignity and individuality of every human being be treated as inviolable.

The Deadening of Economic Labor

Division-of-labor applied to the economic productive process has clearly brought great benefit to humanity and will increasingly do so in the future. It has made possible an economic sector that could produce enough for all humanity and it could do this in a way that would leave everyone free, with time and energy to participate in the cultural life, a possibility that has never been there before. The fact that this is not yet realized is not because the possibility is not there, but because humanity has not yet taken hold of what it has been given as a possibility. But there is a cost for this.

As division-of-labor has evolved there has been squeezed out of the work itself all that which formerly, in the work, nourished the life of soul. It is not possible to have both: the highly productive economic work and soul nourishment in the work. The more economically efficient our labor becomes, the less human fulfillment will we derive from the work itself. Those who work in the economic sphere, producing for others, must now find nourishment for their soul someplace other than in their work.

It is vitally important that a balance be found: firstly, between the need for division-of-labor in economic production with all the advantages that brings to the community, and the bodily and soul welfare of those who must work at it; and secondly, between those whose work lies in cultural life and those who must work at economic production. The possibility must be created for those who work within the economic sphere to fully participate in the cultural life that their soulless work makes possible.

Chapter 11

The Woodcutters and the Creation of Capital

It is an interesting exercise to try to picture all the economic products that we can expect to use, consume, or have during our lifetime. If we do this, we will realize that there is no way any of us could produce even a millionth part of this if we worked alone, no matter how skilled we may be and how hard we worked. The fact that we can have all this is because, in the making of it, very many people work together in the co-operation, or mutuality, of division-of-labor.

In economic life no one can do anything for himself. I have in my time made, among other things, a table. I like to tell people "I made this table." But, economically, is this true? How much of it did I actually make? I did not grow the tree, nor cut it down and saw it into planks. I was involved in none of the work before I went to the shop and obtained the prepared wood. A great number of people had already worked in order that those pieces of wood could be in that shop for me to buy. Nor did I make any of the tools without which I could not possibly have made the table. Nor did I make the screws, glue, varnish, and the other materials used. I should really say: "I, together with many other people, made this table." Or I could say that I finished off, or brought to a certain conclusion, the work of many people. It would be something of great wonder if I could really have an imagination of all the people who in some way contributed to the making of that table.

When we talk of brotherhood or mutuality in the economic sphere, we mean nothing more than that when we divide the work, when we put aside our own needs and work together to produce what others need, then the economic activity of the community itself becomes more productive, then we all can have more than if each worked alone. This principle, that the individual can achieve almost nothing working alone but can become very productive when he unites with others, is fundamental to all aspects of the economic sphere of social activity and should be taken into account at all levels.

This "mutuality," or co-operative working together, is what gives to economic life its particular character and orientation and distinguishes it from the cultural and the rights sectors.

Division-of-labor comprises the working together of two value-creating activities. On one side, the physical work transforms what nature provides into the various products we need to live, work, and play. That is the basic activity, the foundation on which the economic productive process is built. But alongside this, working into it, are all the imaginative and creative talents nurtured in the cultural sphere. They do not themselves produce economic products, but they bring about an enormous increase in the productivity of the labor. Just as cultural life depends on the products of economic activity for the things it needs, such as the instrument for the musician, the canvas and paints for the painter, so in economic activity the producer needs the creativity and imaginative forces of cultural life to make his or her physical activity more efficient and productive.

The Woodcutters and the Creation of Capital

The further development of the economic process of production through division-of-labor can be shown by another simple illustration. Again, it is important that the reader keeps in mind that we are here considering the economic process of production itself. We must exclude all that which, in the thinking of today, is treated as though it were a part of this economic process, but which is in reality quite separate and of a different nature.

Imagine again a simple village community. Everyone needs wood for cooking and for keeping warm. There are ten woodcutters who all work independently of each other. Each goes out to his favorite part of the forest and cuts wood. Each then brings his day's product back to market and there sells it. Let us assume that each cuts 10 units of wood each day so that a total of 100 units come to the community.

Now imagine that one of the woodcutters has an idea. He decides that he will not cut any more wood but will acquire a horse and cart and each day will collect what the others cut and take it to market to sell.

The remaining nine woodcutters do not have to transport their wood, nor sit in the market place selling it. They can now concentrate on cutting the wood and so will, without taking any more time or doing any more work in total than before, produce more wood. Let us assume that they now produce 13 units each, that is 3 more than they did before. The ten between them now cut and sell a total of 117 units of wood each day.

For carting and selling their wood, the man with the cart charges each of the nine 2 units of wood. This is his share of what has become a joint venture. He keeps for himself the value of 18 units, and the woodcutters are left with 11 units each, 1 more than they had before. The community, too, benefits as now more wood is available. Everyone is better off than before.

Through the dividing of the labor, more wood has been produced. This increased production of wood was achieved with the same amount of work as before, so this extra is "profit," some of which goes to the nine woodcutters but, we will assume, proportionately more to the carter.

The question must of course arise as to whether it is right that the carter keeps so much more of the profit for himself than goes to the woodcutters. This is a critical question of our time and will be dealt with later in Chapter Thirteen. For the moment, we are looking at the economic process, at what actually happens, not at what ought to happen, or is morally justified. It is important to see here that profit does arise and that somewhere within the community this can be accumulated as capital.

I have used the term "units" of wood. I could say "units of value." The economic value of the wood could be represented either by the wood itself or by money. In fact, the wood itself could be used as a means of exchange in the community and so become money. One way or another, at this point money must enter the process of economic exchange.

Let us assume that, of the 18 units of value the carter earns each day, he spends 12 on himself – he lives at a slightly higher level of expenditure than the others – and he saves 6. In this way he accumulates units of value, or money. This is part of the "profit" that arose due to his "dividing the labor." This money, as it accumulates, takes on a quite different nature from that which it had in the daily buying and selling of wood and other such products. It becomes "capital." As capital it has the potential to release human creativity, human soul capacities. This becomes clear if we look at the further development of the economic process.

Imagine that another of the woodcutters comes up with a new idea, an idea for a tool that will make the work of cutting wood even more productive. He is someone who has a creative mind and so develops the idea of a kind of saw. Using such a tool, the same number of woodcutters could cut even more wood with the same labor and time, or the same wood with less labor and time.

But an idea of a saw will not itself cut wood. Economically, even the best idea is quite useless so long as it remains in the realm of idea. Before it can become effective, it must be brought down into material substance. Only as a material saw will the idea cut wood. But the man with the idea cannot do this unless he has the means with which to achieve it, he needs a workshop and the necessary tools. For this, capital must be available. Only if he has access to capital can he obtain or create the workshop, or smithy, in which to make the saws.

The man with the idea – I will call him the smith – will borrow the capital from the carter. With this he will set up his smithy and bring his idea down into substance, into the actual tool, the saw. The eight remaining woodcutters will use the new saws to help them cut the wood. That which happened when the carter started working with his cart will now repeat itself: each will cut even more wood than they did without the saws, more wood will come to market for the community, and also more capital will be generated. In the same way as happened with the carter, the smith too will aim to gain for himself a share of the increase in wood, or profit, brought about due to his saw. With this, he will first repay the loan to the carter and then begin to accumulate capital for himself.

At first, there were the ten woodcutters working independently. At that stage no capital was generated. The development of economic activity begins with the practical application of what were, to begin with, creative imaginations – first that of the carter and then that of the smith. Human creative genius, in that it enhances the productive process through division-of-labor, creates capital, which in its turn releases further human creativity. Capital comes into being as an inevitable consequence of human imagination and invention increasing the productive capacity of human labor.

Through this example it also becomes apparent that the function, nature, and value of money changes. Money goes through a cycle of differing states. If these states or phases of money were understood and taken hold of, it would offer an important means of maintaining a balance between the various sectors of society.

As I indicated earlier, I am presenting these ideas from the perspective of *the community as a whole*, not from that of the individual. If this is not born in mind what follows will make little sense.

Purchase Money

When money first comes into existence to facilitate the general circulation of goods it can be called "purchase money." It is what we use when we go into a shop and buy something, or pay for a service. At this level, its value corresponds to that for which it is exchanged. It is the money working at the level of the woodcutters who sell their wood in the market. It stands for the value of the wood they sell and so enables them to purchase another product of like value, or price.

As purchase money, its value in the community is that of the product it will buy. There is nothing in purchase money that gives rise to an increase in value or in productivity – economically, it enables the present to continue into the future in that it makes possible the replacement of that which is bought and consumed.

Loan Capital

When money, instead of being used in purchase and sale, is allowed to accumulate, it becomes capital, and as such it takes on a new potential. Its value within the community is no longer the same as it was as purchase money. The money that the carter lends to the smith has a different quality and takes on a different function than when it first came into being as purchase money in the buying and selling of the wood. Then, its value was in its enabling what was consumed to be replaced. But when accumulated as capital, its value lies in its capacity to release the potential of the person to whom it is lent. It frees the inventive genius of the smith, which then works to the benefit of the community. It enables, not just the continuation of the past into the future, but an increase, a new development, to come about. For the community as a whole, money in the form of loan capital is more productive, and therefore of greater value, than purchase money.

Money does not have a value within the community that is the same wherever it is in the economic process. The value of $1,000 is different when it is in the realm of sale and purchase than when it is lent to a person with inventive capacities as capital. Its value will have a relationship to the capacities of the person to whom it is lent. From the perspective of the community as a whole, it will have a different value if it is placed in the hands of an inventive entrepreneur, an ordinary consumer, or a playboy.

*

Is it correct to call the money that the carter passed over to the smith "loan" capital? If we look at the economic process we see that this money capital, or accumulated profit, taken hold of by the imaginative capacity of the smith, results in it reproducing itself. The original capital, as capital, was used up when he set up his smithy. The money that had been saved no longer exists as money capital. But through the use of the tools created by the smith, more wood will be cut and more capital generated. Capital put into the economic process in this way generates more capital, or can be said to regenerate itself. Due to this fact, any capital passed over to an entrepreneur is, economically, of the nature of a loan. Even if the carter *gives* the money to the smith, the economic process reproduces and repays it. It is therefore correct to call it, and treat it as, "loan capital."

This is one reason why the term "loan" rather than "investment" is used here. The other is that the word "investment" tends to imply that the investing of the money is motivated by the interests of the investor rather than it being part of the normal and healthy course of the community economic process. It might be an investment from the perspective of the individual who "invests" the money to achieve profit for himself, but from the perspective of the community as a whole the reality is that the money is repaid by the economic process.

For any development of the economic process to come about, it must be possible for capital to accumulate. If the carter had spent all his money, or if the increase or profit had been evenly distributed between the carter and the woodcutters and spent rather than saved up, there would not have been a source from which the smith could borrow the capital he needed. He could not have made his idea fruitful, and the community would not have had the benefit of the increased productivity. It must be possible for money – profit – to accumulate somewhere. Whether this should be in the hands of the carter, or the smith, or some other body, will be looked at later. For the present it need only be recognized that the creation of capital is a necessary part of the social economic process.

A crane at work on a building site is another good example of division-of-labor.

The Crane

Passing by a building site at one time or another, many of us have stopped to watch a crane at work. The crane is a good example of those products that have no purpose in themselves but make possible the making of something else.

It can be an interesting exercise if, while actually watching a crane lift a heavy load up into the air, swinging it round and placing it where it is wanted by the builders, one asks oneself the question: "What is it that is actually lifting the load?" It is much more revealing to do this while actually standing there watching the crane at work than doing so abstractly in the comfort of home or study.

One can say that it is the cable of the crane that lifts the load, or the engine that pulls the cable, or the fuel, which drives the engine. None of these answers is incorrect; they are all in a certain way true. And yet do they really give the complete answer? What had to be there before any of them? The crane did not come together out of its own necessity, it did not create and assemble itself.

If one looks at any part of the crane, whether it is a strut that forms part of the tower, or the steel cable that carries the strain of the lifting, or the pulley assembly round which the cable turns, or the parts of the engine, then what one sees is human thought, human imagination and creativity. At every point it is possible to see human thinking caught up into substance, into iron and steel. The size of the nut, the thickness and shape of each strut have all been thought through, each has a form appropriate to its function and purpose. One could even say that each part of the crane is in reality substance-filled thought. The manufacturer of each part of the crane takes substance and forms it into the shape first imagined and thought through by the design engineer.

Ultimately one comes to the perception that it is human thought that lifts the load. That is no less true than it is to say that it is the engine or the burning fuel that lifts it. The crane, before it was built, existed first as thought. But the thoughts themselves could not lift the load; they had to be incorporated into material substance.

The thoughts, caught up in the substance, are no longer active living thoughts, they are no longer creative, they have created. They have died into the substance.

So we can distinguish two quite distinct components of the crane: human creativity, imagination, and thinking on the one side – invisible to sense perception and yet clearly there. On the other side is the physical crane, the product of the economic process of manufacture. Not only has each piece of the crane been thought through, it has also been manufactured. The iron has been extracted from nature, transported, and worked on and so formed through the process of economic production.

The crane has no purpose in itself. It is a tool, a means to something else. It is the building that is wanted; the crane enables it to be built. Within division-of-labor, the crane is the manifestation of the human imaginative thinking that makes labor more productive.

In the economic process, human thinking and imagination are always there at work. To see this, it is necessary first to distinguish between the substance, the physical product, and the thoughts of which it is a kind of distillation. That which can, in the final analysis, be said to actually lift the load, the human creative thinking, was first nurtured within the cultural sphere of social life. It is a gift from cultural life to the economic productive process. Economic activity in its most simple and basic form of labor working on nature is made immeasurably more productive when it is fructified by what comes over from the cultural sphere of society as creative and imaginative thinking.

No machine of any sort can or does come into being of its own volition or creation. Only human powers of thought and imagination can, at the behest of human will, bring them into being. These human faculties are there at work through every machine and tool that we use, or that affects us. No machine exists without them.

The polarity between the cultural and economic spheres of work comes to expression within the means of production in the duality of the *creative human capacity* expressing itself through *manufactured material substance*. A further expression of this duality can be seen between the working of management and the physical work or labor, of those "on the factory floor."

Management and Labor

Most of the actual work or physical labor in economic production lies at or near that pole where there is little or nothing in it that gives inner nourishment to the human soul. It is the very opposite of the work of cultural life. At this pole are all those people who work, for example, in factories or mines and as laborers or construction workers. Even such work as that of a cashier at a supermarket can come close to this pole. But in such work it is important to distinguish between the actual work a person does, which can be devoid of anything that nourishes the soul, and other things which might accompany the work, such as interacting with shoppers.

The work of the entrepreneur or the manager of a business lies nearer the opposite pole. The manager has to bring his creative imaginative capacities to his work, he has to think through the productive process and attune this to the abilities and natural aptitudes of the people who are to do the actual work of production. In this work, the individual impulses and aspirations that arise in the soul can find expression. The manager of a business or factory, although his work lies within the orbit of the economic sphere, is in reality a half-free cultural worker. He is able, within the limits of the requirements of economic necessity, to work out of his creative, imaginative, entrepreneurial potential. It is the person on the factory floor, who must work as the productive process itself requires, who is the true economic worker.

The half-free cultural work includes not only management but also such activities as research and development, publicity, engineering, and design. It is this work that has brought about the enormous increase and improvement in consumer goods and has evolved the technological methods of production needed to produce them. Much of this half-free cultural life – half-free because here human creativity and imaginative thinking are bound within the needs and laws of the economic sphere – is actually more exciting and appealing to many people than much of our cultural life proper, which, compared to what it could be, is today really very lifeless.

It is just because of this that egoism can so easily come to dominate economic activity, and it is just those at this management pole who are in a position to serve their own egoistic tendencies – tendencies that are there in all of us. Many of the most able and creative people amongst us are drawn to this area because there they find work that can be both challenging and creative and so also rewarding in a way that, too often, is not to be found in our present cultural life.

As was shown earlier, the creative imaginative impulse in the human being is rooted, in the first place, in a form of egoism. Something of this egoism must, of necessity, be allowed into the half-free cultural life of the economic sphere, into all that which as management, research, and development brings life, creativity, and improvement to the economic process of production and distribution. But if this egoism is not held in check, if it is allowed to penetrate into the actual process of production and distribution, then it will work destructively and against the interests of the community. I will try to show in the next chapter how, in the working together of "economic associations" and the organs of rights life, this holding back of egoism from the actual economic productive process can be achieved.

The Doctor and the Shoemaker

It might help to give a further illustration. Imagine again a simple village community. There is a shoemaker who makes the boots and shoes for all who need them. One day he falls ill and, in the ordinary course of his illness, would be in bed for three weeks. During that time no shoes would come to the market. This would of course have its effect on the village economy, particularly on all those who need shoes.

Now suppose there is a doctor in the village who has had a good training and thus is able to heal the shoemaker who, as a result, is ill for only one week. This means that for two weeks shoes will be made that would not have been made if there had been no doctor. We can ask who it was that made the shoes during these two weeks: the shoemaker or the doctor? Though it was the shoemaker who physically made them, yet on another level, that of the community as a whole, we must say it was the doctor that made them, or those who gave the doctor his training, or even all the experience and knowledge that came from earlier doctors and researchers that was passed on to him.

Here again we see that cultural life has a direct result in affecting production, but one that cannot be calculated as a cost included in the price of the product. The cost of not only supporting and training the doctor, but before that, of the development of all the experience and knowledge that was incorporated into his training, is too far away in time and nature from any of its possible economic benefit to relate the one to the other. Clearly the contribution of cultural life to economic production cannot be calculated or priced in the normal way.

Cultural life, in that its primary responsibility is to serve and nourish the life of soul of all members of the community, can only fulfill this task if it is free, free from any control or conditions laid down from outside. The human capacity for imagination and ingenuity cannot be produced to order; it will flourish only in a free and active cultural life. But just as economic activity depends on all that it receives, and has received in the past, from cultural life for its technology, for every machine, and for everything that has made it into the highly productive activity that it is, so also cultural life could not exist if economic activity did not supply it with all the products of manufacture that it needs.

The cultural and the economic spheres each contribute to and benefit from the other. But this benefit cannot be calculated in terms of an "exchange." It cannot work that way. It only makes sense and works socially to the benefit of the whole when it is treated from each side as a free contribution to the other. It is a "contribution" or "gift" in the sense that nothing is received or expected back "in exchange," and it is "free" in that each side receives what it does with no obligation for reciprocal service.

The Growth of Excess Capital

When the smith has repaid the loan, he too will start to save money
and so build up capital. Now there will be both the carter and the
smith generating and accumulating capital.

The process will, of course, continue. Another woodcutter will
come up with yet another idea for improving productivity. He, too,
will borrow capital and will also increase the amount of wood cut
by each of the woodcutters. This will continue to repeat itself and
a time will come when, clearly, more wood than is needed will be
produced and more capital than can fruitfully be used up within the
economic process will accumulate. In addition, too many trees will
be cut down and the natural environment of the community will
be denuded. Division-of-labor, which at first greatly benefited the
community, will, if allowed to develop uncontrolled, come to work
to the detriment of the community.

There is always a tendency in human nature to bring the capacities
of invention, creativity, and ingenuity into the economic process in
order to increase efficiency and productivity. Because of this, more
and more products will be produced. This spirit of creativity and
invention urged on by its own necessity, by the lure of profit and the
pressure of the available capital within the system, will, on one side,
create new products that may or may not be particularly necessary to
human well-being, and on the other will generate ever more capital.
Some of this capital will then be used to persuade people that they
need or must have, what is thus produced to excess.

There is a limit to the amount of capital that can be properly used
up in developing or maintaining the economic process of production
at a healthy level. Beyond this level, as more is generated, that which
cannot be profitably invested directly in the sphere of economic
production will try to preserve itself. This is achieved by those
holding the capital "investing" in, for example, land or other such
assets. This forces up the price of land, making it more expensive.
The products of the land will then also rise in price to cover the "rent"
paid on the capital value of the land. It is a natural characteristic of
human nature that when people have capital they will endeavor to
place it where it will increase in value and also give a return.

Within the economic sector itself, an excess of capital comes about when there is more than is needed for the necessary renewal and healthy development of the economic process.

Through the enormous increase in the capital that now floats around within the economic and financial spheres, trying to increase its own value, the economic sector is coming to dominate the whole, to subvert both the rights and cultural sectors to its own values and goals. Clearly, capital should not be allowed to accumulate uncontrolled. The excess must be removed from the economic sector before it can work in a socially harmful way. So long as it is allowed to remain there, those who control it will continue to try, not only to preserve it, but to also make it grow, and so increase their own wealth and power.

If such excess capital, with its inherent striving for growth, is allowed to accumulate within the fabric of society, then it will assume something of the nature of a cancerous growth. It does this, in the main, by treating as an economic product something that properly belongs to the sphere of rights and giving it a capital value, which over time will, it is hoped, increase. In this way the "capital value" of land, houses, shares, cultural property, and other such "investments" are forced upwards to the detriment of the vast majority of humanity. Though the markets in such investments do serve some useful purpose in the economic sector, most of this activity has come to resemble that of casinos where vast sums of money are gambled each day with the sole object of increasing the value of the investment rather than furthering the process of economic production.

How can such harmful effects of division-of-labor be counteracted? How can the excess capital be used up instead of being allowed to accumulate in a way that becomes harmful to social life, and how can the economic process be controlled in such a way that only as many products as are needed are actually produced and natural resources are not wasted?

These questions will be taken further in the next chapter.

Chapter 12
Gift Capital

In the last chapter I put forward the idea of two kinds or qualities of money, *purchase money* and *loan capital*. Further observation will show that there is a third: *gift capital*.

The concept of gifts as a necessary factor within the economic life of society is one that many people may at first find difficult to accept. But if we look at the role of taxes, we will see that much of both the cultural and rights sectors are, of necessity, funded by government through taxes. Is not a tax a kind of gift? An odd example of a gift, to be sure, as it is compulsory and determined by the receiver rather than the giver, but a gift nonetheless. Though a tax might be experienced as a taking of money, it can also be described as giving without expecting to receive anything "in exchange." Politicians, teachers, police, and social workers, funded by taxes, do not provide anything "in exchange." They all provide a service which is not directly paid for, just as taxes are not paid in direct exchange for their public service. On each side there is what can be termed a giving, but since this is not recognized in the administrative arrangements, taxes must be compulsorily imposed by government rather than given by the economic sector itself.

In the last chapter I showed that in the natural course of its activity, the economic sector will, within itself, produce surpluses of both products and capital. If these surpluses are left within the economic sphere of activity they will create real social problems. The excess products must be used up if they are not to accumulate into dead weights, just as excess capital must not be allowed to accumulate, but must be used up.

Economic activity produces these surpluses as a result of the creativity, invention, and management skills nurtured within cultural life. These gifts from cultural life greatly increase the output of the economic productive process within an orderly, secure environment provided by the rights sector. But because what the cultural and rights sectors provide for the economic sector cannot be transferred by way of purchase or exchange, but must, economically, be free contributions, the economic sector must also provide for those in cultural life and the rights sector through free contributions or gifts.

In the rights and cultural sectors there is no such thing as division-of-labor. There may be specialization, but that is something quite different from division-of-labor. Specialization is the opposite: it leads to a deepening of knowledge, understanding, or skills in a particular subject, to an enrichment of the work and a soul satisfaction that is not found in division-of-labor. Between the economic sector and the rights or cultural sectors there can be no exchange, or purchase and sale, as there is within economic life itself.

It is very important that the gift nature of these contributions is recognized as due solely to the nature of the activities of the three different sectors and of the contributions each makes to the others, not to any moral or ethical requirement. By its nature, "purchase" is something that involves the exchange of economic values created within economic activity through division-of-labor. The cultural and rights sectors do not produce economic values, so there can be no exchange of economic values between them and the economic sector, unless the economic sector has first given them money representing economic values. There will be confusion in attempting to see this if money is still seen as something having value in itself and if the distinction is not clearly kept in mind between money arising properly within the economic process, and "counterfeit" money arising through the market in rights which will be discussed in Part Two.

*

In the present circumstances, it is not possible to expect those in the economic sector to have the selfless interest in the community to be able to make the necessarily objective decisions as to how much, and from where, capital is to be taken and given to the other two sectors. Egoism, at present, is too powerful. The leaders in business and industry are not in themselves naturally greedy and self-serving – it is our culture that has made them so. Today it is assumed as normal acceptable behavior that people look after their own interests first. Not only is egoism encouraged in the culture of our time, but the structure of our society is such that it rewards egoism with the possibility of great unearned wealth, as will also be shown in later chapters.

But if the changes to the social structure indicated so far, and the further changes that will be shown as necessary in Part Two of this book, are actually realized, then society will be in a very different situation. Then it will indeed be possible to build a society based on the knowledge that economic activity, by its nature, is essentially based on mutuality, on people working co-operatively together. Then, too, the transfer of capital as a free gift from the economic sector to the cultural life of the community, and also to the rights sector, will come about as of natural necessity. Furthermore, it will be recognized that it is the economic sector itself, as a totality, that should give of its wealth toward what is needed by the other two sectors. This cannot be achieved by individual people working alone; it is the working of the economy as a whole that creates the profit, not individual people.

It will be necessary for certain people working within the economic sphere of activity to come together in what I will call *economic associations*. These will be described more fully in the next chapter. It will then be possible for just those actually involved in the different spheres of economic activity, and who therefore know where money might be taken without doing unnecessary harm to the economy, to ensure that what is needed by the cultural and rights sectors is passed over to them. They will do this because they see that, though each sector is independent of the others, the three also form the unity of the whole. The whole can be healthy and serve the threefold needs of all people within the whole only when each sector also serves the whole.

This will become clearer if we look at actual examples from life.

Between the Rights and the Economic Sectors

Economic activity can only function as it should in an environment
made secure and given form and order by the rights sector. The
various factors and activities such as rights of access to resources,
health and safety, agreements between employers and employees
and between organizations, the role of money, the establishing of
ownership, and the possibility of exchange through purchase and sale
are all made possible through the establishment and administration
of the necessary laws by the rights sector. A police officer, as an
example of someone whose work lies in the rights sector, enforces
the law, investigates a crime, or arrests a suspected criminal. In this,
the officer fulfills a role needed and determined by the community.
Police work is, of course, totally different from economic productive
work in a factory, for example. If a police officer controls a crowd,
arrests a burglar, or protects a person from interference by another,
what he or she does cannot be said to produce a product having
an economic value. The money received as a wage is not given in
exchange for either the work itself or the result of the work.

Like the lecturer spoken of in Chapter Nine, police officers are given
money in order to buy what they need. This frees them to fulfill the
social service they have taken on, that of being a police officer. It
would be a truer description of their wage to say that an individual
contracts to fulfill the role of a police officer within the community
and the community contracts to provide him or her, by means of a
wage, with the money to buy what is needed to live while he or she
does police work for the community. Any other description simply
does not give a true representation of the actual facts. Economically,
the police officer's wage is of the nature of a gift, or more properly, a
contracted contribution. The money received as wage is then used to
buy the products of economic production.

*

If we now look, not at the police officer, but at the police station, the
matter becomes clearer. The police station is of course built by the
labor of workers in the economic sector; it is a product of economic
activity as is also the furniture, equipment, and other consumables
that are part of a complete police station.

In financing the building of a police station, capital, wherever it
comes from, is used up. What was capital returns to the function of

purchase money when it is used to pay the wages of the workers and for all the materials used in the building. As capital, it disappears.

The building materials, the bricks, mortar, and lumber, as products of economic production, are used up in the same way. They become the building. As a newly completed building, it is an economic product. But as soon as the new building is taken over by the police, it goes through a transition. It ceases to be a product having an economic value and becomes a facility of the rights sector, a police station. As a police station it plays no part in further economic productive activity, therefore it can have no economic value, no capital value. In a certain sense, it could be said that it becomes a product that is being consumed in that it slowly deteriorates, is used up, and will one day "go back to nature" and have to be replaced.

Here there might be the objection that the police station, as a building, does have a capital value, even if only a potential one, in that it could be sold for some other purpose. That this is not a true economic or capital value will become clearer when the question of the "market in rights" is looked at in and following Chapter Seventeen.

In that the police station is not used in any way for economic production, there can be no economic return, nor any repayment of the capital, to the economic sector. The police do not generate economic values in the way that economic activity does.

Money that is passed from the economic sector to the rights or cultural sector without any return is, from the point of view of the economic sector, a gift. It passes out of the economic sector without anything being received "in exchange." This is true whether the money is taken in taxes, which are compulsory, or is actually passed over freely by the leaders of the economic sector who perceive that in the long-term the economic sector can continue to function in a healthy way only when supported by the other two sectors.

As *gift capital,* the capital is used up. It is consumed in the building of the new police station, which does not itself have capital value. In that the money pays for all the materials used in the building and also goes to the workers as wages, it returns to the economic sector as purchase money. The cycle in the flow of money is completed:

purchase money → *loan capital* → *gift capital* → (back to) *purchase money.*

Between the Cultural and Economic Sectors

What is true of the police station is also true of buildings of the cultural life of the community. But in a cultural institution such as a theater or concert hall, it is easy to become confused by the fact that a person normally has to purchase a ticket in order to enter, which can lead to the idea that it is an economic purchase. But this exchange is, in fact, of the nature of a gift or contribution. What I showed in Chapter Nine in the case of the lecturer as an example of cultural work is also true of a performer. Cultural activity such as performing or teaching is a totally different activity from economic production; it does not produce an economic product that can be exchanged nor does it generate a profit. Any charge or fee is a contribution, a form of gift, towards the costs of running the theater, concert hall, or school, not the price of a purchase. This is clearer in the case of state-run education, where the costs of running a school or building a school building, like the police station, are funded out of taxes, that is, out of compulsory contributions. It is just as true for private education funded by fees.

Capital used to build, for example, a factory, shop, or railway, goes through a quite different process. The capital used will have accumulated within the economic sector, but in the factory, shop, or railway, it remains within that sector – these are all means of production within the economic process of division-of-labor. The capital put into their construction is used up – as money capital, it disappears. But the buildings themselves become capital – industrial capital. They are a means through which the process of production can take place. The money and the buildings all remain part and parcel of the economic process of production. As such, they create a return on the capital used in their construction. In a properly planned economy, the money earned through the use of the buildings would first repay the capital used up in their construction and then contribute to the creation of further capital.

As shown in the last chapter, from the perspective of those working in economic production, capital used within the economic sector can only correctly be thought of as a loan – it is repaid by the process itself, whereas that passed over to the cultural or rights sectors is of the nature of a gift – there is no direct economic return either financially or in products. The capital is used up and returns to the economic sphere as purchase money.

*

Every building built for purposes of cultural or rights work goes through an important transition, or metamorphosis, at the point when the construction of the building is completed, paid for, and handed over to those who will use it for their work. Just as the gift capital used to pay for it ceases to exist as capital and returns to the economic sector as purchase money, so the building ceases to be an economic product with an economic value, and becomes instead a facility within the cultural or rights sector. This is an important step that is not taken properly into account in the usual studies of social life. It is particularly important in the case of something like a school building. If the idea persists that the building, as a school, has an economic value, then it will follow that the educational activity carried on within that building will be seen as being of a similar nature to an economic productive process. The cost of the building will be taken into account in determining the cost of the education, and so the form of thinking proper to the economic productive process will improperly influence cultural life. The children are then seen as the raw products to which value is added; the 'finished product' should then have a value greater than the cost of the process of adding value. That the child is a living being with a human soul with its own unique biography, capacities, impulses, and longings, will then be lost sight of. This way of thinking is widespread today, and its consequences are plainly visible.

Gift Capital at Work

Within cultural life, money takes on the nature of a contribution, or *contracted contribution,* a quite different nature and way of working than in the economic sector. Money in the cultural sector of society is not "purchase money," nor does it represent a debt owed as it does in economic life. It might be helpful if I brought two examples from actual experience to clarify the use of the word "gift" and "contracted contribution." But it will not be possible within the scope of this book to go into all the many questions these illustrations are likely to raise in anyone accustomed to conventional economic thinking.

I was for many years involved in a small private college of adult education[*]. The students paid fees which consisted of two parts, one for tuition and the other for room and meals. The part of the fee that was for room and meals was clearly a cost of an economic supply; it was a purchase and was treated as such. But the fee for tuition was something quite different. Though a small part of this could be seen as a purchase of materials – books, art supplies, etc. – the bulk was for paying the salaries of the teachers and support staff. In this, there was clearly no purchase, no exchange of economic values; the salary enabled the teachers to buy what they needed to live. It freed them to teach. We thought of this part of the fee as a "contracted contribution." Each student contracted to contribute a certain amount towards the running costs of the college, generally the amount set as the fee. The college in its turn contracted to run the course of study the student would have a right to attend.

Treating the fee in this way opened up different possibilities. It got away from the idea of the fee being the actual cost of a student in the class, which it is not. In reality, the cost of running a course is basically the same whether there are five or thirty-five students. Adding one or more does not materially increase the cost. One could even say that it is the first student who incurs the "cost" of the course, while the others "share" this cost.

If we wished to accept a student from a poorer background we could agree to a lower contracted contribution. This was more realistic than thinking in terms of a scholarship being that part of the "cost" that the student could not pay, and for which an amount had to be found from somewhere else, or taken out of a fund to make up the shortfall.

On one occasion, a married couple who had come to the college to train to be teachers found themselves, during the second year, in financial difficulties. They had arrived at the college with sufficient funds to pay the normal fee, but their bank had later gone into liquidation and they lost much of their money. They could no longer fully pay for their training and so felt they had no choice but to leave the college.

*   See *The Story of Emerson College: Its Founding Impulse, Work and Form* by Michael Spence (Temple Lodge, 2013).

When we in the administration came to consider the situation, we thought of it somewhat differently. They still had enough for board and lodging, but not for the tuition fee. The purpose of the college and of all those who worked there was not to make a profit, but to work with young people and to train, amongst others, teachers. That was the purpose of the college. Certainly the college aimed for a surplus in order to be able to develop the work, but that was not a purpose in itself.

The college would not save any money if these two students left; their completing the course would not cost anything that would be saved by their going. But their leaving would mean that, as far as these two people were concerned, the college would not be able to fulfill its purpose.

Something of this can also be seen in the way salaries were treated. If one sets out to move away from the usual basis of "buying a person's work," then one cannot calculate what one pays a person on the basis of that work. As soon as one arrives at a salary in any way conditioned by a person's qualifications, experience, type of work, or the actual number of hours worked, then one is thinking in terms of the value of the work and paying according to that value – one is paying for the work, buying an integral part of that other person, and that person is then not free.

In order to find a way of paying salaries in a way that avoids any form of paying for the work itself, it was necessary to separate the work from the pay. There was, of course, a certain relationship in that only those who made a full-time commitment to the college could expect to be paid fully. But this full commitment was not defined in terms of hours – some people are simply not able to work at the same intensity or for as long as others. A person who took on responsibility for a certain work needed by the college and recognized by the college as within that person's capacity, would be given a salary, calculated solely on his or her needs, to the extent that that work was a full-time commitment.

Because the faculty experienced their work as entirely separated from their pay, as something they performed out of their own impulse, each came to a sense of freedom, of being free to do the work for its own sake. Due to the fact that it was one's own work, each developed a sense of responsibility for that work and for the work of the college as a whole. Though technically everyone was an employee of the college, in reality each experienced the work as their own, not as work done for someone else. Because of this, individuals were much more flexible and, with less emotional blockages, were able on occasion to adjust their salary needs downwards when this became necessary as the college went through a period of financial difficulties. So too, they would take on extra work when that was needed. The circle of employees, or colleagues as we thought of ourselves, experienced it as *their* college, not themselves as employees doing what they were paid to do. Many students and visitors commented on the warm and positive qualities they experienced in the life of the college.

Of course, a multitude of questions must arise when such statements are made. But this is not the place to go into these, it would lead far beyond the immediate purpose of this book. But the college worked in this way for at least 30 years and continued for a time after I left. What is important here is what was actually experienced by the people who worked in this way and what it achieved in the life of the college as a whole. When this way of working was explained to the students it always had a very positive effect. There ceased to be any question as to the fairness of those with money paying more than those with less or none. In fact some students from richer countries suggested their fees should be higher in the first place. There was also a much greater inclination in the students to pay the fees due rather than find ways of avoiding paying them.

Economic/Cultural – The Balancing of Gifts

All this can be seen as reciprocating cycles of movement in an imaginative picture.

I showed earlier that when the capacities of imagination and invention are applied to economic production, on the one side, labor is made more productive, and on the other, more capital is generated.

Without what comes over from cultural life, the economic sphere of activity would remain static; there would be no development, and no improvement to human levels of livelihood. On the other hand, those who nourish and sustain the cultural life of the community can do so only so long as they are provided with the products of economic activity which they need to live and do their work.

Between the economic and cultural spheres of society there is a reciprocity, a two-way mutuality: each contributes to making the other possible. From the economic sphere of activity flow the commodities needed by the cultural workers, and from the cultural life flows the creativity and ideas that enhance the processes that produce the commodities. That is one side of the reciprocating movement. It finds its counterpart in the money that moves in the opposite direction. Capital, generated by the inventive genius that comes from the cultural life, is passed from the economic sphere of activity back to cultural life as gift. Within cultural life, this gift money is again transformed into purchase money: it returns to the economic sphere in payment for the commodities consumed or used by those in cultural work.

*

In the example of the crane, it is possible to see how the creativity of thinking works into economic life as technology. Each bit of the crane, each screw, pulley, and spar, has been thought through, each is substance formed by thought, or, we could say, each is thought filled with substance. When it has taken the form of technology that enhances the productivity and efficiency of economic production, thinking can be said to have died into substance.

In the cultural sphere, and also in the rights sphere, we see the opposite process. In the example of the building of a police station or school it was shown how the capital brought into being in economic activity and then given over to cultural life is there used up. It is used to pay for the materials needed and the wages of all those who put up the building. As capital it is consumed, it disappears. Each dollar is spent to buy products of economic production. Even the money used to pay the worker's wages ultimately buys commodities, food, clothing, cars, heat, etc. What would have been excess capital if it had remained in the economic sphere has disappeared. Here, too, it is not an unreal picture to say that the capital, as capital, has died into the building.

A simple diagram can illustrate this:

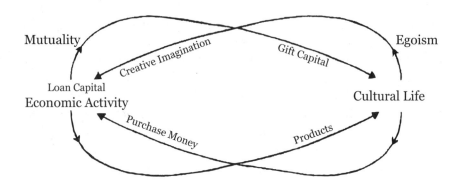

Figure 1: Recripocal Flow of Economic and Cultural Life

This form gives an idea of the flow of the contributions the cultural and economic sectors make to each other, forming reciprocating circles flowing in opposite directions. Like division-of-labor itself, this flow has arisen over time; there is no beginning nor end of each circle.

Within one pole, that of the economy, products are produced. As counter values to these, purchase money comes into being. This moves within the circle of those carrying the work of economic production. Purchase money accumulates as capital: first as loan capital as it unites with the inventive and managerial genius that comes over from cultural life and so fructifies the economic productive process. Out of this union, loan capital evolves into gift capital, which is passed back to cultural life as a counter movement to the inflow of creative ideas.

This gift capital received into the cultural sector is needed by those who carry the work of the cultural life to purchase from the economic sector all they need to live and do their work. What was capital is transformed back into purchase money when used as payment for the products and services flowing from the economic sector.

So both the excess capital and the excess products generated in the economic sphere of activity are used up in a way that benefits, rather than harms, the community as a whole.

Giving form and order to this two-way flow of contributions is all that comes from the rights sphere by way of social structure, regulation and administration. Without this structure, society would inevitably become dysfunctional and descend into chaos.

*

It is not my intention here to go into the corresponding relationships between the cultural and rights sectors and between the rights and economic sectors. But there are of course comparable, though different, contributions and services that flow from each to the other. These will become clear to anyone who comes to look objectively into the threefold structure of social life.

Chapter 13
Mutuality And "Economic Associations"

Before we can know how to bring our community and social life into a form that accords with its own present nature, we must know what that nature is. What I have tried to give so far can be no more than a start, a simple foundation on which anyone can build further who has the resolve and objectivity to penetrate below the surface of life. It might seem at times that I have been over simplistic, that social life, and particularly the economic sector, is far more complex than I have portrayed. But it is just because it is so complex that its foundations and its basic make-up are too often no longer seen. For example, I have frequently used the term "division-of-labor" to describe that which lies at the foundation of all economic activity. Nowadays this phrase is hardly ever used. People think in terms of "economies of scale" and of "technologies," but both of these are a consequence of what is indicated by this term "division-of-labor." In the sphere of economic production it is this dividing of the work that serves to increase productivity. Thinking only in terms of "economies of scale" or of "technology" cannot lead to a sound grasp of the specific factors that make up the productive process. It is necessary to start from these apparently simple beginnings in order to get to the foundations, the essence or basic framework of our present very complex human society.

Egoism and Mutuality

People speak of 'living on' their salary or their pension. But do they? If we are to achieve any healing of human social life we have to look very exactly at the phenomena. We live on the products of other people's work. Money only gives us the power to acquire them, it does not produce them. The money itself will not satisfy any of our actual needs, with the arguable exception of a 'need' for wealth or power. Even then, if there were no others working to produce the things we need and who themselves need money, the money would have no value to us.

We live in the age of individuality, when more and more people come to a sense of their own identity, of their "self" or "I." This consciousness of self awakens egoism. There never has been a time when egoism has come so powerfully to dominate social life. In all earlier times it was held in check by both family consciousness and by a religious discipline which was often very powerful. But these barriers have been falling away and now egoism has been largely freed from these outer restraints.

Alongside this growth of individuality and egoism, the industrial revolution has given birth to an economic life based on division-of-labor, which calls for mutuality and co-operation. Just when there has arisen, within the sphere of economic production, the greatest need for a conscious working in community, human beings have increasingly awoken to themselves as individuals quite distinct from whatever group or family or tribe they may belong to by virtue of birth and blood.

So a conflict has arisen that is deeply rooted in our time. To come to its full productive potential, modern economic activity demands of those who guide it the imaginative creativity that can only come out of egoism. It is these capacities, nurtured in cultural life and kindled initially by a kind of egoism, that sustain and develop division-of-labor. But division-of-labor calls for mutuality or brotherhood, the antithesis of egoism.

It is just those who are impelled by their own egoism to develop the necessary powers of creativity and entrepreneurial enterprise who become the managers and leaders of economic life, from which egoism needs to be excluded. But this egoism must be contained, prevented from working against the interests of the community as a whole. This contrast or conflict is there, it exists and cannot be done away with or suppressed. To a certain extent it must be so, but when it is not understood and egoism is not held in check, it leads to anti-social activities and unsocial structures.

There must be something within the social organism that can allow egoism to work where it contributes positively to the economic productive process but which will not allow it to reach the point at which it becomes destructive.

Center and Periphery

As I have mentioned before, it makes a great difference to our understanding and control of the communal economic life if we view it from the point where we stand individually, or if we view it from the standpoint of the needs of the whole community: that is, if we view it from the periphery. We can act out of the sense that we each have to struggle to make a living, each for him- or herself within the community of human beings where all others also act out of self-interest, where each is a separate center within the economy. Many today believe that only in this way can the welfare of the whole be achieved.

Or we can act on the basis that the economic sector as a whole is responsible for producing all that is needed by the community as a whole, that is, by all humanity.

The single business tends to regard itself as an individual, unique, and free organization responsible only for itself; it sees itself as within, but also separate from, society as a whole. On the other hand, society as a whole will see each business organization as a part of itself, as an organ within itself, interdependent with others providing for the needs of the whole. Both viewpoints are valid within their own fields. Indeed, both are necessary just as each pole of a magnet is necessary to the other. But it makes an enormous difference to the social life of the community if we fail to see the difference and so fail to find a form that provides guidance out of an awareness of the needs of the whole. Due to modern technological developments, humanity now has the ability to provide for every human being on this earth. That there are so many who are not provided for is not because we cannot provide for them, but because we do not have the thoughts and imaginative ideas with which to take hold of economic life and structure it in such a way that all are provided for. In cultural life we start from the impulses and needs of the individual. In economic life we must start from the needs and interests of the whole, from the periphery. The major question now is how to form economic life so that we can bring about this control from the periphery.

This cannot be achieved by rules and regulations issued from the rights sphere, by government. When the forces of egoism in the human soul are as strong as they are today, no legislation or outer authority such as the law will ever get people of themselves to think and act cooperatively, out of brotherhood or sisterhood.

The need to see the economic sphere of activity from the totality can be further illustrated by looking at the factors of supply and demand.

Supply and Demand

In considering the economic sector, it is not enough to think only of the supply and demand for goods and commodities – the supply and demand for money is just as important a factor.

When a producer supplies goods, for example shoes, it is in effect a demand for money; that is the purpose of his activity. This demand or need for money, together with the price that shoes will obtain in the market, will govern what he produces.

Consumers, on the other hand, have a demand for shoes, but whether they buy them will depend on the price and on their need for these particular shoes. They might see it as more beneficial to keep their money, or spend it on something else, or they may not have enough.

Traders stand between the producer and the consumer. They trade money for shoes and shoes for money. Each is part of their "trade capital." For them, the price – that is the price of shoes in terms of money, or the price of money in terms of shoes – is determined by the supply of and demand for both shoes and money.

These three – producer, trader, and consumer – each approach and view a transaction from a different perspective. The producer looks for monetary profit. The trader sees the profit in both the shoes and the money. Consumers see it in the shoes: if a person is to buy the shoes, they must be of more value to that person than the amount of money he or she pays.

It is an incomplete picture if we think only in terms of the supply and demand for commodities. This is only true from the perspective of the trader. It is not true from that of the producer: there we must think in terms of a supply of commodities and a demand for money; nor is it true for the consumer, where there is a supply of money and a demand for commodities. Otherwise we will not perceive the active forces at play in the general circulation of goods and commodities.

This meeting of producer, trader, and consumer, and all that is at work between supply and demand, is not confined only to the point where the goods are purchased by the final consumer. It is to be found at every stage of production where one producer sells to another producer. The shoemaker is a supplier of shoes, but he is a consumer of leather, thread, rubber, glue, and many other products manufactured by others. There may not always be an actual trader in between.

Only a person actually involved in economic life can have a sense of what is at work there. A person standing outside can never do this. Each of these three – producer, trader, and consumer – will view the market differently, each will understand it from their own place in it. Only when these three meet in what I shall describe as "economic associations" will it be possible to rise above the perspective of the individual to an overview of the whole.

Unemployment

There are a number of social problems which we seem unable to overcome despite the best efforts of many sincere and well-meaning people in both industry and government. This can be made clear by looking, for example, at the problem of unemployment.

Imagine that a person starts a business making furniture. We will assume the business is highly successful and periodically has to take on more employees. But a time comes when, for one reason or another, the market slows and sales are badly affected. Production has to be reduced. With reduced sales, and therefore reduced income, the business cannot continue to carry the same work force. Some of the workers are laid off and become unemployed. It may well be that at this same time other businesses are also laying off workers, so there is a real social problem.

Clearly the individual businesses can never solve this question acting alone, nor can even a few do so by coming together. Such a problem is one for the economy as whole. Only the economy in its totality is self-contained, the individual business never is. The individual business may have to solve its problems by getting rid of workers; these workers are then outside the business and no longer its concern. But each individual human being is always a part of, and a concern for, the community as a whole; a person can never be outside of society. The community can never get rid of people, it must somehow take them into account.

If the question of unemployment is looked at, not from the viewpoint of the single organization, which must look after its own interests, but from that of society as a whole, it will be seen in a different light. The single business must see itself as an individual organization, within but separate from society and responsible to itself. But society, the community as a whole, must see itself as a totality of people and see to it that each one has a place within itself; it must see each business or organization as one of many, each part of and serving the whole.

From this perspective, it becomes clear that if there are unemployed people in the community there is a failure of responsibility in that community. If some have more than their share of the products of the whole while others are in need, then the community itself is ailing. This can only be seen in its reality when viewed from the perspective of the community as a whole, not from the point of view of the individual.

Within the community the means must be developed to place on those active in the economic sector the responsibility of providing for the physical needs of every member of the community. It is a failure of the community when people cannot find a place in which they can make a worthwhile contribution to the community and so earn their share of what is produced.

The polarity of viewpoint and interest between the individual, whether a single person or an organization, and the community as a whole, is one of great importance and needs to be taken fully into consideration if a solution is to be found to these problems. The individual enterprise can deal with problems in so far as they relate to that enterprise. It cannot solve the problems of the whole community. For that, there must be some organ that has a consciousness and sense of the needs of the whole.

Associative Working – What Can Be Achieved in a Group

It is possible to form such an organ, but it will need to be founded on a simple, observable fact.

Whether it is an individual or a group, the leadership of a business must in the first place concern itself with the running and development of its own enterprise. It must work out of a form of egoism in so far as the interests of its enterprise are concerned. It is, in a certain way, to the advantage of the community that it does so. But this egoism, while working to the advantage of the single organization, works destructively when allowed to go beyond the single organization and to enter in any way into the economy as a whole.

What cannot be done by the single individual or organization alone can be achieved by individuals working together. When individual producers, traders, and consumers come together, each from their particular place in the economic sphere of activity, then it is possible for something to be born in the group that cannot be achieved by an individual alone.

Each individual brings to the group a view of the economy from their own particular position in it. The baker sees the economy from a different perspective than does the miller, who again sees it differently from the shopkeeper, or the farmer. The baker's relationship to the miller is that of a consumer to a supplier, but to the shopkeeper it is one of a producer to a consumer. They all see the chain of production from their own particular standpoint. Not only will they all see it, but each will act out of the interests of their particular place in the economy. The individual cannot do otherwise. The belief that individuals working in economic life can, on their own, see the whole objectively, or can alone think it through and act out of the interest of the whole, arises out of a failure to grasp both human nature and the nature of economic life as a whole.

But when all these individuals, the farmer, miller, baker, distributor, shopkeeper, and final consumer, come together in the right way, in the right mood of soul, then the group can rise above the egoism of the individual. In the group an "objective community spirit" can arise. In the group an imagination of the whole can develop that the individual alone can never achieve. The group can become more than the sum total of its individual members. Then the imagination of the whole community emerges as though held in the center. Within the group, each individual will share in and act out of this perception of what is needed for the whole.

Anyone who has had the opportunity to work in groups in situations such as just described and who has first observed the individuals outside the group, and then sees what happens when they come together, will know what has been said to be true. That does not mean to say that the group is always able to come to an objective imagination of the whole, but that the potential is always there. Much depends on the mood of soul and the intentions of the members when they come into the meeting.

The assumption that people can only act out of egoistic motives is not sustained by any objective view of life. There are far more people than is often realized who are able and who, deep down in their hearts, wish to work for the community as a whole. But modern life places on everyone the assumption of self-interest, and this overshadows deeper impulses of altruism. Altruistic people are by no means to be found only in the various charitable or alternative organizations. If we assume people to be egoistic or dishonest, this will itself tend to make them so. The opposite is also true. There is good in every human being, and to act on the basis of this conviction will always tend to call it forth.

Among the leaders of society, in business and industry, in the trade unions, in politics, and in other spheres of activity, people are to be found who have remarkable capacities and social impulses. It is not merely a question of morality or charity. What is required is the imagination to see that, from the perspective of society as a whole, egoism within economic productive activity is inefficient, uneconomical, and works against the interests of the community. Altruism, or brotherhood, is an economic factor that leads to productivity. Working cooperatively in this way is a necessity not only for the efficient production of commodities, but also for the understanding and management of every aspect of economic activity. The more one penetrates into the economic sphere, into the actual productive processes, into the interplay of human labor and the creative human spirit and into the creation and flow of money and capital, the more one comes to see that in every aspect of the economic life of the community the single human being working alone can achieve nothing. Even to see and understand its working, a single person needs others.

As we have seen, in cultural life egoism has its proper place. There it does not work destructively in the same way. On the contrary, all art, all creativity, science, and research has its start in egoism. In cultural life it is the individual that is important and central. Everything arises out of individual impulses. But in the economic process of production egoism works destructively.

If we observe life more carefully, all this will become self-evident. When people come together and carry into their meeting a will to work for the whole, then the group can rise above the egoism of the individual members and become aware of the community as a whole. It often happens. But it almost as often passes unnoticed and is not taken hold of.

This transformation, or presence, that comes into a group when people come together in the right mood of soul is of immense importance. Such a group is the only organ that can, firstly, develop a true imagination of the economy as a totality, and secondly, can kindle the will in the individual to act out of the interests of the whole.

Economic Association and the Boundaries to Economic Activity

Those who have consciously worked this way usually refer to such a group as an "economic association," and the way of working as "working associatively." These names do present certain problems. In normal use, the word "association" generally refers to a group with a common interest, one that comes together to gain benefit for those "inside" at the cost of those "outside." This is also true of "co-operatives." It is almost the opposite of what is meant here. But there is no other word in the English language that has a comparable meaning.

Associative working in the sense used here can have no boundaries, no division between those within and those without.

Even when an association is concerned with one narrow line of production, its "objective community spirit" must reach to the whole of humanity. Although its immediate concern may be narrow, it is, nevertheless, a part of, and ultimately concerned with, the whole.

Members of an economic association need to be drawn from those who have expert knowledge and who represent and are actively involved in areas of economic life. They should come from the whole spectrum of production, distribution, and consumption and include people from management as well as from the factory floor. It is very important that they do not come as representatives to look after the interests of those whom they represent, but because they each stand in and have knowledge of a different field of the economy and have come to recognize that all individuals benefit only when the interests of the whole are put first.

Such an associative group should not be set up as a corporate body; it requires no, or only limited, legal foundation. A basis in law could introduce into its work forms that would be counterproductive to its essential function. Its whole essence is that it is formed of people who are themselves active and have authority in different areas of the economy and therefore have expert knowledge; they should freely come together for the purpose of caring for the welfare of the whole by taking specific action in their own place of work.

Economic associations will only work properly if they are given authority and their spheres of influence are held within certain boundaries. These were touched on earlier. The democratically elected rights organization must have a responsibility to set and maintain the limits beyond which the associations will have no control or influence. All that is given by nature – the land itself on which the crops are grown, the raw materials within the land such as iron, coal, and oil, all that grows on the land without human involvement – all this lies outside the area of actual economic productive work. The productive process, and therefore the responsibility of the economic associations, can only begin at the point where economic activity first takes hold of, and in some way transforms, what is given by nature.

I will attempt to show later that nature, the land, and all that it provides is something that rightfully belongs, in so far as it can belong to anyone, to all humanity, or to the people of a particular country which the land defines. It is for the community itself, through its democratically appointed rights organs, to determine the uses of that which nature provides – how much of it may be used for which purpose and by whom. Clearly, members of the economic associations must have no control or influence over this democratic process.

As "sole owner" of the natural resources, the community, through its democratically elected rights organs, can have considerable control over the economic sector in that it can ensure that only those businesses that work in a mutually social way have access to the natural resources. These will include access to the mineral resources within the land, the use of land and water, the disposal of waste, and emissions into the environment. This means that only those businesses participating "associatively" within the community would be able to survive.

The granting and control of the right to use or extract any natural resources would be done by the organs of the rights sector in close discussion with or through the relevant economic associations. Any such rights would be granted to a specific business or organization for a particular purpose, and would, when no longer needed by the particular business, or after a certain time, revert back to the rights body responsible as representing the community as a whole. As will be discussed later, such "rights" must never be subjected to purchase and sale.

This division of responsibility between the rights sphere, with its control over all natural resources, and the economic productive process that needs these resources, gives one boundary to the economic sphere of activity. Maintaining this boundary is essential if there is not to be abuse by those in positions of economic power.

A further boundary that needs to be recognized and taken into account lies between the economic productive process and the human work or labor that drives it, but which is not part of it. The amount of labor to be put into economic production, the conditions of work, and level of wages are all matters that must be determined by the *organs of the rights sphere* – not the economic associations – according to what the community itself feels is right in the existing circumstances of its social life.

A third boundary lies between cultural life and economic activity. The level of activity of the cultural sphere to be focused on further development of the economic process should be solely determined on the basis of the feelings and way of life wanted by the members of the community. This can only be achieved through a working together of the separate and different organs of the three sectors: the cultural, rights, and economic – the economic represented by the associations.

Such economic associations will need to come into being in all the many areas and at the different levels of activity from small single lines of production, distribution, and consumption at village level to those operating worldwide. Due to the nature of the interweaving lines of production that make up the economic sector, the associations will also need to overlap, with some members belonging to more than one.

It will come to be seen that, when such economic associations take responsibility for the overall guidance, management, and conduct of all economic activity, the possibility will arise to bring healing to some of the disorders and aberrations that are so painfully apparent in human society today and that bring such suffering to so many.

*

The economic associations will also be the means by which a control of the flow of capital can be achieved so that it works beneficially for the community as a whole rather than for individual personal gain. If we look back at the example of the woodcutters and the question of to whom the accumulated capital should belong – the woodcutters, the carter, or the community – it is only the associations that will be in a position to provide the answers and to ensure that what is due to the community as a whole is used for the benefit of the community. In so far as the capital arises out of the working of the whole through division-of-labor, some of it must rightly belong to the whole. Only those working in the economic associations will be in a position to apportion it. The carter and the woodcutters should be entitled to keep only as much of it as was directly due to their work or creative ingenuity.

Only people working within economic life itself can be in a position to observe where capital is accumulating and from where it could or should be taken to be passed on as gift. Governments or organs of the state, democratic or otherwise, can never do this.

It will be an important task of those working in the economic associations to maintain a balance between egoism and mutuality. On the one side, there is the necessary input of personal impulses and creative imagination into management, which must of necessity contain certain egoistic traits, and on the other, the actual process of production and distribution, which must be based on mutuality, from which the possibility of egoism and personal interest must be firmly excluded.

Economic associations, or the associative way of working, are the only effective form of management at all levels of the economy if it is to serve the whole of the community rather than benefit only the few. It is, of course, not the right form for the work of either the cultural or rights sectors.

*

For many, these ideas of economic associations will appear unrealistic and completely utopian. This is a natural and understandable reaction. In conditions as they are today they could not immediately be brought into being – that is only too obvious. But before these ideas are completely rejected, certain facts should be carefully considered. Just because the setting up of such associations in the social conditions of today would in all probability lead to failure, does not mean that they would not work well in a different social environment; nor should it be assumed that it is not possible first to build the right environment.

Can We Truly Work out of the Concept of "Society as a Whole?"

Today, particularly in the west, the greater part of our culture, including education, much of the media, and the constant stream of advertising, directs us to think egoistically, to view the world from the particular place at which we stand individually. Egoism is deeply ingrained in our time. And yet it is generally felt that egoism is a negative quality in a person.

But when people come to recognize that social life is a unity formed of three separate and distinct streams, they will also recognize that there is a certain validity to this egoistic approach to the world. Through this they will also know that egoism is only justified to the extent that its opposite, or polarity, is also strongly present in social life. It is this opposite, the mutuality and cooperation that belongs to economic life, that is so difficult to achieve.

What do I mean by the phrase *"from the viewpoint of society as a whole,"* or by *"viewing society from the periphery?"* It is natural to think about something from one's own point of view. Even in considering "society as a whole," we tend at first to think of it from the perspective of our own position in it. But can we truly and realistically think and act from the perspective of *society as a whole*?

Let me illustrate what is meant here with an example. We often refer to wasting money. But when is money wasted? If I spend my money on something that I find does not do what I want it to do, then I might say I have wasted it. But the money is really only wasted from my point of view. For me, it might be a very real waste. I could have bought something that would have been of more use to me. But for the one who received the money it is certainly not wasted; it is still good money.

From the point of view of the community, in this situation it is rather the product of a person's work that could be seen as wasted. Perhaps another person had a need for the article that was of no use to me, so it has gone to the wrong person. Still, the money is not wasted, but continues to circulate. It is like saying that an entry in the accounts is wasted when actually it has just been put in the wrong place.

At that level it is not too difficult to grasp the difference between seeing the event from the point of view of the individual and seeing it from that of the whole. But can we say the same when it is a government that is seen as wasting money – wasting taxpayer's money? If the government spends money putting up a building for a particular function that, due to faulty planning, lack of imagination, or poor administration, turns out to be a fiasco requiring even more money just to keep it running, we say it has wasted money. But the term "wasted money" is a half truth that diverts attention from the reality. The people who do the work and are paid with the money are as much part of the community as anyone else and may need the money as much as the others. Is it a true statement to say that money given to them is wasted money? From their point of view it certainly is not. They may have worked as hard as anyone else for the money. Their work may have been wasted, but it cannot be said that the money paid them is wasted.

To say that the money is wasted leads to thinking that money is a thing in itself and is that which brings the building into being. But the reality is that the vision was faulty, or its implementation was not thought through, and as a result the work was directed to the wrong ends and an opportunity was missed. From the point of view of the whole, this is the reality, not that the money was wasted.

We are not accustomed to thinking in terms of "from the periphery," so to do so can be, at first, a challenge. How do we get to the point where we do not instinctively think first in terms of wasting money, but of human work or labor being made fruitless? Even the government does not think and act from this position, from that of the whole.

This shift in perspective is difficult, but absolutely necessary if we are to bring our economic life into a form where it will serve the needs of all people, not just those with greatest power. There is no other basis from which to begin to take hold of the enormous possibilities for good or harm that our economic life of today offers and bring it to serve humanity. The individual cannot do this alone, only a group of people working in the way here described can do it.

If the leaders of economic activity could really reach the point of thinking instinctively from the whole, from the periphery, then problems such as unemployment and the pollution of our environment would be approached quite differently. But so long as we think only from the place where we each stand within the whole, and the three sectors of society are confused as one, these problems will continue to exist and the poor, the unemployed, the degradation of the environment, and the domination of humanity by the giant financial and industrial institutions and conglomerates will continue to be with us.

Part 2

Chapter 14
Money –
Its Nature and Creation

Money is one of the most powerful and all-embracing forces at work in the world today. It touches, with very few exceptions, every human being, and has a more universal control over people's actions and ways of life than anything else. We are largely unconscious of the influence that it has over us, while the effects of this influence can be seen in the language we use, our ways of thinking, and in our feelings.

What is this money that today can have as powerful a role in human affairs as religions did in the ancient past? A single photograph of a tree will never give us a true picture of the whole tree. To be able to form a true idea of the tree we must see photographs taken from many different positions and then, through our powers of imagination, transform these into a concept of the single whole.

So too with money; to acquire any true picture we must look at it from many different directions. We will then come to see that it is almost impossible to arrive at any certainty, or come to definitions or perceptions that have constant validity. Money is a moving target, and understanding it requires a mobile thinking.

*

Although money is not itself a separate sector of social life, it plays an increasingly powerful role in our society and reaches far beyond the economic sector out of which it arose. It has become a far greater influence and power in our lives than is generally realized or acknowledged. Money permeates *all three* spheres of social life, often in ways that bring great suffering and harm.

For many people, the words "economy" or "economic" immediately bring to mind thoughts of money. Certainly money is closely connected to economic activity, but it reaches far beyond it. As I have shown, money arises out of the combined working of the human creative spirit and human labor, it facilitates the economic process of production and distribution, and brings flexibility and movement into social economic life; but money is not itself what produces the products we use.

We tend to see money as a value in itself. We think in terms of living on an income or on a pension. We think that we have something because we have paid for it, that it was the money that somehow produced it. Stopping there, we do not see that we actually have something because other people have labored to produce it. We do not think of what lies behind the money, what gives it value, or what it represents.

The quality and nature of money varies depending on where within the economic cycle it appears, and indeed on whether it represents an actual economic value, or an apparent but unreal economic value. From the point of view of the individual, it may seem unimportant how the money was acquired or what lies behind it; its reality seems rather to be what it will buy. But if we are in any way concerned for the well-being, not of the individual but of society as a whole, it is immensely important that we see beyond the actual money and understand what lies behind it.

Money in Society

There is an increasing tendency for people to see the money they are paid as that which gives them their identity or dignity. Not to be paid for work done, or to be paid less than "the going rate," is often experienced as a loss of personal worth.

I knew someone once who worked for a particular charitable organization that was not in a position to pay him what he could expect for the same work elsewhere. He actually wanted to work for that particular organization, and what was offered was enough for him to live in reasonable comfort. So he had agreed to do the work for that salary.

But after a while he could not continue. In the course of his work he would meet other people in the same profession as himself.

Although they could not know that he was paid less than themselves, he himself did know it and it gave him a feeling of inferiority, of loss of worth. He felt this so strongly that he had to give up the work he wanted to do and find other work that would pay him what he felt corresponded to his value, although the work itself would not be as fulfilling. It was not what the extra money could buy that was important to him, but what it gave him as confirmation of his personal worth.

Many people today judge their worth as a human being by the money they earn. This can lead to their being unable to work unless they are paid for the work. It is sometimes as though it is the money that switches them on, just as we switch on a machine. This is a phenomenon that is increasingly observable today, and is something that should worry anyone who is concerned for individual freedom.

Money has a tendency to hide the reality, to distort the truth. We see this in its most pronounced form in the fact that humanity's attention has become focused on money, yet has lost sight of what lies behind it. How often when we buy something does our consciousness reach beyond the price we pay to the work and activity that had to happen in order that what we are buying could be there in the shop where we buy it? When we switch on an electric light or heater, are we aware as we do so that at that moment there are people working to keep the generators going so that the light comes on or the heater gives out heat?

It is essential that this masking tendency of money be perceived. When we do so, we will be able to work with money in a healthy way, and so begin to heal our social life. Seeing through money, we will begin to recognize those transactions that do not, in fact, involve an exchange of economic products. We will find that many of the exchanges involving money today consist of the buying and selling of what are properly *rights*, rights that should be granted on the basis of the equality of all people, not sold. Only when we can clearly see the true nature of such a transaction can we start to correct it.

What is of greatest importance today is that we learn to see through money to the realities of social life: to the human labor that lies behind even the simplest things that we use, to the gifts of nature to which all people have an equal right, and to what can emerge out of the free and creative human soul that itself must be free.

The Corrupting Voice Within Money

Many years ago I inherited some money that I was not expecting. It was not a great amount, but I felt considerable gratitude for it. It meant that we as a family could do something we could not otherwise have done. After looking at a number of options, we decided to build a room onto our house. The money would be just enough for that. The room would greatly improve the quality of our lives and we all felt grateful for the legacy.

But as the room neared completion, I came to see certain other small improvements that it would have been good to have done had there been a little more money. Then I became aware of still other things that we could have done. I found myself imagining that the legacy had been bigger than it actually was. What if I had had one less sibling so that more of the inheritance had come to me? It was then that I awoke with a certain shock to something I perceived in myself. Whereas I had at first been very grateful for the gift, for being able to build the room onto the house, this feeling of gratitude had been transformed into a kind of resentment that it had not been more, that what there was had to be shared. This pulled me up with a jolt, and I tried to look into myself to see what had actually happened.

I became aware of something like a voice, a voice that whispered in my ear "what if it had been more?" It was a very persistent thought that I felt had been put into my head. *What if it had been more?* It showed me all that I could have had or done if only it had been more. The money had awakened greed within me.

It would have been easy to have slept through this event and to have remained unconscious of what had entered into my thinking. It was as though it came from outside, that someone had whispered in my inner ear what could have been done with more money. How often does such a voice whisper to us and do we remain asleep to our hearing it?

There is always inherent in money the temptation to want more, to get something for nothing. Money can offer a life of ease, of not having to work. It gives us power to do what we want, to have control over others. It can take hold of us in such a way that it distorts all our better impulses and feelings. This is most apparent where the money comes without having to be worked for, such as with inherited money, capital gains, or money won in the lottery. It often plays havoc within families when there is any opening for dispute over inherited money.

After careful observation of oneself, it is a rare person who finds they have never heard the whisper of such a voice.

*

I showed earlier how money, or monetary value, arises in the economic process, and I illustrated the three forms of purchase money, loan capital, and gift capital. I will now try briefly to show something of the evolution of money from its original form as "substance value."

Its Origin in Substance

Until very recently what was used as, and thus became, money was either a material substance that had intrinsic value such as gold or silver, or it was an economic product that had an economic value in itself such as the wood in the example of the woodcutters. Someone who received wood in exchange for what he had made or grown, instead of burning it, could have stored it. Then, at a later time, he could have exchanged it for what he needed from someone else.

The substances that have been the most widely used as money are gold and silver. But there have been times when others such as tobacco have filled the same role. An illustrative example of a precious substance being used as money is the old English "penny." Gold and silver were originally measured in "troy" weights – 5,760 troy grains made up one troy pound weight; 24 grains was a penny weight. A penny weight of silver became also a penny of money – 12 pennies were a shilling and 20 shillings a pound (24 x 12 x 20 = 5,760), so one troy pound of silver by weight was one pound value in money. When a person sold something he had made, he received in exchange something that had value in itself, the silver in the form of a coin. The coin was worth its content of silver, and silver its weight in silver coins.

In purchase and sale there was once a far greater consciousness of the value of both what was given and what was received. By value I mean, not the monetary value, but the social/economic value that arises out of the process of production on the one side and the inherent value of the gold or silver given in exchange. In those earlier times, production included a considerable degree of individual craftsmanship. This gave a human and personal value on the one side, and, on the other, the money, whether gold, silver, or tobacco, had an inherent and transparent value in itself. We can say that the focus of consciousness was on the values of the two things exchanged and their reciprocity. The products were of course much simpler and the activity involved in their production more transparent than they are today.

At the next stage in the development of the financial system what happened was this. People did not find it convenient or safe to always carry their silver or gold with them, so they deposited it with a goldsmith, who had a safe of some kind, or a "bank." They received from the goldsmith a receipt, the receipt being for so much gold.

It came about that often in large transactions, instead of going to get the gold and handing that over, it was the receipt for the gold that was handed over and accepted as payment. At a later date, and in order to facilitate this, these receipts came to be issued in the form of bearer promissory notes – "I promise to pay the bearer on demand the sum of ... ." These words still appear on all United Kingdom bank notes.

But now something became necessary that was not so important before – confidence. There had to be confidence in the receipt, that is, the person receiving it had to be confident that there was actual silver or gold behind the receipt and that they could collect it if and when it was needed. The name of the goldsmith or "bank" issuing the receipt had to be known and be one that inspired confidence. Although in a transaction only paper was handed over, there was still a feeling of the reality of the gold or silver for which the paper was a receipt.

The Emergence of the Present Financial System

The next stage is a very important one that added a completely new dimension to the nature of money and brought about our present financial system.

The "bankers" up to now had issued a note of receipt only on the actual receipt of new coin, that is, of actual silver or gold. (I shall in future use the word "gold" to cover all the various substances that have at different times come to be "money.") At this point, the sum total of the receipts in circulation was equal to the actual gold in the bank vaults. If everyone holding a receipt went to the bank there would be enough gold to cover all the receipts; everyone would get their gold.

But the bankers came to see that, so long as there was confidence in the system, people did not come to collect their gold, but traded the receipts. They observed that never more than a small fraction of the deposited gold, less than 10%, was actually taken out at any one time. Nine-tenths of it remained permanently in the bank.

They came to realize that so long as enough actual gold was retained in their vaults to meet the needs of anyone wishing to withdraw deposits, it would be possible to lend out at interest some of the nine-tenths to anyone who could use it profitably. It was, of course, essential that all people who deposited their gold with the bank continued to feel confident that they could withdraw it whenever they needed to. Confidence in the system was essential if it was to function properly.

What happened then was that when the banker lent the gold to a borrower, the borrower would hand the gold back to the banker as a deposit, (or deposit it in another bank within the banking system) and ask for a receipt. There were then in circulation more receipts than there was actual gold in the banks. The difference was made up by what was "owed" to the bank by the people who had borrowed the gold. The total of the receipts in circulation was equal to the total gold held in the bank plus the amount of gold lent out and owed to the banks. The consciousness of there being gold behind the receipts, or money, was still there, but it began to recede.

The next stage, which in the main came about during the first third of the twentieth century, was that the gold disappeared from behind the money. This happened when the law was changed and it was no longer possible for people who held receipts (money) to go to the bank and ask for their gold. The paper receipt itself became money, but an abstract money that had only a debt behind it. In the meantime, the coins had lost their gold or silver content and had become "token" coins.

What started off as a "receipt" for gold has now itself become money, but with nothing standing behind it except debts "owed" to the bank. What is more, money is now only partially in note form, and very largely nothing more than an entry in a book or a computer. The "I promise to pay the bearer on demand the sum of ... " has in most countries disappeared from the notes or it has become a meaningless phrase. The *substance* has gone and been replaced by *debt*.

Here we see a complete process of abstraction: in its historical development money has been separated from its original substance. The gold, for which the money was a receipt, has been replaced by *debt*, by a negative, and the abstract receipt itself has become the value, the money.

The consciousness that up to very recently looked for a balancing of two values, the gold on one side and the product of a person's work on the other, now looks for a balancing of two abstractions: it sees the value of the product, not in the product itself or in the human labor that produced it, but in the numerical amount of the money asked as the price. Just when money has lost all its substance and has become a complete abstraction – a number on a piece of paper or an entry in an account book or a computer – we have come to focus most closely on it. We are increasingly determining values of all kinds, even sometimes of life itself, in terms of this money.

*

The evolution of money from substance to abstraction should not be seen, however, as a negative development. On the contrary, this transformation was necessary and has been instrumental in creating the possibility of freeing human beings from the situation where the few can enjoy a cultural life at the cost of the labor of the many. But it has also made possible much that is destructive to the health of society. It has released forces that have been taken over by egoism and greed, and so has once again enabled a minority to exercise power and dominion over the majority.

To achieve the possibility of freedom, human beings have to become aware of the true nature of money and consciously take control of it. Money is not a natural phenomenon; it has come into existence through the agency of human activity, albeit without conscious thought or planning. At present, it is out of human conscious control. It has taken on a life of its own and takes some people into its arms and excludes others. But we can, through conscious human thinking, take hold of what we have created and transform it to serve the needs of humanity.

Our evolved financial system led to the expansion of "credit" in a way that the dependence on a substance such as gold could never have done. It is this that made possible the enormous and rapid expansion of the manufacturing base, of technology, and of the economic infrastructure during the later part of the twentieth century.

If the substance value has disappeared from money, if money is now something without tangible form, a number on a piece of paper, an entry in the accounts of a bank or other financial institution, then what is it that gives it reality?

On the immediately practical level, if when a person makes a coat and takes it to market he is to accept payment in money from which all real value has disappeared, that has in fact become an abstraction, two things are necessary. First, he must have confidence that when he wants to buy something from another person the money will be accepted in payment. And if, instead of spending it immediately, he places it in a bank or savings fund, he must have confidence that when he needs it he can get it back.

The second is something that must come from the rights sphere. This is the making of the abstract money into "legal tender." The use of money is then backed by law and payment of money in settlement of a debt cannot be refused. When it was the gold itself that was used as money, no such law was necessary.

The Creation of Money

Imagine that a manufacturer needs money in order to expand his business. He has some capital but will need more, so he arranges an overdraft facility[†] with his bank.

Building work then commences. At a certain point the manufacturer will have used up his own money, and for the purposes of this example we will assume that his bank account falls to zero.

† An 'overdraft facility' is a kind of short-term loan, or credit line, arranged with a bank, that allows for a business or individual to continue to withdraw funds from their bank account after the account has reached "$0."

The builder presents his next invoice for, say, $20,000. The manufacturer gives him a check for this amount. The builder presents this to his own bank, which enters a credit of $20,000 in his account. The paid check goes to the bank of the manufacturer, which marks his account as overdrawn by that amount, so that the manufacturer now owes the bank $20,000.

For the builder who receives it, this is real money. He can spend it in any way he likes. He can pay his workers with it, draw it out as cash, buy a car, or go on holiday. For him it is money, even if it is only an entry in a book.

But it is money *newly created*, money that did not exist before but has been created "out of thin air." If for the builder it is actual money, where did it come from? On the manufacturer's account it is a debt, money owed to the bank, one could call that negative money. But it is money that is backed by the future, by the profits of the economic production that the new building will make possible. Although the banker may take a mortgage on the buildings as security, there still has to be confidence in the capacities and the future earnings of the manufacturer, for it is these that will repay the debt.

The manufacturer has a debt, but, on the other side, he has the new building.

Here we see a loan, or, more correctly, newly created capital, made possible not out of past savings, the accumulation of past profits, but out of *future profits*. It is, in reality, the lender's confidence in the *future* potential of the borrower which stands behind the money that is lent. This is an important point.

The manufacturer first used capital that was accumulated by saving the profit created earlier within the manufacturing process. Behind this capital was all that went before to bring it into existence. Then he borrowed further capital, capital that did not come about through past earnings and savings, but on the basis of confidence in future potential. Behind this new capital is debt, or negative capital. Future earnings will go towards, not replacing capital that has been used up, but towards canceling out a debt. The repayment of the loan gives substance to the money that was earlier "created out of thin air," for which the new building now stands as balance.

There is a question that we should now ask: Should the building itself continue to have capital value, and what are the social consequences of this? This important question will be taken up within the further course of this study.

*

In the future, if we are to organize money in a way that enables it to be used for the benefit and the support of all humanity, then something else will be necessary. In earliest times people perceived the inherent value of what they created, and they related this to a substance such as gold, the value of which was actual and widely recognized. Later it came about that the inherent value of the product of human labor was lost sight of and only its abstract monetary value was perceived. Now we have to learn to look beyond the abstract money, not to a substance, but to the human and personal activity that stands behind the product, to that which the money represents in any particular transaction.

The Three Coats

What is it that money tends to conceal? Let us look at three transactions in which the same sum of money, $200, buys a coat.

The first coat: Imagine that a carpenter makes a table. This involves a certain amount of work not only by the carpenter but by all those unknown others who felled the trees, prepared the wood, and made the tools and other materials used in its production. The carpenter sells the table and receives money in exchange. She then decides that she needs a coat, so she buys one from the tailor. This is paid for with $200 of the money she received for the table.

The second coat: A student is given a grant to enable him to study. He must of course protect his health and he finds that he needs a coat. He buys one from the tailor with $200 of the money given to him as a grant.

The third coat: A person owns a house with a big garden in an area where it is difficult to obtain permission to build any more houses. Despite this, she applies for permission to build a second house on the land and the request is granted. As a result of permission being granted, the land goes up in value and she sells it at a profit. We will assume there are no other factors that have affected the value of the land, that the increase in value is entirely a result of the granting of a building permit. The landowner then decides to buy a coat. To do this, she hands over to the tailor $200 of the money from the profit on the sale of the land and receives the coat in exchange.

In each of these examples the amount of money paid to the tailor is the same. What difference can there be between one sum of $200 and another? It is always just $200. But if we only see the $200, we remain on the surface and do not see the socio-economic reality behind the money.

Behind the money the carpenter gave the tailor was the table that the carpenter had made, a product of her work that had gone to someone in the community. The community owes her something of like value in exchange. The money signifies this. Money does not have value in itself, it stands for a value that has been created and given and indicates that a like value is owed in return. When the carpenter pays for the coat, she actually completes the transaction: in exchange for the table, she has received the coat, something that others in the community had produced and that she needed. What we see here is in reality *an exchange of values within economic life*, the table for the coat. But when a coat is bought, too often only the money is seen, the table is lost sight of.

What lay behind the money the student gave for the coat? He himself had produced nothing. But what of the future? The student may well become a doctor and heal people, or an artist who inspires others. In the future he may well benefit the community. There, behind the money, is the act of the freeing of the future potential in the student. There must be confidence in his potential, in the capacities that he will develop to the benefit of the community. Here we see a purchase of a coat with *money given to cultural life*.

What lies behind the money which arose as profit on the land? The "profit" arose out of the permission that the community itself gave. The landowner has contributed nothing out of her own activity to the community. The money arising out of the profit on the land does not represent anything that she has, or will in the future, give over to the community. She receives a product of the work of the community – the coat – but gives nothing in exchange. The community owes her nothing. There is, then, something false in this exchange. When someone is in possession of money, it should indicate that they are owed something by the community. Though the landowner hands over money for the coat, she has not, in economic reality, paid for it. Because she receives a coat, but gives nothing real for it, a debt is created – she still "owes" for the coat. But this is hidden. Something that should properly belong to the sphere of rights – permission given by the community – has been "sold" as though it were an economic value produced by the landowner.

That there are transactions where, in reality, nothing is given in exchange for the product of labor has consequences for the social life of a community, even if these are not at first easily seen. The cumulative effects, however, of these untrue transactions are becoming ever more apparent. This issue of the purchase of "rights," which now forms an increasingly large part of what is too often thought of as "economic," will be gone into at length in later chapters.

Did the $200 Produce the Coat?

In all three illustrations a sum of $200 was paid for the coat. We have just looked at what lies behind the money, but where did the coat come from? Is there any consciousness of its origin present in the transaction? In each case there is no indication, in the price of $200, of the true nature of the transaction. On the contrary, the price has a tendency to cast a veil over the reality by encouraging us to think that we are able to have what we buy because we pay money for it. We assume that, if we pay money for something, then we have the right to have and to own it. We give to money a role of absolute power as arbiter of a person's entitlement to own and dispose of what he pays for. It is enough to give money for that which we wish to buy. In our minds the money encompasses and even supersedes all other responsibilities.

This point was illustrated for me some time ago when my wife was teaching a number of students to make dresses for themselves. One of them wanted to cut her cloth in a particular way, but my wife saw that it would be wasteful of the cloth, and that the same could be achieved without the waste. When she told the student that she should not waste the cloth by cutting it that way, the student replied "the cloth is mine, I paid for it, so I can waste it if I want to." This student was generally a responsible and considerate person. In this case, she was only expressing how we as a society generally think today, she was a young person of our time.

We fail to see that we have something because, in the first place, others have worked to produce it. We fail to perceive and remain conscious of what is actually "exchanged" when we pay money for something. And we fail to consider what it is that gives us the right, through the money, to have what we buy.

We enforce this way of thinking when we say to our children: "Don't waste that, it costs money" instead of: "Don't waste that, many people had to work to make it before you could have it."

Chapter 15
The Ownership Of Land

As land and the substances within it are a foundation for and play a major part in the economy, it will be good at this point to look at the place of land within the social life of the community.

A Right to a Share of the Earth

Does birth into life on Earth give with it a right to a place on the Earth, to walk over the land, and to a share of what the Earth provides? Are all human beings co-owners with equal rights to the Earth, or are wealth, birth, and inheritance the deciding factors as to who shall have access to the land, to work it, to walk over it, to own it? Is ownership of the land rightly a matter of *economics*, of money, or should it be one of *human rights*, separate from money? Is this a question where democracy has a proper role in establishing the procedure whereby land, and all that comes with the land, are allocated in a way that takes into account the rights and interests of each person as well as those of the community as a whole? Or is it truly just that those with access to money, however acquired, should be able to appropriate the land to themselves? And should they and those who have inherited land through birth continue to hold it not only for their own personal use or enjoyment, but, just in the holding of it, be able to increase their wealth?

Today we hear much talk of democracy, and of human rights. There is a claim to moral leadership by countries who claim to be democratic. But democracy is only just beginning; no country can yet call itself truly democratic. It is not sufficient to lay claim to being democratic purely on the basis of the leaders being elected by universal and equal vote, when those leaders then make their decisions under the influence of unelected groups of people, groups with economic or other interests. True democracy must require not just that the leaders be elected democratically, but that the laws and the social structure of the country be themselves a reflection of the feelings and opinions of the people, opinions in which every person's sense of what is just and right is given equal weight. No country can yet lay claim to that. No country can claim that all its laws are a true reflection of what is felt to be right and just by the people of that country.

Most of our laws come out of, or are formed in ways that belong to, the ancient past. If the common feelings of what is fair, right, and just that live in people were listened to, and all laws made to be a true reflection of this, would our laws be as they are? Surely in a community where the sense of right and justice was developed in a healthy way it will not be possible to lawfully "own" land in the way that it is today; it will not be possible for the few to gain wealth at the cost of others. Land will be seen as something belonging to all people, to humanity as a whole; something that no one person or group of people can own to the exclusion of all others. A person or organization might be given a right to hold and use it, a place to live or work, perhaps to the exclusion of others, but this will be different from ownership and will have certain appropriate limitations of time and use placed on it. It will be allocated through some form of democratic process, not by money to only those who can afford to buy it.

*

Land, the surface of the earth, including the minerals that lie within it, is not something that has been produced by human activity. Over vast ages of time it has been there, formed and moulded by powerful forces from the depths of the earth and by the sun, wind, and rain. How is it possible for a person to "own" this? The Earth is given by God or by Nature, and human beings are born onto it. Not only does it provide the "space" on which each person can be and live, it is the foundation and source of all our physical and much of our soul needs without which we cannot live. Our food, clothes, tools, and housing all have their origin in the land. If all of humanity is absolutely dependent, for their very lives, on *land*, how can it be appropriated for private ownership by the few?

While the population of the world is steadily growing, the land on which all humanity must live is coming to be "owned" by fewer and fewer people, and by corporations and institutions which are themselves owned, or effectively owned and run, by a comparatively small number of people. This is also true of the resources within the earth.

Meanwhile, there is a growing recognition that all people are equal and have equal rights irrespective of differences due, for example, to color, sex, creed, birth, or abilities. But should there not be included amongst these "rights," to which all people have equal claim, a right to a place on the Earth, and an equal claim to the resources of the Earth? Is it really felt to be fair and just, and in line with modern democratic principles, that a person born into poverty, into, for example, an inner city culture, and without any particular capacities to earn money beyond the average, should have no right to a place on which to have or to build a house and create a home for his or her family – while at the same time others, through birth and inheritance, may own many thousands of acres?

*

If a person makes something, for example a table, then it is accepted as socially and morally right that this table belongs to the one who made it. The law confirms and upholds this. The maker of the table owns it and can do with it as he or she pleases – keep it, change it, sell it, destroy it, give it away – by virtue of the fact that it is a product of his or her own creative activity.

It is also lawful, in a similar way, for a person to own land. One can own a piece of the Earth – a mountain, field, or river can be "owned." Here again, an owner can, to a great extent, do what he or she likes with it; the owner of land can hold it for personal and exclusive use, can exclude others from it, change it, and even spoil it for future generations. This, clearly, is not due to the owner having created the land, as was the case with the one who made the table. The land – the mountain, valley, field, or river – is a part of the surface of the Earth, an inheritance from that which created both human beings and the Earth for their habitation.

We must, of course, make a distinction between the actual land, the earth, rocks, and natural vegetation, and the products of people's work on the land, such as crops on farmland, and also the land on which people live or that they might require for other necessary and reasonable activities of life. In such cases, even preceding the law, there is a general recognition of a moral justification for some exclusion of other people. There is no such justification in owning part of the Earth *per se*.

The law that creates the possibility of buying and owning land did not arise through any democratic process but came into being in quite other ways. That a person can "own" a portion of the Earth is a denial of what must surely come to be accepted by the vast majority of humanity as a fundamental human right, a right of every person to a place, a fair and reasonable portion of the Earth onto which he or she was born.

The Origins of the Law of Land Ownership

The possibility of legally "owning" and holding land as we do a commodity is comparatively new in human evolution. In earliest times it was simply seen as God given, it was the land on which a particular people or tribe lived. This relationship to the land has continued on in many peoples until quite recently.

The idea of owning land brought by the white settlers as they moved west across North America was something that the Native Americans had great difficulty grasping, it was not something that existed in their thinking. For them, land – the earth, stones, minerals, and waters that form it – and all that lives and grows on the land, the plants, insects, birds, and animals, are the creation of God the Creator. How can they be *owned*?

So too in many parts of Africa the various colonial settlers moved in to "own" and farm what they had taken by force – that which had formerly been open tribal land. The native peoples had no concept of owning land. They lived on it. The Europeans arrived with their structure of laws, which included the "rights of ownership." This structure they imposed on the indigenous people. That which could, perhaps, best be described as common land was now occupied by the new arrivals, who established their ownership of it according to their own alien laws. This has provided genuine grounds of resentment in parts of the world, particularly in Africa, where former colonists continued to own land long after colonization had come to be seen as wrong and had ended.

In Australia too, a form of rights life was forced onto a people who had since ancient times lived according to a quite different sense of "right," one that had its source in a perception that each person was a member of the community or tribe and was placed on the land by the creator who created human beings and created the land for them to live on.

With few exceptions, it is possible in all parts of the world to trace the holding or occupation of land back to forceful acquisition or conquest. Since ancient times people have been attacking and overrunning others and taking their land. What was originally taken and then held through the superior power of the conqueror came in later times to be regarded as a "legal right." The necessary laws were brought into being so that what was first acquired by conquest and held by force could then be transformed into a "right of ownership," established and enforced by law.

*

Within the scope of this book it is not possible to indicate other than very sketchily some aspects of how the present structure of law relating to the ownership of land has arisen through the evolving course of human social life. A deeper study of the course of history, particularly legal history, will confirm what can here be only indicated.

As I have already shown, in former times the structure of society was that of the pyramid, with the leadership at the top and the masses forming the base. God, who created the people, had also given them the land. Their leaders, appointed by and acting on behalf of God, were the guardians of this land determining its use in the best interests of their people.

Then there came a time when the connection with divine wisdom was lost, when the leaders could no longer rely on the people recognizing their divine right to lead. As their authority diminished, in order to maintain their place at the head of the pyramid, they came increasingly to rely on earthly force rather than divine authority.

For this, the leaders, the pharaohs, kings, emperors, or feudal lords, depended on the support of their immediate followers.

In return for this support, as land came to be fought over and won through force of arms, the leader would allocate some of the conquered land to those who had assisted him in his conquest. This allocation of the land was still seen as in the nature of the giving of a "right" to the use of the land rather than the granting of ownership.

As those who supported the king received land or the right to land, so they in turn passed on some of this to those who had, in their turn, supported them. This right to land could also be made to provide an income as they could charge a rent, or a share of the produce of the land. At the bottom were still the peasants, the servants and laborers.

There was no written law as we know it today, only ancestral law as it had evolved out of the past. This worked so long as there was a strong group soul consciousness that held people together within the social order.

At what could be called the next stage, although there was no clear demarcation between stages, there came a time when it was no longer felt to be acceptable to hold land purely on the basis of the king's authority or the strength of one's followers. As society evolved, and the group soul consciousness gave way to individual consciousness, those who had received the right to hold land came to look for greater security of tenure than this provided. They were no longer satisfied to remain at the mercy of an unpredictable king or of the threat of invasion by power-seeking neighbors. Those who held land sought to establish a more permanent and secure right to it. In England, Magna Carta, which King John was forced to sign by the Barons in 1215 and which included clauses dealing with the protection of holders of land, was an important event in the course of this development.

But security of tenure was not enough. There also arose the need to establish procedures for such processes as transferring the right to the land to other people in exchange for money or services, of dividing the land, or of bequeathing it to descendants. Out of these needs came the possibility in law of owning the land. So people came to think and act in terms of "owning" land as opposed to holding the right to it. Those who owned it came to see that they could raise money by selling it, and so there arose a market in land.

It was the aristocracy, the landowners, the descendants of those who held the land through divine right or conquest, who came to write the law. They did this in a way that would establish and preserve their own position in society and their holding of the land. The rest of the population, those who were not members of the aristocracy, were increasingly excluded. For a time, peasant farmers continued to have access to common land, but as new improved methods of farming were developed, the landowners, in order to adopt these new methods, were able to bring about the necessary legislation to enclose for their own sole use most of the remaining common land. In England, this reached a certain culmination in the eighteenth and early nineteenth centuries.

The legal basis for land ownership came into being in a form that secured the continuation of the previously existing system; that is, the one that arose out of, and could only be justified as consistent with, ancient theocratic pyramidal social structures. The laws that have brought private ownership of land into being are not the product of a democratic process.

Although there have been ideas of democracy ever since ancient Greek civilization, it has, until very recently, been considered appropriate for the leading or property-owning classes only. Not until late in the eighteenth century, at the time of the French and American revolutions, did thoughts turn to the inclusion of all people, though in the United States that did not include people of color or any women until much later. Universal suffrage did not emerge until the nineteenth century for men and the twentieth century for women. Today, democracy still means little more than the recognition of the right of the people to elect those who govern them, and to change those elected after a certain period of time if they so wish. There is still little consciousness that democracy must come to mean very much more than just this.

The Market in Land

In this way, through the creation of the necessary laws, land became subject to personal ownership. It acquired capital value by reason of the fact that the possibility arose for it to be sold on the market. It is now generally assumed to be in the natural order of things that land is bought and sold. But, as has just been demonstrated, ownership of land is in reality a right, but a right that has become subject to the working of the market economy through the way law has evolved over a long period of time. If democracy is to be the basis of law and the establishment of human rights, then there must be a clear separation between the sphere of rights and the sphere of economic productive activity based on division-of-labor. *Rights* must come to be seen for what they are.

If one buys a piece of land today, one can generally expect to sell it at a later time for a higher figure. This is one step in the ongoing increase in value that had its start in the past. There have, of course, been fluctuations; over the years the price of land has gone up and down, but in the course of time it has gradually increased from nothing to what it is today. In some parts of the world this process has been going on for hundreds or even thousands of years, in others it started only very recently. But if something that is not a product of economic production is given economic value, and the money so created is spent, then a debt is created. This is something that has major repercussions in society today. This will be discussed more fully in the next chapter.

Today we see only the money. We feel good about the capital value of our land, but we do not see the true nature of this value; we do not see that behind its capital value there is a hidden debt. Sometime in the future, when another generation comes to recognize that land use is a matter of rights and should be decided purely on that basis, they will have a huge debt to clear. They will have to somehow absolve this debt before the land can be freed from the clutches of the market.

Chapter 16

The Two Economies, Capitalized Debt, and Compulsory Gift

At times when the financial markets have been in crisis, it has often been said that the "real economy" was still in good shape. If the "real economy" was not in crisis, then what was in crisis must have been an "unreal economy." What is this "unreal economy," and why is it unreal?

Within the economic sphere, a "product" is something that is produced from the substances and forces of nature through the shared work of production based on division-of-labor. These products are then distributed by means of purchase and sale facilitated through the medium of money. The sale/purchase transaction is the culminating act or completion of the economic process that begins with division-of-labor.

In the first part of the book I considered money only in so far as it arises within the cycle of production, distribution, and consumption based on division-of-labor, and in its three roles of purchase money, loan, and gift capital. But today money has taken on a role that goes far beyond this. Money has, for example, taken over the function of allocating such "rights" as access to and use of land and natural resources through the mechanism of purchase and sale. "Permission" granted to one person or organization by government bodies and the "right" to engage in certain profitable activities can often also be passed from one person or organization to another via the market through the medium of money.

A "right" is quite different from a product of economic activity. According to *The New Oxford Dictionary*, it is "a moral or legal entitlement to have or obtain something or to act in a certain way." In a democratic society, a "right" or legal entitlement can only be established through the democratic process, that is, when it is the community itself that wills it to be so.

The right of producers to own the product of their work, and the right to give or sell that product to another, is a right because it has been recognized as such by our society and has been incorporated into the law. Not all people have come to such a right of ownership. In some earlier societies, whatever a person made was seen as belonging to the community, not to the individual who made it.

In the sale of an economic product, it is not the ownership of the product which is sold but the product itself – it is exchanged for another product of equal value, or for money that stands for such a value. It has been established by our society and incorporated into the law that when such an exchange properly takes place, ownership also passes from the seller to the buyer, just as the ownership of the money passes from the buyer to the seller.

If a person is hungry and buys a banana, it is the banana that is eaten, not the ownership of the banana. The ownership, which comes at the same time as the purchase, merely gives the person the right to have and to eat the banana. A product that is the result of economic activity, and the ownership of that product which is established through the law as a result of the community's sense of what is right, are two very different things. The important question then must be asked: *What happens when the right of ownership is treated as a product and traded through purchase and sale in the same way that true economic products are?*

If the land is not a product of human economic activity but is given by nature, or by God, what happens if it too is treated as capable of being owned and traded in the same way that an economic product can be owned and traded? In nearly all earlier communities it was the right to hold or use land that was given or allocated, not the land itself. Land was not "owned" in the way it is today.

When a right of ownership, or a right to hold and use something, comes itself to be treated as a product capable of being owned and traded, then a situation is created that has profound social consequences: alongside the market of economic products proper there comes into being a market in *rights*. A second, "unreal economy," has come into being.

The activities of each of these two markets create monetary value. In each, the money looks the same, but what lies behind the money is very different. Behind the money of the "real economy" are all the actual commodities produced through the dividing of the work in division-of-labor. This money always represents an actual value; it represents a credit owed to the holder for a value he has given. There is no such product behind the money created in the "unreal economy," no actual, created value; instead, a debt is created, a debt that someone else will have to pay at another time.

In order to earn money in the "real economy," a person must, in one way or another, contribute to the production of products or services, that is, products or services needed by others. The money workers receive relates to the commodity values they have helped to produce. What they can earn in this way is limited by what they can produce – this money is hard-earned and has a value commensurate with the actual product of their labor.

It is quite different in the "unreal economy." There, much of the money "earned" bears very little relationship to work, or the product of work, actually done. It does not represent, or stand for, an economic value contributed to the community. A person who buys shares or land as an investment may have done some research as to where to invest his or her money, but that work is solely for one's own benefit. Once the shares or land are bought, the buyer can sit back and hope the value rises, which, in the main, it probably will. The monetary value acquired in this way is not founded on something the buyer has had to work to produce; it comes as a gift. There may have been luck or a certain risk involved, there may have been considerable work in research, but, here again, the individual did not create any monetary value. The value came from the ups and downs of the market, not from any productive process to which he or she contributed. This work mainly benefits the individual investor, not the community. Because the money is unearned, it takes on a different quality from earned money. Less value will be placed on it; it is "cheaper," because it did not have to be worked for. Acquiring money in this manner, one will quickly come to expect a much higher income than those who work to earn each dollar.

In the "real economy," it is not so easy for a person to gain wealth far beyond what others achieve. Only through hard work and creativity, perhaps aided by a bit of intuition and good fortune, do those rare ones rise above their fellows, but even then the difference will not be so very great. In the "unreal economy," on the other hand, once a person acquires the first piece of capital to invest, the growth of wealth can be rapid and without much effort.

The person who obtains money through the increase in value of land or shares, and uses this to pay for the product of manufacture, receives in exchange for this money the product of other people's work. In the exchange, there is the implication of an exchange of equal values: that the money handed over stands for a value economically equal to that which is received. But from the viewpoint of the interests of the community as a whole, this is not so. The money given came into existence of its own accord through the particular legal conditions of our society today; behind it stands no economic value. It is false money. True money is that which stands for value created, especially when work is made more productive through division-of-labor.

At present, a person who has need of access to something that is properly a "right," such as a right to hold and use land or to the resources given by nature, must buy it. Most of us face this problem when we buy a house. In the price of a house there are almost always two elements. There is the actual cost arising from the economic process of building the house. That is the true economic cost. On top of this is that element of the price which relates to the right to own or to live in a house in that particular place.

This "unreal economy" based on the legal structure that makes it possible to own and market rights is already a major factor in the social life of today and is growing fast.

Visible or Open Debt

If money is to properly fulfill its role within economic activity as an order on the products produced, then it must be created within that economic activity as a counter-value to those products. Money, in its role as a means of exchange, is an "I owe you," a note of credit. In so far as it is a credit, there must be the balancing debt or debtor. Just as in any proper accounting there are always two balancing entries, the debit and the credit, with money as a credit there must always be somewhere the second factor, the debt or debtor.

The tailor who makes a coat and sells it on the market receives money in exchange. He has handed over to the community the product of his work and instead of receiving in return something that he needs of like value, he receives money. He has not yet received the true counter-value to the product which he sold. The money is not a value in itself but stands for the fact that the community owes him a counter-value to the coat he supplied. This counter-value represented by the money is a debt of the community. The money stands for, or indicates, this debt. As "a promise to pay the holder," it can also be passed on to another, for example as a loan, gift, or in the payment of taxes.

In the normal course of the economic cycle of production, distribution, and consumption, all the money held by people or organizations should in this way represent values that are owed to them by the community or its individual members. If this were the case, debtors and creditors would always be in balance, and the existing debt would be visible or open debt.

There can be certain variations, or developments of this fundamental relationship. When a bank lends money to a manufacturer, for example, that money does not at its creation represent anything real; there is no economic value behind it, no product created in the past for which it stands. The money is created out of nothing. It comes into being as an entry in a book, an overdraft (see Chapter 14). When the manufacturer pays for something with this money, what is given in exchange for what is bought is not money that stands for any created value – what stands behind the money is a debt to the bank. It is a debt of a different nature, not one the community owes to the manufacturer, but one that the manufacturer owes to the bank and will have to pay in the future.

This borrowed or loaned money enables the manufacturer to produce products in the future. These products are passed on to the community in exchange for money. The manufacturer is now a creditor of the community, the money signifies this, but also a debtor to the bank. The bank will be repaid, and so the debt and credit cancel each other out.

Counterfeit Money

A person who needs money might decide, instead of going to all the trouble of making coats or tables, to just print the money. If someone prints money which is so exact a copy of "real" money that it cannot be told apart, what is there in the one that makes it "real" and legal tender but is not there in the other? What is different in the two that are outwardly exactly the same? They are both bits of printed paper. The one stands for a certain actual value and as such is real money. At one time it stood for gold or silver, then later it came to stand for debt, a debt of the central bank authorized to issue such notes and standing behind it. The other, the counterfeit money, does not represent any such debt or value; it is false in that it purports to do so.

Normally we obtain money by somehow earning it. We might, for example, render a service or provide a product in exchange for which we receive money that represents the value given, an acknowledgement of a debt owed. This debt is always there behind true money. Even if a person has been given the money, has stolen it, or won it in a lottery, it is always possible to trace it back to the person who did earn it and gave it its present value, its authenticity. If the money has been borrowed, then the promise to repay it in the future, the acknowledgement of one's debt, stands behind the money and gives the borrower the right to use it. Behind true money there is always this actual value that has been created and which gives it authority. In counterfeit money, though it may be outwardly exactly the same, there is no such value that has been supplied and for which it stands.

If the counterfeiter uses counterfeit money to seemingly buy a product or pay for a service, then something has been obtained without real payment. There will still be something owing, something unpaid. Someone has received something from the community but given nothing in return. A debt is created. It may be a debt that is lost in the general round of buying and selling, but it is there within society and will have to be paid at sometime in the future – if not by the counterfeiter, then by the person holding the counterfeit money when the fact that it is counterfeit is discovered.

Hidden or Capitalized Debt

In the example of the landowner buying a coat (Chapter 14), the increase in the market value of her land was due to permission to build being given by the local authority representing the community. The landowner sells this land and with part of the hypothetical profit buys the coat. The profit – the increase in the value of the land – is not something resulting from her work; it does not represent any value the landowner has created or earned and passed on to the community. It is newly created money – value that has no true economic value behind it. So the money handed over to the tailor in exchange for the coat cannot represent anything owed to her by the community. Though the money might appear to represent a debt owed to the landowner, this is a false representation, it is counterfeit, for she is owed nothing. In reality, she gives nothing in exchange for the coat.

Because she has bought the product of other people's work but has given nothing of real value in return, the value of the coat is still owed, a debt has been created. This debt, the counterpart of the coat, is carried in the increased value of the land and, as such, is taken forward into the future. It is of the nature of a mortgage on the future. It is a hidden debt as in counterfeit money, but unlike the counterfeit money, it is perfectly legal. The debt is hidden in the capital value of the asset – it is what I will call a "capitalized debt."

In society today there are vast amounts of such hidden or capitalized debts being created, debts that have their effects, and which others or future generations will at some time have to settle.

It might help to give a simple example to clarify the underlying principle involved.

In social life there are many occasions where it is necessary to restrict or control activities such as building developments, the discharge of environmentally damaging waste, or the acreage of a particular crop that a farmer may grow.

These restrictions may be imposed in a number of ways but will probably involve the issuing of some kind of license, permit, or quota.

For simplicity, I shall use the word "permit" to cover all these terms. These restrictions are normally imposed by government bodies but can in some instances be imposed by private bodies.

Whatever means are used, they are generally in one of two forms. The permit can be issued to, and limited to, a specific named person or body; that is, it cannot be transferred to another person or organization. Alternately, it can be issued in such a way that it is transferable, that is, it can be passed to another person or organization at the will of the holder. For example, a driver's license, for obvious reasons, must be specific to the named holder of the license, but a permit allowing a farmer to grow a given acreage of potatoes might be one that is transferable to another farmer. If the authorities are trying to limit the quantity of potatoes produced, they will not be concerned with who grows them, only that the total does not exceed the desired limit.

For the purpose of controlling the particular activity, it may make little difference whether the permit is specific to the named person, or applies more generally to whoever holds it from time to time. But when such permits are transferable, there are consequences for society as a whole that are not usually intended in their issuing. Where a transferable permit makes possible an activity that creates profit, the permit itself will acquire a monetary value through the possibility of it being transferred by way of sale to whoever will pay the highest price. Such a permit will acquire a value which will be a multiple of the profit that it makes possible for the person holding it.

Imagine a situation where farmers find that there is considerable profit in growing potatoes. As a result, too many start doing so, with the consequence that the market in potatoes becomes completely distorted. The authorities then decide to control the production by limiting the quantity that each farmer is permitted to grow. To do this in a fair and just way, they issue permits giving the acreage on which each will be permitted to grow potatoes in future years.

To make these permits transferable might well be administratively the simplest way of achieving their purpose. When a farmer wishes to stop growing potatoes, he may then pass his permit on to another without the authorities having to be involved, apart from registering the new grower. But is this the most socially responsible way of achieving the desired ends? In the first place, the licenses will be allocated to farmers in a way that is intended to be fair and just. But, once issued, they can be sold to whoever will pay the highest price. The distribution will then be by means of who can afford to pay for them, not by what is fair and just. Those who have money will be able to buy the licenses and thus increase their incomes. Clearly, here is a situation where what is properly a social right is passed from one person to another by means of purchase and sale, rather than through any form arising out of the democratic process.

Further Debt is Created

The giving of permission or the issuing of a permit is, properly, a responsibility of the rights sector of social life. The permit allows the holder to do what is permitted; in this case, it permits the farmer to grow the stated acreage of potatoes.

The farmer to whom the permit was issued may decide later to sell it. The permit, as originally issued, cost nothing. In selling the permit, the farmer makes a profit. This profit has not arisen out of any economic activity – again, monetary value has been created out of nothing.

Though it cost nothing, through being given the permit the farmer gains monetary value. The permit becomes money itself when it is sold. In the sale, the farmer transfers to another person the permission, or right, to grow x acres of potatoes and receives for this a sum of money. The farmer receives money for something that was not a product of his own activity, but a permission given by the community. The buyer now has the benefit of the permit. Although he has handed over cash, the buyer still has the monetary or capital value of the permit. There has been an increase in the money supply.

Imagine now that the farmer, the former holder of the permit, buys a coat with the money received from the sale of the permit. The money paid in exchange for the coat is money that was created "out of thin air." It does not stand for any true economic value. Although quite legal, it actually works within the community in the same way as does counterfeit money – another debt is created.

This debt is not lost – it is carried forward, unobserved, in the capital value of the permit. The counterpart of the profit made on the sale of the permit is carried forward in the increased price of the permit – the capitalized debt that someone else, or society itself, will have to pay sometime in the future.

The second holder may, after a time, sell the permit to a third person. If the price of potatoes has risen in the meantime, the permit may well have gained further value; so not only will he get his money back, but he will make a profit. The permit might be sold again many times.

Suppose that for some reason, the authorities decide after a time to discontinue the restrictions placed on the growing of potatoes so that anyone may then grow as many as they choose. The farmer still holding the permit finds that it has become worthless. This buyer will have lost whatever money was paid for it. In this loss, he is in fact paying off the accumulated debts carried forward in the capital value of the permit. The final holder actually pays the debt incurred by the first holder when he bought the coat as well as any further debts incurred in the same way by later owners. This would also be partially the case if the marketable value of the permit falls though it is still required for the growing of potatoes.

What is illustrated in this example is comparatively simple and might appear to be of no great importance in itself, but it is a useful illustration of what is happening on a more far reaching and complex level in those areas where what are properly *rights* are treated as though they were products of economic production.

In the money, the particular qualities of the transactions are obscured so the difference is not seen – the difference between a commodity that is a product of economic activity, and a right that is treated as a commodity.

Money created through an increase in asset value can also be used to buy more assets, making further unearned income possible for the holder of the assets. This unearned income – unearned in the sense that no real product or service is provided in exchange for what is received – is today the most important factor in increasing the wealth of the rich, widening the gap between them and the poor, who must earn their money through their work.

Along with capitalized debt, there is a second important element that contributes to the increasing divide in our society between the haves and the have-nots.

Rent or Compulsory Gift

Whenever something like land, which belongs properly within the rights sphere of social life, makes possible an activity that itself generates profit, there will always be a tendency to create *rent*, i.e., to charge for the benefit or use of the right by those having control of or "owning" it. Here I am looking at a right that is rented as opposed to one that is sold.

Imagine a person owning a house with a large upstairs room that has a wide window overlooking a boulevard along which a parade is to pass. It is his house, so of course he has the right to invite whomever he likes to watch the parade from this room. He might awaken to the idea that he could make money by allowing people to watch the pageant from his house on payment of a fee.

Here he is clearly selling a right – permission to sit in his room and look out of the window. What he charges is a "rent" rather than the purchase price of a "commodity." The difference is important. Wherever rights are owned it is possible to charge rents, and there is always in human nature the tendency to create and charge rents.

In such a simple case as this there can be no objection, it does no harm. But in other situations it can have a very profound effect on the fabric of society. This is most easily seen in the situation of a farmer who must pay rent to the owner of the land.

The landlord who owns the land, as landlord, plays no part in the actual productive process of growing and harvesting the crops, so any rent paid cannot be in exchange for any economic reciprocal value. The contribution that the land makes towards the production of the crop is one that comes from nature, from the land itself, and from the sun, wind, and rain, not from the person who owns the land. The crop is not improved by the payment of rent. From the viewpoint of the economic productive process, the rent can only be described as a compulsory gift, something that the farmer is compelled to give, but for which, economically, nothing is received in exchange.

If a farmer is to receive a *true price* for a given year's crop (see Chapter 4), then the price must be sufficient to cover all the farm's needs as well as those of all the people who work on the farm. But to this "true price" must be added the contribution to the landlord, who does no productive work on the farm. After meeting this added cost, the farmer may be left with less than the true reciprocal value of the farm's product, and so suffer hardship, or else the price of the produce must go up and those who buy it will have to pay more than its true economic value. Either way, there is a disturbance of the ordinary course of the economic process.

This can be made clearer with another simple picture, one that has quite often happened in poorer, less developed societies where there is weak or corrupt government. This will illustrate again the "compulsory gift" nature of rent. Such a situation is well illustrated in the Japanese film, "Seven Samurai" (and in the American version, "The Magnificent Seven.")

Imagine a community of peasant farmers. Any government is far away and takes little interest in them as they are a simple people too poor to pay taxes, so there are no police or other civil security. In the hills nearby there is a gang of robbers. These every year descend on the peasant farmers and rob them of a portion of their harvest. The robbers do not take everything; they always leave the farmers enough for themselves. It is in the robbers' own interest that the farmers continue to farm, because the robbers will continue to depend on them for further supplies in the years to come.

The farmers then have for themselves only a portion of the product of their work. The other portion goes to the robbers who make no contribution to the work. Their nature is that of a parasite. Each year the farmers have to make what can only be called a "compulsory gift" to the robbers.

A landlord cannot legally be called a robber; charging rent is fully within the law. The legal structure of society creates the system where land is treated as a salable commodity and so given monetary value. A person who has purchased the land and paid this value is then legally, and some would say morally, justified in charging a rent to obtain a return on his or her money. Economically, the landlord makes no contribution to the actual production of the crops but does receive a portion of the produce, or the monetary value, of the work of the farmer. It is quite possible for a person who owns enough land to not have to do any work but live entirely off the productive work of others who do.

If the landlord carries out work that improves the land in a way that increases the yield, then any rent covering this is a purchase of those improvements, which are themselves the products of economic activity. It is important to differentiate between what is simply a rent connected to the granting of permission to use the land, and one that is a contribution towards the actual costs of improving the productivity of the land, even if both are called rent.

All products of economic activity based on land, such as farming, forestry, and mining where it is possible for rents to be charged, will tend to increase in price as opposed to those depending more exclusively on the manufacturing process. This tendency will also be there when farmers themselves own their land, as they will take into their calculations the need for a return on the capital value of the land, in addition to the income from the actual work of farming.

*

The market in rights provides the opportunity for creating monetary value, or "profit," on two levels:

- through the trading of the right itself, "capitalized debt" is created which will be borne by other people in the future
- by the creation of rents, or "compulsory gifts," through which prices of products are forced up

The holder of a marketable right with capital value will generally consider this right to be a capital asset. Today, a very large proportion of the wealth that people own, or that is included in company accounts under assets, is actually the marketable value of rights, not the accumulated monetary values of profits arising out of the manufacture and sale of the products of economic production.

The world of finance in all its complexity is something created by human beings. It is not God given, nor is it a fact of nature. It is not something that has been brought into existence through enlightened and clear thought and planning but has emerged through history and has been given shape according to the evolving nature of humanity. By simply awakening to its real nature, we take the first step towards healing the injustice inherent in the buying and selling of rights.

Chapter 17

The Structure and Ownership of Business

Through the ages, there have always been people who have come together with the intention of carrying out some particular joint enterprise. In order to do this they have had to agree on the necessary arrangements and on their responsibilities, and so have established certain rules and codes of conduct. They have brought into being a body of agreements, rules, and regulations within which they worked together. Frequently their joint work affected others within the wider community, so after a time the community itself set rules that gave further structure and bounds to their work. In this way a framework of laws, agreements, and regulations evolved governing the way people joined together to work at a common enterprise. Different legal structures came about, offering various possibilities for achieving different purposes. Amongst other such frameworks thus developed are those that give structure to present-day business enterprises.

Today, what in English law is called a "limited liability company" is by far the most common form used for business. The actual law and constitution of such a company varies from country to country, but the basic structure is common to most. I shall use the word "company" to indicate this basic common structure or form.

The law that gives legal form to our present company structures has evolved over millennia, and, like the law pertaining to land, it evolved for the most part within a society that had little or no idea of democracy. Those who had the impulses and abilities to start new enterprises were invariably members of the leading circles of society, those at the top of the pyramid. This was also the class or level within society that decided on and created the rules and regulations of that society, the legal framework within which such initiatives could develop. The ordinary people, those at the lower levels of the social pyramid, were there to serve the leaders; their interests were the interests of servants and as such were expected to be consistent with those of their masters. The legal framework reflected this hierarchy.

By the time ideas of democracy entered into government and most of our current law, the basic conceptual structure of the company had long been established.

The social structure that put those who were born to lead at the head and those born to follow at the lower level may well have been right for an earlier form of group consciousness. We can see that even in very recent times remnants of this still existed. People born and brought up on the land or in the immediate social vicinity of the big manorial houses and ancestral families did not always question the rightness of the lord of the manor being where he was and of their own place as his servants. That was the created order of things. They did not feel the need to be treated as equals with those above them in the social order. They might have questioned whether the nobility properly fulfilled their role, but not have been inclined to question that role. This can be seen too in the way some in England, particularly older people, still speak of the queen. They speak of one to whom reverence is due by the fact of her hereditary right to the throne, which has come down through the generations from a divine origin. For many people, something of this is still felt and comes to expression in a reluctance to consider doing away with the monarchy.

But the consciousness that made the hierarchical social structure of former times possible and even right has changed. Now human beings feel themselves to be individuals *first*, and only secondarily as members of some ethnic group or family. There is a growing demand to be free, to be recognized and treated as an individual distinct from but equal to others. The pyramidal structure may have been right for its time, but it no longer has a place in human social life. The equality of all people is a demand of our time, and democracy is a requirement arising out of this.

Owners and Employees

At present almost all economic organizations have a basic twofold structure: the owners and the employees. The managers, who lie in between, fall into one or the other of these two groups; they are owners or employees, and often both. This twofold structure is derived from the old pyramidal framework of society with the head at the top and those who labor at the bottom.

Why is it that in our society those who put in the capital – and often nothing more – are thereby the owners, while those who do the work of production, who actually make the products or provide the services, have no ownership over that which they produce? The law that establishes this ownership is founded on a much earlier, pre-democratic, sense of social right. The question that is in urgent need of attention is this: If we followed a truly democratic process, one where every person's opinion was given equal hearing, would we arrive at the same structure of company law that gives ownership of the company, its products and any profit, to the person or people who put in the capital, capital that they probably did not themselves create, rather than to those whose actual creativity and work produced the products and thus also the profit?

If it is the provision of money, or capital, that establishes ownership, then we should be able to find the justification of this in the capital itself; not in the forms of ancient times but in how the capital itself came into being, that is, in what stands behind the money, and in how the particular holder came to own it. As was demonstrated earlier, under our present system monetary value, and thus capital, arises in one of two ways:

First of all, capital arises in the economic process of production through the division-of-labor. As I will show in more detail in the next chapter, this capital arises through the joint work of the community as a whole, not through any one person or business working alone. There may be justification in a person who has saved money rather than spending it, lending it to a business and earning reasonable interest, or even being given a share of those profits actually generated by the loan. But, where the capital arises out of the activity of the whole community, there cannot be anything in the capital itself that justifies an individual's owning a business as well as the products and profits generated by those active in the business.

Secondly, as was shown in the last chapter, capital is also created through the "market in rights." In that this money is created through "compulsory gifts" or backed by "capitalized debt," there can be nothing in it that justifies ownership.

There is nothing, either from within the economic process itself, or from any common view of what is morally right, that justifies this arrangement whereby it is through capital as such that ownership is established over the natural rights of the people whose imagination and creativity brought the business into being and also over those who actually do the work of production. It is, after all, just these or others like them who probably brought the capital into being in the first place, not those who have come to "own" it. This should become clear in the following chapters.

*

There is some justification in the twofold structure of owner and employees in the initial stages of the life of a business. An individual with enterprise and ingenuity may decide to start a business making a particular product. He carries the impulse for the new venture within his own soul. His is the imagination and the drive to start and keep it going. He puts in the money to set it up, he carries the risk of it all going wrong. But this can only be true in the pioneering stage of a new enterprise.

Because he cannot do all the work himself, he employs workers to carry out the operations to achieve his goal. It may well be that those who he employs do not want to have any other input into the business than the work they are employed to do, that they do not want to worry or even have to think about the business itself. This attitude is a holdover from an older form of class consciousness, which, though often rejected today, is still deeply ingrained in our habits of thought and in our patterns of social behavior.

The idea that the employed worker might actually be thought of as a joint producer with the entrepreneur is still in its infancy. Nevertheless, economically, it is a joint undertaking. In addition to those who bring their physical labor there must always be those who bring the creativity, imagination, and leadership. What is produced is the result of the joint but separate contributions of the different people bringing to the work their different capacities. The product is a product of their co-operative work and thus must surely be seen as belonging to both. This is the essence of the division-of-labor.

*

Basic to the development of our present company law was the perception of labor as a commodity subject to sale and purchase, a perception founded in a time when human social life was largely based, for its economic needs, on differing forms of slavery.

Law and the Ownership of Labor

Slavery goes back to very ancient times, back to a time for which we have no written records. It is something that has been practiced at different times in nearly all parts of the world and continues in some parts of the world right up to the present day. In order for slavery to exist, there had to be a basis in law allowing for the owning of slaves. Such law would arise through the acceptance of the institution of slavery by the people, or the leaders of that social group. Quotations from religious documents, including the Bible and the Koran, have been used at times to justify the practice of slavery. The slaves themselves, in nearly all cultures, have been people from other countries or tribes, often captured in war or in other forms of conquest.

Whatever form the law took, it created the possibility of one human being owning another. The slave owner, by way of buying and owning the slave, also owned the labor of the slave. The slave could be hired out, in which case it was really a sale of the labor; the labor became a commodity as was the slave himself. This might appear to be a distinction of minor importance, but when, over time, slavery came to be socially unacceptable and was abolished, the commodity nature of labor continued.

In the feudal systems of Europe, slavery as such largely disappeared, but something of it continued in other forms such as serfdom, and in the peasants being entirely subject to, and confined to, the lands of the lord of the manor. They provided their serfs with labor in return for certain rights to the use of land and security. But they were largely unfree in that they were bound through the land to the lord of the manor. They could not leave or change their occupation.

As the industrial revolution emerged and the first factories came into being, the peasants were gradually forced from the land into the factories. These laborers were not bound to the factory owner as they were to the former landowners. In theory, they were not compelled to work, to sell their labor, but were free to work or not to work. But in practice these factory workers were not truly free, the alternative to working being starvation for them and their families. Though the worker was theoretically free by virtue of not being a slave, the labor was still purchased in the old way, retaining its commodity nature. A remnant of slavery survived.

So the idea of labor as a commodity was established in human consciousness. It entered deeply into human thought and has continued to affect the social fabric of society right up to our time.

The industrial revolution transformed the way we live. People have now come to think deeply on the social questions of our time. Social and economic thinking have become sciences. Social upheavals have resulted from different theories about the causes of the social ills that have followed on from the industrial revolution. But in all this, from Adam Smith and Karl Marx to thinkers and social scientists of today, there has been an almost universal assumption that human labor is something that can be bought and sold. Both sides of industry, labor and management, have argued and fought over the price of labor, but both have based their positions on the same assumptions – that labor is a commodity that is sold by the worker and purchased by management and thus has a price.

Up until recent times this was true of all thoughts concerning the employment of manual workers. But in the "professions" and in top management there was not the same relationship of purchase and sale between the employer and employee. This professional work was a kind of continuation or development of the vocational work of the former leading classes – those who could be classed as "gentlemen" in the older meaning of the word, or the aristocracy. In earlier times, people knew that they were following their profession because life had to have meaning and purpose. This could only be achieved through active participation in some sphere of professional work. Their salary or income was not a purchase of their work; it was more of the nature of an income on which to live while they did the work. It came with the work but was not for the work.

But over time this has changed. As the social or class distinction between manual and professional workers has diminished, as the focus on money with the standard of living it makes possible has intensified, as technological and financial fields of activity have gained momentum and changed social behavior, and as people have become aware of themselves as individuals, the idea of one's work, whether professional or manual, being something that one sells for the highest price possible has spread to most spheres of human activity.

This change has occurred over several centuries, but has been particularly rapid in just the last few decades. Today people have largely forgotten that they often actually need, out of their own life's path, to do *their* work. Instead, they have come to think in terms of working for money, that all work has a commodity nature and must be paid for. For many, this causes some confusion. There is something not entirely true in their acting as though they worked for the money and demanding a higher price for that work, when they actually feel a love for the work, or that in doing it they fulfill some need within themselves.

The way of thinking that bases itself on the assumption that work is a commodity and that in a factory, shop, or restaurant the relationship between owners or management and the workers is one of purchase and sale rather than of joint work or production, has taken deep hold in the fabric of human social life. It has taken such deep hold that it is accepted as though it were an immutable law, a god-given fact of nature. But it is not. It is something that has arisen in the course of human history, from the old relationship of owner and slave at a time when human beings had a very different form of consciousness. I showed earlier through observations of the economic process that the true relationship between all those engaged in economic productive activity is one of mutuality, of co-operation or joint work. If it had been this relationship that had taken hold and become the basis of social structure and of law, our whole social life today would be very different. Since this is not the case, however, this basic shift must begin now, so that it can come to be fully realized in the future.

The legal structure that gives form to the great majority of both commercial and service organizations has arisen out of a duality: the owners and those who sell their labor. It might help here to look at some examples of how different businesses have come into being and particularly at some of the related factors that have given form to our present social structures and relationships.

The Cloth Manufacturers

The law giving form and structure to what we now have in the limited liability company evolved out of needs that arose when people associated for purposes of business and trade. The following example is one that may help to illustrate this.

Imagine a situation – not uncommon in 18th century England – where there are a number of cloth and garment manufacturers. They need substantial and regular supplies of cotton, but they all experience difficulty and uncertainty in the existing suppliers. Though they compete in the weaving of cloth, a number of them decide to unite their efforts so as to obtain more certain and regular supplies. To do this, they agree to pool their resources in order to buy a ship and to commission a captain and crew who will sail to America, purchase the cotton, and bring it back. They each put in a share of the capital needed to cover all the costs of the venture. It would not be necessary that each put in the same amount; it is a natural form in such an arrangement that those who need more cotton put in a proportionately larger share of the capital.

At this early stage, it is a simple co-operative venture to obtain the cotton they need for their factories. The individuals come together for their mutual benefit in a venture that is separate from, but of benefit to, their main businesses. They draw up an agreement outlining, among other things, what each will contribute by way of capital and their rights and share of the proceeds of the venture.

The money capital they put in is used to buy the ship and to pay all other set-up costs. This means that no one will be able to "get their money back," unless the ship is sold and the venture brought to an end. But, even in such an event, it will be very unlikely that any member will get all their money back. The money each puts in is not a simple loan, it is more of the nature of an investment. If it ever does become necessary to stop the venture and sell the ship, they will each get back a share of the proceeds. The purpose and benefit for which the manufacturers undertake this venture is to obtain the supplies for their businesses at a lower price and with greater regularity than they can achieve by buying them in the market. In this way, they increase the profitability of their main businesses – that is the intended return on their investment.

What starts as a small mutual co-operative venture might later, if successful, grow into an organization with a second or even a third ship, not only bringing back cotton, but also taking over to America various manufactured cotton products. The next step could be the development of a transport business carrying other materials and trade goods not only to and from America but also to other destinations. The business will then have developed from one that solely obtained the cotton needed for their main businesses by those who set it up, to one that does business in its own right, and makes a profit on that business. What, in its origin, was a mutual arrangement between people in which each was entitled to a share of the cotton in proportion to their contribution to the costs of the venture, has become one where each owns a share of the business and of the profits. Each has become a shareholder.

What happens now if one of the founding partners comes to need his money back? The others do not want to have to give up the business. He might then sell his share to one of the other original founders if there was one who wanted to increase his shareholding. But what if this is not possible? He could then try to find another buyer, but this could be difficult as long as there was no marketplace for the trading of such a part ownership of a business.

The Market or Stock Exchange

In the middle of the eighteenth century in the City of London, it came about that such a person who wanted to sell, or buy, "shares" in a business would go to a certain Jonathan's Coffee House. There he would tell a waiter that he was looking for a buyer for his "share." The waiter might, in a similar way, also hear from someone else who was looking to buy shares. The waiter would bring the two together, and probably receive a small commission. This was the beginning of the stock exchange. In the London Stock Exchange those who carried messages were, until quite recently, still called "waiters."

For such a market to function successfully, something else would have to have come into being. A legal framework would have to have been created that established that the shares traded represented actual ownership of the business in question and that the shares and all the rights attached to them could be passed from the seller to the buyer in exchange for money. This also called for a legally recognized company structure.

Such a market, or stock exchange, also gave confidence to people considering putting money into a venture by ensuring that, should they come to need it at a later date, they could recover their investment, or more or less of it, by selling their share. After a time people also came to realize that, in addition to the dividends, they could sometimes make substantial gains through an increase in the monetary value of the shares.

*

What started as people coming together as partners in a joint venture is later incorporated. This is a significant step. The group of people working together under some sort of mutual arrangement now becomes a "company" of people owning the business, which has an identity and activity of its own separate from those who own it.

So the law established the limited liability company. Instead of a group of partners working together in a "partnership," the enterprise becomes a corporate body with a group of directors managing the business of the "company" as servants of the shareholders, who are the owners. The directors are appointed by, and act in the interests of, the shareholders.

In the market, the value or price of a share does not depend on the original capital invested, but on the prospect of future profits that can be expected as dividends on the share.

Those who later bought shares in the shipping business did not need to be cloth manufacturers. Having the money to invest, they may have simply seen that there was a prospect of earning a good return on their money. They would not have been interested in the cotton as such, but in the profit to be made on the sale of the cotton, or whatever other cargoes the ships might carry. These later investors would see the venture as one that makes a profit rather than one that enables manufacturers to obtain cheap supplies.

Due to its historical genesis, the law which governs the incorporation of this enterprise at the same time assigns and restricts ownership and control to the shareholders. The work, skills, and commitment of the original venturers, and the labor of those who do the actual work of the company – in this example, the sailors who risk their lives on the seas and in foreign lands – is not recognized as in any way on a level with those who put in the original capital or those who later replace them through the purchase of their shares. Ownership and control is passed on via the market in the shares, even to those who at a later date buy the shares with no other interest than to benefit from any growth in the profits. It is the logical continuation of that which started as "owner and slave."

In this picture, in miniature form, we can see how the legal structure of a society is formed. It was the class of people in positions of power and leadership, such as those who founded the shipping business, who also came to write the law. They wrote it according to the needs of their own positions and businesses.

A look at another picture, one of a business formed within this law, might shed more light on the nature of this legal structure.

The Furniture Maker

Imagine that an individual employed in the office furniture trade develops ideas for new designs, which he feels are more appropriate to the needs of the market. He decides with his wife to set up his own business to make the furniture. To do this, he will need a workshop, tools and materials, and he will need to employ skilled workers to help him. He and his wife each have some capital of their own, but to make a good start they will need quite a lot more.

There are a number of family friends who have confidence in this young man. They recognize his abilities and are prepared to back him with their money. They can do this in one of two ways. Firstly, they can lend him the money, secured by the property. He will pay them interest, which may well reflect something of the risk they are taking. Provided his business is successful, in addition to the interest, he will repay the loan over an agreed period. Once the loan is repaid, their involvement is ended. Their "profit" is limited to the interest they receive. The capital they receive back is the amount they lent. In this way, the furniture maker retains ownership and thus full control of the business he founded and into which he continues to put his life's work.

The other possibility is for the friends to go in with him as joint owners of the business. They might well prefer this if they are confident that the business will grow and the profits increase over time. The risk might be greater, but as shareholders their gain could eventually go well beyond what they could expect from a simple loan.

Each puts up a share of the capital needed and thus "owns" a share of the business. Instead of interest, they will receive a dividend, that is, a share of the profits. The founder himself, like the others, will have a share in the ownership of the business, but only to the extent of the share of the capital he puts in, it will not be "his business." The company is owned, and so ultimately controlled, solely by those who put in the money, not by the one who initiates it, nor by those who have the knowledge, abilities, or skills and who do the work. If the founder puts in less than half, then the others jointly will have the majority vote and thus ultimate control. (In certain circumstances it is possible to avoid this, but what I show here is generally true.) For the actual work the founder does in directing and managing the business, he is an employee and will receive a wage or salary, probably including a share of profits.

I will assume for purposes of illustration that the founder himself cannot put up over half the capital needed to retain control, but his wife also puts in some and so jointly they are able to retain control.

So we see three groups of people: those who do the actual work of making the furniture; the directors, in this case the founder and his wife who were the original initiators of the work, who had the creative imagination to bring it into being and manage it; and finally, the shareholders, those who had capital and who, having confidence in the founder, were prepared to back their confidence with their money to make the venture possible. Except for the founder himself, they take no part in the actual work of the business.

The business is successful. The founder pays his workers generously, and they in turn feel a certain commitment to him. He has designed good furniture and he inspires his workforce to produce reliable top quality products that sell well. Much of the profits are put back into the business, which expands. After a few years, on the basis of its good record, it is able to borrow money from the bank to enlarge its premises and buy new machinery. More employees are taken on and the business generally enlarged. The bank loans are repaid out of the increased income.

*

Let us assume that the initial capital put into the business was made up of $1 shares. So a person who put in $2,000 would have been issued two thousand $1 shares. After a time, the business has expanded to the point where the profits are such that the company is paying an increased dividend of around 10 cents per $1 share. So the person who put $2,000 into the venture at the beginning is now receiving some $200 per year in dividends.

The increased dividend, and also the expectation of further growth in the business, will result in a rise in the marketable value of the $1 shares to, say, $1.50. The original investment of $2,000 will now have a market value of around $3,000. In addition to the dividend for the year of $200, each person who put in $2,000 will have made a potential profit or an increase in his capital of $1,000 over the first few years. So long as he leaves his investment in the company, this remains as potential profit. He will realize this as cash and be able to spend it when he actually sells the shares.

I have shown here two quite different sources of gain: the dividends which arise out of the profits generated by the activity of the business, and the increase in the market value of the shares, which arises out of the perception of the shares as a profitable investment. To the individual investor they will both be profit – money that can be spent or used to reinvest. But for the community as a whole there is a very real difference between the two.

The dividend arises directly out of the actual productive activity and represents a real value, but a value that is passed to the owners of the shares rather than to the people who created it. For those who work in the factory it could be seen as a compulsory gift that they are obliged to make to the owners, something like the rent paid to the landlord discussed in the last chapter.

The other source of profit, the rise in the price of shares, is the creation of money value that does not represent anything real. It is money that enables the owner to buy something without earning it and is backed by capitalized debt, as shown in the example of the person who sold part of his land and bought a coat.

Of course the value of the shares might have decreased rather than increased, and so the holders of the shares might have lost some of their money. That was a risk they took in order to support their friend in whom they had confidence. It would have meant that their judgment and confidence was at fault. But, over time, share prices have tended to rise, and it is the general assumption that they will continue to do so.

*

All those who originally supported the founder may eventually sell their shares. We will assume, as is normally the case, that the people who buy them, the new shareholders, do so as an investment, not because they are interested in supporting or protecting the business. They will be interested only in the capacity of the business to make a profit. They could even exert pressure on the founder to make cheaper or less robust furniture because that will bring more immediate profit, and thus also immediate gain in share value. But so long as the founder, whose impulse, skills, and initiative it was that created the business, is in control, they will not be able to make any changes against his wishes.

But now the founder's wife dies. In her will she has left her shares to her son. He is not interested in the business, nor in following in his father's footsteps. If he chooses to vote with the other shareholders, or to sell his shares, his father will have lost control. Let us assume that he sells his shares. Unless the person who buys them supports the founder, the other shareholders together will now have a majority vote and so have ultimate control. They will have the power to appoint new directors, to change company policy from the original primary purpose of making good quality furniture to one where the primary purpose is to make a good profit and, through this, to increase share value. They can even remove the founder.

The people who now have control are people who themselves have contributed nothing to the business, neither by way of work nor of capital; they bought their shares from other people who perhaps also had little direct interest in the business except as an investment. It is quite probable that some of the shareholders are not very familiar with the business, nor even sure of what it actually produces. They may have little or no concern about how the changes they wish to make will affect those who work in the factory.

For purposes of overall control, the founder, whose initiative the business is and whose capacity and genius has guided it to prosperity, counts for nothing unless he also owns shares, and then only to the extent that he does own them.

All the others, those whose work actually makes the furniture, on the sale of which the profits are made, have no say in the control or running of the business. They may spend a great portion of their lives in the business, working hard and with commitment to its ideals, but receive no more than "the cost of labor." This will be seen as just one of the costs of the business paid out of income, income that is actually created through their work. The income and profits of the business belong to the shareholders, not to the people whose work produced them, and if share value can be increased by making some of the workers redundant, then the shareholders have the right to do that.

The problem is highlighted in this example by the son, who has himself contributed nothing to the work of the company, and who, solely by the fact that he has inherited shares, and for no other reason than to serve his own lifestyle, is able to bring a change about in the company that has very serious consequences for the lives and families of those who may have worked for the company for many years.

This example shows something in the structure of our society that cannot be justified on any grounds of morality, equal human rights, or democracy. Nor does it make economic sense. This is so obvious that most people do sense it. But it seems that we are presently incapable of righting the injustice of the situation.

*

In the course of the evolution of economic production and trade, people have come together in their different ways to do business. According to their interests, they have created the legal framework which now determines our social forms. So it has come about that people own shares, not because they put money into the venture, but because they bought the shares from people who did. It is only the original shareholders, and those who buy shares of a new issue, who actually put money into the company.

A person might think that he has put money into a particular company, but in most cases this is not so; a share is usually bought by paying someone else for it. All the increases (and losses) in value that normally accumulate over time are passed on to the sellers of the shares, not to the business. For example, a $1 share might eventually be sold for $10. Only the original $1 will have actually gone into the venture, the remaining $9 having been shared between all those who have bought and sold the share since then. It cannot be claimed that a person has put money into a particular business, unless they put it into brand new shares when they are first issued.

The share, or a part ownership of the business, has come to be treated just as though it were a commodity in the same way as a table is a commodity. But in reality it is not a commodity, it is a "right," a right given by law to the shareholders to own and control the activities of the company and of those who work in it, and to keep for their own use the profits of the company. We need to see these things exactly as they are. There can be different kinds of shares, but this is the basic form from which all are derived.

Chapter 18

The Single Organization and the Economy as a Whole

In studying the cycle of economic production, distribution, and consumption in the worldwide context in which it now operates, it helps to bear in mind something I indicated earlier. Economics has a complex and ever changing nature. It is impossible to define or grasp the economic sphere as such at any one point with ordinary logical thinking. Very seldom is it possible to say anything about economics that is *absolutely* true; it can only be said that something is true at one particular point, but that as one moves in one direction or another what is true in the one place ceases to be completely so a little further over.

*

From the point of view of any single commercial organization and of all those involved in it, the business itself will be seen as an individual activity with its own name and identity, separate and distinct from all others. But the activity of manufacturing any particular product does not stand in isolation, it is closely connected with and dependent on very many other activities that must precede, accompany, and follow it. It stands within a process of which it is a component, a nexus where different streams of activity meet and again separate into further streams and in other directions.

From the perspective of the economic life of the community as a whole, the single business is but one point of activity within a network of interdependent activities involved in the production, not of any one particular product, but of *all* the multiplicity of products used by human beings.

The single company or manufacturer will see itself as the maker of the particular products that it makes and sells. Each piece will probably have the individual manufacturer's name on it. But is it a complete and true statement of fact to say that a particular named manufacturer made a particular product? In reality, very many people and organizations other than the one that has put its name on the product will have been involved in its production. The single business does not and cannot exist in isolation – by itself it would achieve nothing, it could not survive.

If we look again at the example of the furniture manufacturer, this will be seen clearly. Those working in the business may see themselves as the producers of their particular office furniture, but they will by no means be the only ones who have contributed to its manufacture. All those involved – from the planting of the trees to preparing and delivering the wood, from the mining and extraction of the metal to the making of the screws, hinges and other metal parts, all the people who contributed to the designing and making of the tools and machinery and who produced the power needed to drive them, and those who produce the many other materials needed – the glues, polishes etc. – all these were also involved in making each piece of furniture. That is the nature of division-of-labor, all economic activity is mutual, co-operative work.

All the materials that we saw enter into the factory on the one side, the wood, metal, cloth, glues, polishes, screws and nails, the heat and power as well as the tools and machinery and the building itself, are all products of other producers, each of whom see themselves as separate and individual, but who are in fact also dependent on and connected to other producers. The completed furniture then goes out from the factory where it is made. At this point, there will be still other organizations active, from the publicity agents, shipping firms, wholesalers, and shops to, finally, the customer. The waste products, too, have to be disposed of, otherwise they will accumulate in the factory. It might even be that some of the furniture goes to one of the suppliers of the furniture company.

So we see a network, an infrastructure of productive units stretching across the world, each interlinked, each serving and being served by others, each playing its part in interweaving chains of production, each benefiting from and supporting others. Each is a consumer of what others produce and a producer of what others consume. It is impossible to calculate exactly how many people and organizations contribute in some way to the production of any single product – table, light bulb, or loaf of bread – all of whom play their part in enabling the price to be so much lower than if a single person or business had to make the whole. The work of production is divided out amongst a vast group of people involved in making not only the one product, but also all other manufactured goods and commodities.

Profit – A Wider View

The world economy is itself the whole, the unity. There will be no understanding of any part of the economic life of the community unless this is recognized. The multiplicity and low prices of the vast array of commodities that are now available to us have been made possible by the cumulative effect of division-of-labor through this merging of all smaller economies into the one world economy. The profit that any single commercial organization makes is due to the fact that it is a part of this whole. In this new economic world organism, no one organization can make a profit other than as a part of the whole, and that profit can only be seen as part of, and due to, the profit of the whole.

According to the working of the market, producers will have to pay a certain price for their inputs, and will sell their products at another. These prices, together with actual operating costs, will determine the share of the total profits. Between the interests of the individual and of the whole there will always be a tension. The individual will try to buy cheap and sell expensive so as to increase his or her profit, that is part of human nature. The interests of the community as a whole will lie in keeping a certain harmony between the various producers, and between the producers and consumers, with regard to the prices and so also to the creation of profit. This can be achieved only through the working of the economic associations described in Chapter Thirteen. The market plays its part in guiding each step in the cycle of production, distribution, and consumption, but for that to happen in a healthy way it must be not only a free, but a balanced market. The maintaining of this balance in the interests of the whole can only be achieved by the economic associations.

Any organization that attempts to stand alone, to be self-sufficient outside the whole, will find that it cannot compete on prices and will fail. This is the misleading aspect of the term "self-sufficiency." It is misleading because if the truly global nature of the economic life of the community were to come to full expression it would be beneficial to all humanity. Our present "global" corporations bring harm to world humanity due, in part, to the fact that they strive to be global, but to be so outside the actual global economy. They are "outside" to the extent that they strive to be self-contained and self-sufficient.

To be self-sufficient means to perform, within a single organization, activities of production or distribution which, on the basis of division-of-labor, could contribute to and benefit from the cheapening effect of the mutually shared working of the global economy if performed by another organization specializing in that activity. Through their size and power over the market, global organizations are often in a position to overcome any adverse effects on themselves. But of course the consequence for the rest of the world is that the cheapening effect of the division-of-labor is reduced, so prices will tend to rise.

*

To form a more complete picture of what plays into economic life, one must look still further at all that plays a part in the cheapening process that creates profit. It will then be seen that part of the profit arising within the economic sphere is due to factors to be found beyond it. The creative imaginations that create the technology and the organizational and management skills that play so large a part in developing and refining production all have their source in cultural life. Looked at purely from the standpoint of the whole, it will be seen that activity within cultural life also contributes to the creation of profit within economic life. Without an active and vibrant life of soul in the cultural sector, there would be no innovation or new development in the economy.

The rights sphere of social life also plays its part. Without stability and an ordered environment where people can get on with their work in peace and security, where agreements can be made and if necessary enforced, and where work and property are protected, economic activity could not function smoothly and continuously and profits would not be generated as they are.

There is another factor that is easily forgotten but which is an essential factor in the production and distribution of goods and contributes to the lowering of prices and the creation of profit. This is all that comes from the past, all that is, so to speak, a gift from people now dead. A large part of the infrastructure of a country – buildings, roads, railways, and ports – was built by earlier generations. Many of the tools used today are further developments of what was first invented by people of former times; so too, much of the knowledge of materials and techniques used to make today's products.

If one is able to enter fully into the wider picture of the totality of the economic sphere of activity as separate from, but sustained by, the cultural and rights spheres, then, when viewed from the perspective of that whole, the question of shares (also known as *stocks*), profit, dividends, and wages will be seen to have much wider ramifications than when viewed, as is normal, from the immediacy of the actual situation of the individual person or organization.

Profit – To Whom is it Due?

Profit arises within the individual activity of a business. From the perspective of the individual business and of those who work in it, this is profit created through their own activity and therefore belongs to them. It will increase or decrease according to the hard work, efficiency, and creative thinking of the people who work in the business. But from the perspective of the whole, of which the single business is but a part, profit arises, in the main, due to the interweaving of all businesses in a mutual sharing of the total work of production through division-of-labor. An individual business may, through the particular ingenuity and hard work of its people, create profit beyond the norm, but seen from the point of view of the economy as a whole, the profit the single business makes is only its share of the profit created through the work done in mutual co-operation with all others through division-of-labor. From this perspective, it is not due to its work as a single organization working apart from the others.

From the standpoint of the whole, to whom then does this profit belong? Should it belong to the shareholders? to those whose work actually creates it along with the products? or to the wider community including the consumers without whom there could be no profit?

Putting aside the law as it stands, within the framework of the whole as just described, can it truly be asserted, either on the basis of the actual process of production and creation of values or on a basis of equity, that the profit should belong to the shareholders? A reasonable return on their money is certainly justified for those risking their capital. But within the economic process of production, this can be justified only in proportion to the contribution their money makes, within the totality, to the creation of that profit. Economically, there is no rational justification for them to have anything more, even if the law may allow it. Paying out more must come at a cost to others who have played their part in the productive process.

The existing arrangements as established by law are dependent on two assumptions that have no basis in reality. First, it is assumed that work, whether physical labor or creative-imaginative work of the soul, is an input to the productive process of the same nature as other inputs and, as such, is purchased and paid for as an expense – the fact that workers are living human beings who contribute through their work is not considered. Second, it is assumed that – because everything that contributes to the productive process, and thus to the profit, is an input purchased, and is thus owned by the shareholders – the shareholders therefore have a right to the profit. These assumptions have already been discussed and shown to be unfounded in reality. The shareholders do no more than put capital into the business, or, to be more exact, those who originally bought the shares put money into the business; later shareholders may have paid a greater or lesser sum for their shares, but their money did not go into the business.

It is not easy to get away from the present deeply ingrained way of thinking that bases itself on the assumption that those who put in the capital rightfully "own" the business, that they "buy" the labor or work of those employed, which is seen as an expense like other inputs to the factory. It is essential that this social form be seen as what it is: a distorted remnant of an old theocratic form of society. If in our social thinking we are to rise beyond the outdated conceptions of old theocratic societies and base our society on the recognition that all people are equal and individual, then we must also see that those who actually do the work in mutual co-operation with others must own the products of their own work. Those who put in the money do no more than contribute to this co-operative work.

The mutual co-operative working between the individual and society as a whole is at the very foundation of the economic sphere of productive activity. The question as to what part of the profit is due to the individual and what to society as a whole can only be decided at any particular time by the people themselves working associatively as previously described.

Under our present system, vast amounts of wealth that should by right go to those who create it go instead to those who contribute little or nothing to its production. So, while the community is in great need of more funds for education, hospitals, and much else, and while those who work in the factories, supermarkets, and offices receive only enough for a modest standard of living, there are those who can enjoy the benefits of huge wealth without having to work because the system gives them the profits.

What has just been shown is based on equity and on economic realities, not on beliefs, emotions, or political ideology.

The Nature of Invested Capital and Ownership

I showed in Chapter Eleven that when capital is made available to the human creative spirit to enable it to work into the economic productive process, human imagination and creativity will make that process increasingly efficient and productive. The economic process will then, out of that increased productivity, regenerate or repay that capital. Just as it is the productive process that repays the loan, so it was the productive process that created the capital that was loaned in the first place.

For this reason, capital put into the economic process must properly be considered as having the characteristics of a loan, no matter how it is treated in practice. It increases profit in a way that can quite correctly be said to repay itself. This is true in any situation where the purely economic process is allowed to function out of its own natural laws – that is, if all other unconnected pressures and influences are excluded.

The phrase "capital put into a business" here includes loans as well as all that is normally meant by the term *investment*; but the word *investment* carries implications of the kind of return on money that might currently be expected from shares in a business, not from simple loans. That which within the framework of the economic process is in reality nothing other than a loan, has been transformed into something totally different – money that can buy ownership in a business. This possibility of ownership brings into the economic sphere something which is alien to its nature and which works against its healthy functioning in mutual co-operation – that is, it opens the door to egoism.

The whole basis of the economic productive process, the very foundation of the division-of-labor which gives it its enormous productivity, is the working together of all involved in the one universal economic organism and mutual activity – the very opposite of that which leads to ownership, the holding on to something for one's own exclusive benefit. There can be no doubt that if the economic sector of social life was able to function entirely on the basis of its own nature there would now be no poverty – enough could and would be produced for all humanity. But instead of mutuality being the guiding factor, egoism and self-interest, the natural offspring of ownership, have come to be the dominant factors driving the production process.

Just as the economic productive process has evolved to the point where, if allowed to function on the basis of mutuality, it could provide a reasonable standard of living for all humanity, the egoistic forces in human nature have taken control. Through the continuation of old social forms, these forces have diverted to their own use and control what should have been available to all humanity.

*

If, instead of being able to buy shares in a business, it were only possible to lend the money, the whole basis of the financial support and the working of the economic sphere of activity would be transformed. A loan is a form that belongs and is true to the economic process itself.

In contrast to share ownership, which continues into the future without any time limit, a loan will be repaid within a certain period so that the transaction comes to a natural completion, after which there are no further commitments between the parties. What comes from the past is completed, and the business can go forward into the future, unencumbered by the past. Ownership and control remain with those who initiated and carry the ongoing work of, and responsibility for, the enterprise. Whether it is right that this should be shared between all those who do the actual work, physical or imaginative, is a separate question, but in the loan it does not pass to the person with the money.

The loan plays its part in the productive process and is then repaid by that process. It is fair and reasonable that the lenders receive not only their capital back, but something of the profit that the loan helped to produce as well as some compensation for the risk factor. This is received in the form of interest. The loan could be for a shorter or longer period of time, depending on the nature of the particular productive process into which it is put. Economically, its timing should be adjusted to the time it takes to recreate itself within the productive process. This applies regardless of whether it is an individual or a bank that is lending the money.

The value of the loan remains constant in that it is always the amount outstanding at any time. Unlike a share, its value does not change and so does not artificially create wealth. The only benefit to the lender is interest on the loan, which could include a reasonable share of the profits the loan made possible.

*

What I have put forward so far in this chapter comes out of observing the economic sector, firstly, as *separate and distinct from* but given form *by* the other two sectors and secondly, from the standpoint of society as a whole, not from that of the individual.

But, if one sees society as a unity and assumes that "the greatest social good is achieved when individuals pursue their own self-interest," then one arrives at a very different picture, that of the market economy of today with its dominant rich on the one side and the great masses of poor and dispossessed on the other.

From the imagination of the economy as one world whole, let us look again at the present form of the individual business.

Shareholder Value

As I showed in the last chapter, a key factor in our present company structure based on share-ownership is that the profits are owned by the shareholders. Not only does the owner of a share receive a share of these profits in the form of a dividend, but as a result of an increase in the dividend the market value of the share itself may increase, giving added value to his or her capital. There are then two possible sources of income, the dividend and the increase in the market value of the share.

There are many factors that play into the market value of shares. Anything that gives rise to an idea that sometime in the near future the business will increase its profits or expand will itself bring about an increase in the value of the shares. Share prices can rise simply because there is a belief in the market that they will rise. In the same way they can also fall.

In the main, the share price will be a multiple of the expected dividend. What this multiple is will depend on a number of factors including current interest rates and the perceived prospects of the company in the future. For purposes of illustration and simplicity I will ignore other factors that may affect the price and, for this example, will consider it solely as a multiple of the expected dividend and, for purposes of illustration, will assume it to be 15. This means that the shares of a company paying a dividend of $1 per share will be valued on the market at around $15. A person buying such a share for $15 with a dividend of $1 will be getting a return of around 6.7% on his investment.

If, at a later time, the dividend rises by 20¢ to $1.20, an increase of 20%, the share value on the market will also rise by a similar, though not necessarily identical, percentage. This means the value of the share would rise from $15 to around $18. So the shareholder will benefit by an increase of $3 in the value of his share due to this increase of 20¢ in the dividend. On his original investment of $15 he now receives a dividend of $1.20 plus a gain of $3.00 in the market value of his share, a total of $4.20, or a return of 28% rather than the original expectation of 6.7% in looking at the dividend alone.

As soon as there is an increase in profit, or even an expected increase, the market value of the shares will rise. It is then that the investment becomes highly profitable. But it will only continue to be so for as long as the increase continues to grow. As soon as the profit levels off again, even at the higher level, the sole income will once again be the regular dividend. If the high profit is a one-off and the next year drops back to the earlier level, then the share value will also drop back, and what is gained the one year, if the shares are not sold in time, will be lost the next.

*

Shareholders of public companies are generally not involved in the actual work of the companies they own; they have no interest in the people who work in them, in their products, nor in the customers. But they do have ultimate control, and their sole interests are the dividend and an increase in the value of the shares. Clearly, shareholders will be very happy with managers of their company who are able to increase share value. Indeed, increase in shareholder value has become the main measure of the success or worth of the management of a company by the shareholders and therefore also by the financial markets.

This puts great pressure on management. Within our present legal structure, their responsibility is to their shareholders. It is in the interest of the shareholders, and usually of the managers themselves as shareholders, to concentrate on bringing about a perceived increase in future profit or company growth. Anything that may be thought to increase profits, even if this is only short-term, such as the laying off of workers, taking shortcuts on safety and environmental pollution, moving to areas of cheap labor, and producing only low standard short-lived products for the mass market, may be seen as the fulfilling, by management, of its responsibilities to its shareholders. Unlike the employees, customers, and the wider community, the shareholders' commitment to the company can be very short term – they can sell out at any time they think the value of their shares has peaked and may be about to decline.

This also places on management a temptation toward fraud. There are, for example, ways by which clever accounting practices can be used to give a false picture of the profits of a company. This can be done by carrying over current expenditure to a future year, or by bringing forward future sales into the present year's accounts.

There are also ways to manipulate the accounts so as to take certain kinds of expenditure "off balance sheet." Though the great majority of companies and corporations do not give way to such temptations and are more or less honest in their accounting, there have been in recent years many bankruptcies of huge organizations, such as World Com and Enron, which have been due in part to just such malpractices in their accounting. While some shareholders were able to sell out in time and so make huge fortunes, very many others, mostly the small shareholders and pensioners, lost much, if not all, of their life's savings.

The sometimes excessively generous remuneration, bonuses, pension rights, and other perks paid to CEOs and top managers are considered as justified so long as they attract and reward those with the necessary experience and skills to bring about increase in shareholder value. From the viewpoint of the other workers in the company and of the wider community the amount of these payments might be seen as excessive and out of all proportion to the work they do. But from the point of view of the shareholders who stand to make huge gains through such skills, these sums will not be seen as out of proportion to their gains.

*

Of the two forms of income or profit by which shareholders expect to gain from their shareholding, the dividend, or share of the profits, is money behind which stands actual economic value, but the shareholders themselves contribute little or even nothing to the creation of this value. Like rent, it can also be called a "compulsory gift." What the shareholders receive beyond what they rightfully "earn," others have to forgo out of that which is due to them.

The increase in shareholder value, to which so much effort and so many brilliant minds are now committed, is unreal money value – counterfeit money – that has nothing real behind it. Against it, "capitalized debt" is created, debt that others will have to pay.

Chapter 19
Have We Earned What We Buy?

Money as Power Over the Work of Others

It is in the nature of our present time, and of the form and structure of our society, that before we can provide ourselves with even the most basic necessities, we must first acquire money. Only through the medium of money can we obtain food and other necessities of life for ourselves and our dependents. If we do not already have the money, then we must somehow earn it, we must work to do something that someone else is willing to pay to have done. If we cannot provide what others need, then so long as the community provides no other way, we must of necessity "sell" our labor, sell something of ourselves; we are not then free – the only alternative is to go without, to become destitute and starve.

This situation gives those with money power over those who do not have it, power over their work, and so over their lives. The assertion that a person is free to sell or not to sell his or her labor is beneath rebuttal. If we have no money and no independent way of acquiring it, then, because of the way our society is formed today, we must of necessity sell our labor to someone who will buy it.

*

From the point of view of the individual, the money a person earns, or is paid, is very real. It provides a certain freedom to buy some or all of those things that a person may need or want. If we earn enough, it can give us a sense of well-being and increase our standing or prestige within the community. It can also give us the power to influence or control others.

From the perspective of the community as a whole, the money that constitutes the wage is of no value except in that it is an order or requisition on the products of other people's work to the value of that money. The person with the money can execute this order, can buy something with it, or it can be passed on to someone else for that person to use. We can give it as fees to a college for our child to attend, give it to a charity whose work we want to support, we can save it for another time, or something else entirely. But the primary characteristic of money is that it is an order on other people's work.

This aspect of money as an "order" or "requisition" that carries within itself a certain compulsion has arisen through human evolution, and is inherent in the development of the division-of-labor. It has come about that the human being can now no longer provide for him or herself; we cannot solely survive on what we as individuals, or even as single families, or even together with an immediate circle of friends, can produce. In both soul and body, the human being has changed, we have grown beyond what we were in earlier, more primitive, times. We could not survive on what sustained a person then. We are dependent for the necessities of life on the products that our present highly developed economic and cultural activities provide. This is especially true in the more "developed" parts of the world.

Pay as Share of the Community Product

If, in a closed community, every person in that community worked equally at economic production within division-of-labor, then the true wage that each would be entitled to – the reciprocal value for each individual's contribution to the total production – would be an equal share of the total that was produced by all. The system would be seen as right and just when the money each received as a wage was the amount required to buy this equal share.

Actual life is of course much more complex than this. There are many factors that affect what each can contribute, and also what each needs, but this concept is helpful as a starting point, a foundation on which to build our economic science.

Clearly, there are very many people who cannot contribute to the work of economic production but who do need a share of what is produced. There are those who are too young or too old to work, and there are the sick and disabled. Something must be taken from the total production for them. Then, as the community develops separate cultural and rights sectors, the people who carry that work will also need a share. Economically, they produce nothing. But the creativity, imagination, invention, order, and security that they foster go also to those active in economic production who need and benefit from them both in their productive work and in their individual lives.

This can be seen by way of another picture. Imagine, again, a simple village community in which all the villagers work in the fields or in the further economic elaboration of the products of the land. A time comes when they feel that something more is needed. If there was a priest who could bring cultural nourishment for their soul needs and who could also provide an education for their children, the lives of all would be richer and the community would develop. So they invite a priest to come and live in their village. But if the priest is to do what they want of him, he cannot himself also work in the fields to produce what he needs to sustain life. The other villagers must do this for him. So each does extra work in the field allocated to the priest, or perhaps each gives him some of the produce from their own field.

So the villagers free the priest from having to work in the fields. Economically, what the priest receives must be thought of as a gift or a contribution from the villagers – the economic workers. This gift frees him to do the cultural work that is his vocation and is wanted by the community. It might also be that the community feels that such a priest may have certain needs that they do not have, in which case they may decide that he should actually receive as wage more than they do. What the workers would now receive as wage, or as the true price of their produce, would need to be their equal share of what is produced, minus that portion that goes to the priest.

All that which must go to others such as the children, the aged, and the sick who can make no contribution to the work of economic production can be brought into the calculation in the same way. From the point of view of the community, what must be striven for is an arrangement whereby each person receives, by way of wage or gift, the money that equals the agreed upon share of the total produced.

The relationship between the economic worker and the cultural worker is illustrated in this simple picture. What the cultural worker produces, whether priest, teacher, pop singer, poet, architect, or writer, is not a product of division-of-labor, but is something that serves the life of soul of the members of the community.

What the cultural workers receive from those who value their particular work and contribution is, economically, a gift to free them from having to work in economic activity. Here there can be no exchange of reciprocal values. While the economic worker, through the process of division-of-labor, earns the counter-value to the product of his or her work, the cultural workers earn what the others do for them, the economic work they do not have to do themselves.

Much the same thing can be seen in the relationship of the economic worker to the worker in the rights sphere.

It should not be thought that what is said here suggests that all people should receive the same wage. People are different, their capacities and their needs are different. Some make very important contributions to the life of the community, others are not able to do this. Some are committed to working long hours in service to the community, while others prefer to limit the productive work they do in order to have time for their own pursuits. None of this is right or wrong, they are facts of community life. It is not unreasonable that people who work hard and long, and through whose work considerable benefits accrue to the community, should receive more than others who do no more than a basic share of the work. It is often true that those who work hard and long have greater needs for what the community can provide, but it should make a difference if the object of the long hard hours of work is for the individual's own personal benefit or for that of the community.

Though it may be justified that one person earns more than another, it must nevertheless be felt to be justified because the social structure that brings this about has arisen out of the will of the community, because the members of that community feel that it is just and fair.

If a person is sick or handicapped, or for some other reason is unable to work, it is generally accepted in our society today that they have a right to the support of the community and should be given a share of what is communally produced. There is also a general sense that a family with many children and a low income has a similar right to receive some assistance from the community. If this is so, is it such a far step to say that, if two people have the same needs and do the same work, one possessing considerable ability and stamina while the other does not, they both should receive an equal or similar share of the total that is produced?

Whose Work Produces What We Buy?

The working of economic activity is very complex; it does not follow simple or logical paths that can be understood through definitions or rational thinking. We have to develop the ability to grasp it through imaginative thinking, a thinking that can take hold of something that is never still – that is always in a state of movement, of change, of growing and declining, where effect does not simply follow cause. This becomes apparent as soon as we go beyond simple barter or exchange.

No person working in a factory makes a product on his own. Nor is it meaningful to identify the particular contribution each makes to the whole. It is in the sharing of the work, in working in mutual co-operation that the profit arises, not in working separately. A factory is a joint working of many people, each at their own particular place. In the factory it is not possible to say that any one person creates any particular economic value; the work of the individual and the creation of value can only happen in the context of the whole. This is work that in the true sense of the word can be called co-operative. And it is true of all the people concerned, whether working on the factory floor or as chief executive.

This working together in mutuality is the very bedrock of division-of-labor. It is just this working together that makes the work so productive.

As I pointed out in the last chapter, not even the single factory stands alone; each is a part of the whole, part of a network in which each is interlinked and dependent on all others. Production is a joint effort between many "independent" factories and businesses. They, in turn, are part of and dependent on society as a whole. Alone they could produce nothing. Economically, no single factory, business, school, museum, or police station stands alone.

Within this working together there are some who make a larger contribution to the total than others: those, for example, who carry responsibility, who worry and do not leave their work behind them when they go home at the end of the day, and those who bring creativity and imagination to the productive process. These are the people who, in the normal run of the work, bring about improved productivity, rather than those who do no more than their work on the factory floor. But it is also true that, without those on the factory floor, nothing would be produced. It is also relevant that the nature of their work means that they gain from that work a far greater sense of fulfillment and soul satisfaction than the people who labor on the factory floor can find in their work. Then again, it may well be that in order to develop and sustain the creative and imaginative abilities they need for their work, they require a different and more fulfilling lifestyle. On the other hand, those whose work gives no nourishment to the soul must find that elsewhere – the community may feel it owes them at least that.

This brings us back to the question: should all be paid an equal wage, or if not, on what basis should wages differ and how should the differentials be decided? This question does not arise so long as we continue to think in terms of one person buying the labor of another in the market place. But as soon as we look at the inherent co-operative and mutual nature of the economic process and put this into the context of the recognition that has come very powerfully into the consciousness of people today – that all people are equal, have equal rights, and a right to be free – then we must ask it. But the answer is not simple. We can start with questioning whether there is any justification for some earning so much more than others as happens at present.

If we look, for example, at the actual work of those who are often referred to as key workers, such as teachers, police officers, bus drivers, firefighters, and nurses, we will see that, through their work, they and many others like them make an essential contribution to the welfare and even survival of the community as a whole. Their work requires skill and dedication; it is very often hard and sometimes dangerous. We all, in one way or another, depend on them for our well-being, health, and safety – without their hard work, our social life would all but disintegrate.

Over against this we can look, for example, at people who, through their work in the various financial markets and institutions, can accumulate for themselves vast wealth. This wealth gives them power to acquire a very large proportion of the products and services of society as a whole. Is the work they do and the contribution they make to society so large that it justifies their receiving so much more than teachers, police officers, and others like them? When we weigh these things, we cannot but come to the perception that it is completely out of proportion, that there is something deeply wrong in our society.

This is not intended to be a moral judgment of individuals who find themselves in a position to "make" or "earn" a lot of money – most of us would do the same. It is the structure or form of our society that makes this possible which is here being questioned and that needs changing. If society were structured according to what is felt to be morally right, then people would come to act in a moral way.

Do We 'Earn' Money, or Do We 'Earn' What We Buy with Money?

This divide between those who receive very little from the work they do and those who receive many hundred, or even many thousand times as much, is one of the most pressing social problems of our time. What must deeply concern any reasonably socially minded person is not only the size of the gap, which is by any standards very wide, but the fact that the gap continues to widen. How is it that in our enlightened, democratic, and economically developed world some people are able to acquire enormous wealth with all the power and control over others that this gives them, while others earn comparatively little, and still others not even enough to support themselves and their families? Do the rich "earn" their money? Do the poor receive what they have "earned?"

How is it that, at a time when it is possible to produce enough for all humanity, there are still so many that have to suffer poverty and wretchedness while others can have so much more than they need, than they can actually themselves enjoy? How is it that the lifestyles of an affluent minority are able to affect the Earth's environment to the detriment of all humanity, that the right to "do business" and to "make money" takes precedence over the well-being of whole populations of those who themselves have no such possibility? This can be looked at as a moral question, and it is one, but it is also a practical socioeconomic one and will be looked at here as such.

*

Deep down most people do feel that something is fundamentally wrong when relatively few individuals are able to acquire vast sums of money, amounts which are far beyond anything reasonably comparable to what the majority of people earn. But so long as people are not able to see beyond the money itself and are thus unable to come to any sound foundation from which to question these high earnings, they will find it difficult to offer any thoughts that may lead towards a solution of the problem, nor will they have the means to understand or justify the feelings of injustice, anger, and frustration that well up, often quite strongly, within their souls. Such expressions as "fat cats" arise out of just such feelings, and, because of their inability to justify them, people become emotionally frustrated.

In the economic thinking of today, it would be absurd to assert that, if people sell their skills for a high price, they have not earned the money they are paid. Similarly, according to today's dominant thinking about economics, it would be unreasonable to claim that, if a manufacturer is able to buy labor and materials cheap, and sell products expensively, the profits earned are not the manufacturer's own. Or to state that if a singer makes an album that sells a million copies, she has not actually earned the money she receives as a result.

However, based on a true and sound observation of the actual facts of social life, and particularly of the economic productive process itself, we may begin to make such claims with authority. Today it is almost universally common to think in terms of people working for, or earning, money. The money one earns is an entitlement to acquire as much of the available products and services as it will buy. But is this meaning of the verb "to earn" true to the actual economic process? Is it the money that one "earns," or is it the products that are bought with the money? In current thinking, one is seen as *earning money,* which is then used to buy what one can afford, rather than as *earning the products and services themselves*, i.e., what the money enables us to buy. The difference may be subtle, but it is fundamentally important. If we approach this question from the perspective of the community as a whole, then we will come to think in terms of people earning their share of the total produced by the community.

Take, for example, the situation where someone buys a product for $1,000. If we look only at the money, we will see the payment of $1,000 as the justification for the acquisition of the product. But, if we look not at the money but at the work the individual performed to earn the $1,000, and set this over and against all the work of the many different people who worked to make the product, we will come to a different, fuller and more nuanced, picture. It could be that we see that the person has not actually earned what she bought, or perhaps that in the $1,000 she has not been paid what she earned.

If we look no further than the money, then it is not easy to say that we do not always earn what others agree to pay us. But if we look upon the money as an order on other people's work and see how much work those others have to do in order to supply us with what we wish to buy with the money we are paid, then we can come to a very different answer to the question of whether we have earned what we are paid. We can ask whether our contribution to the community is really so great as to justify so many others having to work to produce what the power of our money demands of them. From the point of view of the community as a whole, what is paid as remuneration is by no means solely a matter for those immediately concerned, for the person or organization that pays and the one who is paid. The money gives the recipient power over others and thus has an effect on the whole community.

If we only look at the money, then whatever lies behind it and gives it its value within the social life of the community as a whole remains hidden – the money becomes a thing in itself, the possession of which justifies the obtaining of what it will buy. But if we look more closely at what the money stands for, then we can know whether it truly represents a value or contribution from which the community has benefited and which justifies the community providing reciprocal products or services of like value.

We can look again at the examples of the three coats given in Chapter 14. In the first example the table stands behind the money that buys the coat. There it is clear that the making of the table has earned the carpenter the coat: we can see both the table and the coat and that they are of a like value. The maker of the table has earned what he is paid, and can buy what he has earned.

In the second example it is not so clear. The student has been given the grant because there is confidence in his future potential; the community might well receive great benefit at some future time. In this it can be said that the student has, or will, earn the coat. But what stands behind the money with which he pays for the coat is not clear. How did the person or institution that gave the money come into possession of it? We might have to go far back to find what it actually represents, and that can be lost in the total mix of money.

The matter becomes clearer again in the third example. Someone buys a coat with profit made on the sale of land, profit that arose solely out of being given permission to build another house on the land. This money buys the coat that the tailor worked to produce. If we look only at the money with which the landowner pays for the coat we may well say that she is justified in buying it, she paid the $200 asked – it was her good fortune that the price of land had increased through obtaining permission to build. But from the perspective of the community, the landowner has neither created nor provided anything that is of benefit to the community as a whole or any one member of it. It cannot be said that the landowner, in this case, has earned what the money will buy, the coat, the fruit of other people's labor.

Chapter 20
Who Pays?

Almost daily we see highlighted somewhere in the media social problems to which there appear to be no solutions. But we often do not see the true nature of these problems because we do not look beyond the money involved. Money has taken on the properties of a veil through which we no longer see the actual economic realities.

Let me illustrate this by considering, as an example, something that is a very real problem in society today, and particularly acute in London. There, as in many other cities around the world today, people doing essential work such as nurses, teachers, train drivers, police, and firefighters, are often unable to buy even the cheapest and most basic houses for themselves. Society could not function without people such as these doing the important work they do. Surely in such an economically advanced and productive society as ours, one that lays great stress on the equality of all people, it cannot be accepted that the share they are justly entitled to in return for the real and actual contribution to society they make does not include the provision of such a basic need as a reasonable place in which to live and raise their families. This in a city where there are others, making little or no comparable contribution to the welfare of society, who can afford to buy and live in houses costing many millions of pounds. That this situation is accepted as the natural order of things is confirmation that the old forms of class, though now based on wealth, still live strongly in our social consciousness, and that democracy and a sense of equality and justice have still a long way to come. How has this state of affairs come about?

The reality is that if the wages such people as nurses and firefighters received were a just and fair share of the total community product, and if it was only the actual economic cost of building that they had to pay, they could easily afford to buy a house. But, as has been shown, both these conditions are distorted within the structure of our society due to the fact that rights have been assigned attributes that are appropriate solely to products of economic activity. Due to the "compulsory gift" element behind such factors as rents and dividends, wages are forced below their proper economic level; added to this, the "market in rights" forces up above their true economic cost the price of assets such as houses.

Imagine that a piece of undeveloped land is purchased by a developer who builds a number of simple houses, which he then sells. For the buyer, the cost of each house will have three elements:

1) the true economic cost of the actual building of the house including any reasonable profit to the builder

2) the cost of the land on which the house is built, i.e., the capitalized debt passed on in the price of the land

3) any additional profit made by the developer arising out of the tensions of the market which may well push up the marketable value of the house. Like earlier profit on the sale of the land, it too will bring about the creation of capitalized debt that would be added to the earlier debt and carried forward in the price of the house.

The houses may be bought and sold several times, generally increasing in price each time.

Later, when a nurse or other such worker wishes to buy one of the houses, what is the "price" she will have to pay? It will, of course, include the original economic cost of building the house. If that were all, she could probably afford it. But, in addition to this, she will have to pay an amount to cover all the capitalized debt carried forward in the price; that is, she must take over the "debts" incurred by previous owners and accumulated in the price of the house. This represents all the profits that the different owners have made ever since the land first acquired a monetary value and which are now capitalized in the price of the house. This can be a very substantial sum of money, several times the true economic cost.

This means that, if she is to buy the house, she will have to find a large sum of money in order to take over and carry forward the burden of the capitalized debt. We can assume that she will have to borrow this money, so she will also have to pay interest on it. She will receive no benefit or advantage from the sum she pays on this capitalized debt, aside from the remote possibility of someday selling the house without needing to buy another and thus keeping the profit. But if the cost means that she cannot afford to buy the house in the first place, then she can only be a loser.

The cost alone of carrying this capitalized debt could be a major obstacle to her acquiring her own home, but it is made even more difficult, or impossible, by an additional factor. She will have to find this money while being paid a wage that is itself well below what it should rightly be. Her wages, already below what they would be as a reasonable share of the total produced, are reduced even further by what I have described as "compulsory gift" (see p. 183 ff.).

The result of these factors means that many of those who carry the essential work of our society today are prevented from acquiring a decent home in which to live and have a family. This is the social cost of the fact that the legal structure of our society is such that many are given the possibility to buy the products of the work of others without themselves giving anything real in exchange.

So too, anyone who follows through this line of study will come to understand why many people from the cities are able to move into rural areas to buy a second, or even a third, home thus pricing out of the housing market local people whose families may have lived there for generations. There are now villages and rural areas in beautiful parts of the country where the cost of houses has risen out of all proportion to the local economy and what local people can earn. Rich people from the financial centers move in and buy up houses for their weekends or as holiday homes, forcing up prices to many times their true value and completely outpricing local people. This is a symptom of a deep sickness within society.

*

Although the capitalized debt held in land, shares, and other such "assets" tends always to increase, there are several ways by which some of it is, from time to time, reduced, repaid, or dissolved.

Just as when asset values increase, the owners make a profit offset by the increase in capitalized debt, so when they later decline the current holders lose money. In this way there is a paying off of the debt. This is the most immediately apparent instance of the debt being repaid.

Inflation, too, pays off such debt. Those who hold money during inflation become very aware that their money loses value; it buys less than it would have done when they earned it. This decrease in value is a way of paying, or making up for, earlier debts.

The constant increase in the money supply with cheap money, created through the market in rights, tends to devalue earned money. Though this devaluation is a paying off of the debt, it tends to force up the value of the rights on which it feeds. This is because when there is a threat of inflation there is a tendency for those with money in cash to buy non-cash assets such as land, shares, and bonds, which preserve value against inflation. This inflates the prices of the assets, which further devalues money and at the same time creates additional profit for those who hold the assets. Those involved in the real economy, in the actual work of manufacture and distribution of commodities and the provision of services, as well as all those dependent on fixed wages, pensions, or their cash savings, are the ones who suffer. *They* must pay the price of inflation, thus contributing to the paying off of debts incurred by others.

To the extent that assets continue to have monetary value, debt is carried forward into the future.

The question must be asked: Is it conceivable that these accumulated debts stored up in the monetary value of land, shares, and all other such marketable rights, debts that grow ever greater despite periodic reduction in value, can just continue to increase *ad infinitum*? Is it blindness that prevents people from seeing the impossibility of this, from seeing that there will inevitably come a time when this is no longer sustainable? Or is it a conscious or unconscious shutting out of an uncomfortable truth because in the short-term so much is to be gained by those in the right places? In so far as it is thought of at all, is it put aside in the hope that it will not happen "in our time," that it is something that a future generation will either deal with or suffer disastrous social turmoil when it resolves itself?

Is it not a case of 'what goes up must eventually come down?' It is clear to anyone who sees the present situation that it cannot continue upwards indefinitely. Must we allow events to take their natural course until disaster strikes, or can the problem be taken in hand in a conscious and controlled way? The growing divide between the rich and the poor, between those who have access to the land and the resources within it, and those who must of necessity work for them but with inadequate return, will not be tolerated indefinitely. Change may come through peaceful means achieved through human reason, but history shows that it is more likely to come through financial collapse or through strife and violence. The more that ownership is confined to fewer and fewer of the super rich and to powerful organizations, the less acceptable will it become to a greater and greater section of humanity. Something will eventually shift the whole value-creating movement into reverse. The demand for equality and human rights, accompanied by the recognition of the individual and of deeper human values, grows ever stronger.

*

A large part of what is and will be paid out as pensions is the profit arising out of and dependent on a continuing upward trend in asset values. This exacerbates the worry, fear, and even panic when there are steep declines in the markets. But because, historically, prices have always bounced back again, these recessions have been temporary, and so confidence of a continuing rise in the future continues to reassert itself. This confidence, together with the lure of gain, is what makes people turn from selling to buying, actually bringing about the recovery they hope for and believe in – this confidence is what causes prices again to rise. A day will come, however, when the confidence will not return. The markets will continue downward and the consequences will indeed be dire. There have been speculative financial bubbles in the past that have burst causing great hardship and misery for very many people, but they have been local affairs within individual enterprises, countries, or banking systems. Now we are fast approaching a single worldwide, interrelated financial system.

The Markets and the Price of Oil

When anyone tries to buy a house, the cost is considerably inflated by both capitalized debt and compulsory gift. But this distortion of the true economic cost of products goes far beyond just the price of houses. It affects all aspects of life. I will give another example of how the great majority of humanity are forced to pay an amount over and above the true economic cost and how a minority are able to accumulate this overpayment in the form of huge unearned wealth. I refer here to the cost of oil and of everything deriving from it, including gasoline. Oil plays an enormously important part in all our lives; it is used extensively in the generation of electricity, in industry and in agriculture, and as raw material for the production of many substances such as plastics. The price of oil, and so also of gasoline, has very little relationship to the true economic cost, the cost of extracting it from the earth, refining, and transporting it.

The last dramatic fluctuations in the price of crude oil occurred in 2008. That year, the price climbed from around $60 a barrel in early 2007 to just under $150 a barrel in July 2008, after which it fell back down again. A decade before that, the price was not much more than $10 a barrel. Presently, the price for a barrel of crude oil hovers around $100. These fluctuations have little connection to the actual cost of production; they are simply the outcome of the working of the market, a result of the tension between supply and demand. As demand for oil increased during 2007 and the early part of 2008, particularly from emerging economies such as China, the price rose. But the supply did not increase as it could and should have done according to the advocates of the market economy. While the doubling of the cost of oil brought great hardship to a large part of the population of the world through increased prices in a great range of products including many of the necessities of life, particularly food, it also brought even greater wealth to those who benefitted from the increase. The beneficiaries included not only the oil producing countries and their sovereign wealth funds[‡], but also, of course, the oil processing and trading companies and their shareholders.

[‡] A sovereign wealth fund (SWF) is a state-owned investment fund investing in real and financial assets such as stocks, bonds, real estate, precious metals, or in private equity funds or hedge funds. SWF's invest globally; most are funded by revenues from commodity exports or from foreign-exchange reserves held by the central bank.

This was a clear example of the "compulsory gift" demanded from the majority for the benefit of the few. Sovereign wealth funds are, in the main, accumulations of money resulting from overcharging. We should clearly see that much of the vast wealth of the oil producing countries and of individuals connected to the industry is not earned income but the accumulation of compulsory gifts of what great numbers of people have earned, often through hard work under soul-destroying conditions. This wealth is now buying ownership of property, businesses, and even sports teams, often in the countries that have provided them with their wealth. Increasingly, ownership of sections of our economic and financial institutions is passing out of the control of those directly connected with them as they are bought up by the sovereign wealth funds of other countries who have no other interest than making money. This is a problem that is still in its early days but will increase in the coming years.

Large sums of money are accumulated from compulsory gifts, not only through the market in oil but from many other such sources. These are formed into "funds." These funds are then used to buy a wide variety of assets worldwide including land and controlling stock in large and often nationally important businesses. The demand for assets itself forces up the value of the assets, thus creating capitalized debt on the one side, and increased monetary value in the funds on the other. Some of these assets generate compulsory gifts themselves, so funds grow ever bigger through interweaving spirals of money creation by way of compulsory gift on the one side and the increasing value of assets offset by capitalized debt on the other. They develop life forces of their own that are focused on growth. The managers of the funds are employed solely to care for the funds, to make them grow. Their responsibility is to their employers, whether they are owners, shareholders, private investors, pensioners, or governments owning sovereign wealth funds. Their task is to sustain growth through careful investment and the buying and selling of assets; it is not to concern themselves with moral judgments or the interests of the wider community. Some of these funds hold assets valued in the hundreds of billions of dollars. They are slowly acquiring land and controlling interests in major businesses and so gaining the power to change the very nature and legal structure of the society which provides the monetary values on which they feed.

With their self-sustaining focus on their own growth, these funds take on parasitic lives of their own within the social body of humanity, lives akin to those of cancerous growths.

Today there is as much dogma concerning the sanctity of "the markets" as there ever was in the past concerning religious beliefs.

But given our present form of thinking based on the idea that human society is a unitary whole with a pyramidal structure, there is really no alternative to the market for controlling the economy. Human egoism and greed is too powerful. The only alternative is first to recognize the threefold nature of society and to begin to form it accordingly. Only when the recognition of the threefold nature of society takes hold will it become possible to start working along the lines of the economic associations I described earlier, and to establish socially healthier economic forms.

Chapter 21

The Social and the Anti-Social

Mutual Societies or Partnerships

A study of the recent demutualization of some of the old mutual societies illustrates clearly the nature of the money capital created through the marketing of shares and reveals how this process has been a substantial source of capitalized debt. It shows at the same time how certain organizations, set up in ways that accorded very closely to the needs of the mutual co-operative nature of economic activity, have been taken over by forces of egoism and reformed to enable a few to benefit from the labor of many others.

Throughout history, in times of hardship, people have come together for mutual support. Long before government-run social services came into being, people formed groups to help each other during sickness or unemployment. Those that came together agreed among themselves to each put a certain amount of their earnings into a common fund. Then, when one of them became ill or suffered hardship, there would be money available to help that person through the hard times.

As the number of members contributing to the fund grew, one or more might eventually be appointed to hold, or possibly invest, the money. They or others would be empowered to make any necessary decisions regarding the payment of benefits to those who fell ill or lost their jobs.

Such a mutual society consisted of its members, who were bound by the agreement that they themselves had drawn up and agreed upon. This was not a business or a trading organization; there were neither dividends nor sharing of any profits. It was a simple mutual arrangement that did not have an existence as a body separate from its members. All monies held in the fund and accumulated from investments were held solely for the benefit of members who fell on hard times. All monies gained through investing the capital became part of the fund, except for an amount that might be needed to pay the administrators of the fund for the actual work they did. The fund belonged to the members, and its sole purpose was the mutual support of the members. This was an early form of mutual insurance.

Another form of mutual society was connected with housing. Very often, people living or working together at a particular locality found that as individuals it was difficult or impossible to save enough money to buy a house, or to buy the land on which to build one. Nor was it possible at that time for most ordinary people to borrow money. But, if every week each of them put an agreed upon amount into a common fund as a loan, rather than as a gift as in the case of the welfare fund just described, then the fund would grow into what eventually would be a substantial sum of capital. There would then be the possibility for individuals to borrow from the fund in order to buy a house. It also helped people to save money – they could get back the money they had put into the fund when they needed it, possibly with interest.

This was a mutually held fund, that is, one held by joint agreement. Each individual who joined the group and deposited money into the fund was a member of the group or society. The members would appoint one or more of their number, or even employ someone from outside the membership, to hold and invest the monies in the fund. All decisions were made by all members jointly, or by those elected or appointed by the members for that purpose.

As the group or mutual society grew, interest came to be charged on all borrowed money and paid to those that lent it. Any administrative costs were covered by charging those who borrowed money a slightly higher rate than that paid to the lenders. It was not in the original purpose of the fund to generate profits nor to pay dividends to the members; it was not a business, but a circle of people mutually supporting each other.

No one *owned* the fund, and no one owned the group or society. The society only existed through the members who jointly formed it and jointly held the money put into it by the members, plus any interest earned.

These two examples illustrate what was, and still is, the basic nature of the "mutual society." This form originated in the late eighteenth century out of the industrial revolution. Nearly all the older building societies and insurance and pension funds started in this way. Partnerships of specialists such as accountants, architects, or lawyers are also frequently based on a similar mutual structure; they come together to mutually benefit from sharing such services as offices, expertise, publicity, or a well-known "name."

The structure of the mutual society, where there are no outside "owners" taking a share of any profits, is one that is ideally suited to organizations of the economic sphere of activity, based, as it is, on the mutual co-operative work of those actually active in the enterprise. In such a mutual economic society, it was the people active in the organization who owned it; there were no shares to sell, and thus no capitalized debt was generated.

Demutualization

It is a sign of our times that in recent years members of many of these mutual societies, which in some cases have grown enormously since their first founding, have come to see the possibility of achieving considerable financial gain for themselves by "demutualizing" the society or partnership. "Demutualizing" means transforming it from a mutual society providing a service for its members into a business owned by the former members in order to generate profit, shared out as dividends, for themselves. This profit could be created by making the services available to a wider public and increasing the charge for these services. Although profit is always attractive, it has not generally been the primary aim of the demutualization of the societies. The objective has been to achieve something that the profits or dividends make possible.

Merely distributing the profit to the members would create little or no advantage as it would be in large part a case of the members paying higher fees so as to receive the money back as profit. But what was enticing was something else. As was shown earlier, anything that creates profit can itself acquire a capital value provided that it is also tradable. Membership in a mutual society cannot be bought or sold; it is not tradable, so it can have no marketable or capital value. But a share in the ownership of a profit-creating asset, such as a business, is marketable and will achieve a monetary value relative to its potential to pay a dividend to the owner. So where membership, which has no capital value attached to it, is transformed into tradable shares of ownership which do have capital value, the recipient of the new shares finds himself – without himself having to do anything to earn it – the owner of capital value. This capital value comes into being solely because, and to the extent that, people will be prepared to pay to own the dividend-paying shares.

This shows clearly how the structure of our laws relating to ownership offers an opening for the egoistic desire for financial gain. Instead of a group of people arranging matters mutually between themselves to the advantage of all, there are now two groups, each primarily concerned with their own interests – owners and customers. While the profit may be a genuine product of commercial activity arising out of an actual contribution of one party to the other, the capital value that that profit leads to represents no such contribution or service.

The total capital value of the shares issued (or the monetary value created) on the demutualization of the building societies in the U.K. during the mid-nineties was reckoned to be more than £18 billion. None of this value represented money put as capital into the new companies, it was all newly created monetary value in the hands of the new shareholders. I know – I was one of them.

The money the members put into the mutual society had changed in quality: it had become a salable capital asset with the potential to increase in monetary value through sale on the capital market.

Normally, in a limited company, the share value does in part represent actual capital put into the company, and only the increase in value of those shares is newly created monetary value. But in the demutualization of the mutual societies the new shareholders paid nothing for their shares. The shares, as a right of ownership to what previously could not be owned, were newly created and given to the members. This makes the situation much more transparent. A *right*, in the sense that membership bestows certain beneficial rights on the members of the mutual society, is transformed into the *ownership* of a share in what has become an economic-financial business. The former members now become owners of a transformed enterprise. While it continues to give the same service as before, the company now charges more for that service and pays the profit to the new owners. These owners, who have themselves put nothing into the new company that they had not previously put into the mutual society, now receive dividends payable on the shares they own. More importantly, through the entitlement to the dividends attached to the shares, the shares immediately acquire a capital value and can be sold at a profit on the market.

What came into being for the purpose of enabling people to help and support each other has become transformed into a business with a focus on making financial gain for the owners.

If the owner of a share sells it, he receives money in exchange. The share that he hands over is not something that he created through his own work, it is a legal right, a right, amongst other things, to a share of the profit created through the work of others. He has contributed nothing to the creation of that profit. Any loan or deposit he may have put into the former mutual society, which is now held by the new business, is still a repayable loan on which interest is paid – that has not changed.

Here again, when he uses this money from the sale of his share to pay for the products of other people's work, what he hands over is very similar to counterfeit money, only legal. Though he has not himself printed the money, it is just as newly created out of nothing. The money appears to stand for a value when in fact no such value has been given.

It might be argued that it is not new money because the money already existed – it is the money that the buyer had earned and passed to the seller of the shares. Here it is important to differentiate between "money" and "monetary value." Actual money, whether as cash or an entry in an account, is not a value in itself but something that stands for, or represents, an economic value that exists elsewhere. The money that a carpenter holds, received in exchange for a table, stands for the value of the table – the economic value created through the carpenter's work within the division-of-labor.

But, unlike the table, a share is not a product of someone's work, it is a right of ownership which, because it is tradable, acquires monetary value behind which there is no real economic value. The buyer of the share hands over money, but he does not part with monetary value: he still holds monetary value in the share, even if, in reality, it is a false value.

The following is another simple illustration which can throw further light on the nature of the economic sphere.

The Tunnel

Sometimes a manufacturing or construction company produces something that is not used up or consumed in the normal way, but has a certain permanence. In such cases the product of human activity becomes one with the land and nature. Tunnels, land reclaimed from the sea, roads, railways, and some buildings are examples of this.

Imagine that a company is created for the purpose of building a tunnel through a mountain range and then maintaining it. The tunnel will enable private and commercial vehicles to save considerable mileage on their journeys between two major areas of population and industry. It is a huge undertaking requiring a great deal of money for which it is felt necessary to raise both investment capital and loans. The subsequent cost of maintaining the tunnel will be comparatively small, so loans will be repaid out of income from charging those who use the tunnel.

This company will not be manufacturing a product in the way that clothing or furniture manufacturers do. Simply put, it will dig a hole through a mountain and then charge people for allowing them to pass through it.

Before it can do this, the company will have to obtain permission from the government. Because of the very considerable cost of the project, it will also need to obtain from the government some sort of guarantee that no one else will be given the right to build another competing tunnel for a certain period of time. We see here a very important working together of two separate sectors of society. The rights sector has to create the right environment in which the economic sector can operate in order to build the tunnel. Its responsibility is to the interests of society as a whole, not to the company, except in so far as that too is a part of society. In giving the company the monopoly for a certain period, the rights sector will first need to establish that the tunnel is itself in the best interests of the public, and then establish that granting the monopoly is necessary for the achievement of that end. This was a particularly important factor in the building of the Channel Tunnel beneath the English Channel.

Society itself has to create the conditions within which it will be economically viable for the company to build and operate the tunnel.

Once the tunnel is built, those who use it will have to pay a fee for doing so. This is a proper economic activity and will have to be paid for accordingly. This charge will, in the first place, go towards the ongoing cost of maintaining and operating the tunnel, and then towards repaying the loans. It is entirely reasonable that those enjoying the benefit of the tunnel should each pay a contribution towards the cost of its construction, including interest.

Assuming everything goes according to plan, a time will come when all the loans, together with the interest, will be repaid. The lenders will then have no further interest or lien on the tunnel.

A person who put his money into the venture by buying shares will not expect a large return on his money until the loans have been repaid. But, once these are cleared, the income that had been used for the repayments will go to increasing the dividends paid to the shareholders. As a result, the value of their shares will rise. When they spend this unearned money, the amount of capitalized debt (see p. 179 ff.) accumulated within society will increase. Although they may not have put any more capital into the construction of the tunnel than those who lent their money, nor incurred very much greater risk, they will, in all probability, over time, reap benefits far greater than the lenders – they will be rewarded for being the owners of the tunnel.

These shares may be sold many times over, but for as long as the tunnel continues to serve the community the "owners" of the shares, whoever they are, will expect to receive a fee from all those who use it, even though they themselves have contributed nothing towards either building the tunnel or maintaining it. This becomes clearer if one looks to the person who, one hundred years later, inherits shares.

Once dug, the hole is there, and there it will remain, like a fact of nature. The tunnel is not a product that wears out and has to be replaced. It is built by the people of one generation and continues to serve the people of future generations. All those who planned it, built it, and invested in it will eventually pass from the earth. Future generations will have it as something bequeathed to them by a past generation. The tunnel as a hole in the earth becomes part of the land. But "ownership" continues on for as long as the tunnel exists. (I questioned the right of any person to own land in Chapter 15).

Is there any economic, moral, or democratic justification for a legal system that gives to a person of a later generation the right to charge others for permission to pass through a tunnel built and paid for by people of an earlier generation?

Surely there must come a time when such a construction becomes the property of the community as a whole, like the land itself. If someone writes a book or a play, or composes music, the copyright belongs to the author and then to his or her heirs, or to those who have bought the rights to it. But this right lasts only for a certain period of time. These rights eventually pass into the public domain, they become the property of the community. If this is possible for such works, why not for others such as the tunnel?

It is different for the ongoing work of maintaining and operating the tunnel. That is a work that belongs properly within the economic sector. Once the construction costs are paid, the charges for using the tunnel should be sufficient to cover all the maintenance and operating costs, that is, the actual economic costs.

This example shows a further boundary to the rightful activity of the economic sector. Clearly there comes a time when a "product" has been fully paid for, when the total cost of production has been repaid. At that point it should rightly be passed out of the economic sector and taken over by the rights sector. If this does not happen, as is often the case at present, then it becomes a further source for the creation of money for the owners, as well as the counterbalancing capitalized debt placed on society.

*

In each of these two pictures, the mutual society and the building of the tunnel, it is possible to see, on the one side, a socially healthy structure of economic activity that works in a way that is beneficial to society as a whole, and how something coming in from outside the economic process proper takes a parasitic hold on that activity. The product of that beneficial activity is then transformed into something that works against the best interests of society.

If one looks deeply into such activities, one will come to observe how this parasitic element is entering ever more strongly into human social life.

The financial centers of big cities all around the world are filled with organizations and individuals – stock, futures, and options markets, merchant and investment banks, land development companies, financial and legal consultants, accountants, tax advisors and others – somehow engaged in the creation of false monetary value, or legal counterfeit money.

Only a decreasing proportion of the activities of financial institutions such as the stock markets are involved in the promotion or facilitation of true economic production and trade. In most cases it is no more than a small part of their work that contributes to actually producing the goods and services that people need. Generally, this is estimated as being not more than ten percent – some think considerably less.

A very large part of the work of people in the financial centers is simply the creating of monetary value without any counter-value in actual products or services that are of benefit to the wider human community. Huge sums of money are created that enable a portion of society to enjoy a very high standard of living, derived from other people's work, without themselves contributing anything of value in return.

A fund manager, for example, may work harder and for longer hours than, say, someone making furniture or growing grain, but what is the fund manager producing? It is not work itself which justifies "earnings," but the product of the work, goods or services that are useful or wanted by others. From the point of view of the community, the work of the fund manager produces little or nothing of actual value. On the contrary, this work may be to the detriment of the community as a whole: The fund manager guides and assists people to "make money" through the buying and selling of "rights," is paid by receiving a percentage of the money created, and then buys with this money what others have worked to produce.

The counterfeiter, too, may work hard, but this does not justify the purchases made with the counterfeit money. To create money without providing a product or service as counterpart to that which the money will buy is to live off the work of others without giving anything in return.

What is said here is not intended as a moral judgment of the individuals involved, but of the system that has come into being that makes this possible, that in fact encourages it. The problem is that the present structure of society, and the way of thinking it gives rise to, leads people to treat money as a thing in itself, to act as though in some way money itself creates what it buys.

*

Debt, properly used, can and does fulfill a necessary function within the community. In Chapter 14 I indicated how debt was rightly created when the manufacturer borrowed money from the bank. There, it was the manufacturer who benefited from the money thus created but also the one who carried the liability for the debt – he owed the money to the bank. The manufacturer would eventually have to clear the debt, therefore it was not a debt that continued into the future for others to pay.

Where financial or economic debt of any kind is created, as it must be in the proper running of community life, it is essential that it is set up in a way that clearly indicates its nature as a debt, and that a particular organization or individual carries responsibility for it and sees that it is cleared within a specified time.

As the rate of production and trade increases, it will be necessary that an increase in the supply of money is maintained. But it is a very different thing if, instead of allowing this to be haphazardly achieved through the market in rights to the benefit of a few and at the expense of many, it is done consciously and in a controlled way in accordance with the needs of the economic life of the community as a whole. This can only be done by those in the economic associations in conjunction with the banks. They are the only people who will be in a position to see and understand the need for an increase, or a decrease, in the money supply, and see also the consequences of having too much or too little in circulation. In an environment where there is no money to be made out of "ownership," this could be achieved quite easily, for instance, by controlling the borrowing of capital from the banks. The manufacturer who wished to expand would only be able to borrow money, and the bank to lend it to him, within the guidelines laid down by the economic associations in conjunction with the organs of the rights sector.

Where, as at present, any necessary increase in the money supply is left to the market, it is the individuals who own the tradable assets or rights, the increase in the price of which brings about the increase in the money supply, who thereby own the new money. They 'supply' this new money to the community by purchasing for themselves goods and services provided by the community. The owners of the new money benefit from it, but the community carries the debt which lies behind the new money, not those who create and spend it.

*

The structure established by our laws and the social behavior we have inherited from the past have led to our present financial system. This system makes it possible for some to live off the work of others without themselves contributing anything to those others in return. This must be seen clearly for what it is, no matter how many of us may ourselves, at some time or other, benefit from this possibility. In nature, an organism which lives in or on another, deriving its nourishment from the other without rendering any service in return, is called a parasite. Insofar as a person benefits personally from the creation of money through the market in rights and thus is able to buy what others produce without providing anything in return, that person is living as a parasite on the others. This is an uncomfortable truth about our society, but, until it is recognized, one major cause of much of the poverty in the world today will not be understood or properly dealt with. This must come to be seen and acted upon as an objective economic fact, not just a requirement of some moral teaching.

Because a person acquires money in, what are at present, quite lawful ways, we do not question that person's right to what is bought with that money. We are so caught up in the apparent rightness and, one can almost say, the sanctity of money, that it dazzles and blinds us to its reality.

Though we see the greed, the manipulation, the injustice, and the exercise of power and lack of concern for others which all too often lie behind great wealth, we ourselves can easily become caught up in its powerful allure, its promise of paradise on earth. We see the luxurious houses, the expensive cars and personal jets, the lifestyle of the tremendously wealthy and all that can come with it, and those who are not appalled are often fascinated and somehow comforted that such things are possible. These figures of great wealth are perceived, or presented, as almost god-like "Beings." They have reached a paradise to which we too long to find our way. They have achieved a state of grace to which we also aspire. Work is something that has to be done by those who have not yet reached that state.

But all this is an illusion; we must come to see the situation clearly for what it is.

On the other hand, we can come to resent the wealth and lifestyle of the super rich. But resentment also falsifies the picture and clouds our judgment. No healthy change can ever be achieved where illusion *or* resentment have any part in the motive that drives it.

Chapter 22

What About the Future?

The purpose of this book has been to demonstrate what happens when we observe the social life of humanity from a fresh perspective, free of the pre-conceptions that largely dominate today's social and economic thinking. Looked at in this way, the threefold nature of society and community life is soon evident. Within the scope of a single book, however, it is hardly possible to give more than an indication of this threefold nature, and much that has been touched on has not, of necessity, been developed fully. The further development of the perceptions I have shared is left to others who, one hopes, will have the impulse and the energy to take them much further. Those who do will find confirmation of their validity and soundness. No one person working alone, however, will be able to achieve a true working-picture of the whole of society. Only when people come together from different areas of work, and with different perspectives on society, will it be possible to arrive at a deeper understanding of the whole.

Society has created within itself many serious faults that are now leading to disastrous misunderstandings, conflicts, and aberrations. There are the more obvious problems: the ever-widening gap between the enormously rich and the desperately poor, the growing domination of the important aspects of life by financial and economic interests, the increasing ownership or control of the surface of the Earth and the resources within it by proportionately fewer people and institutions, and the failure by governments and industry to do anything more than tinker with the causes of climate change. In addition to all this, there are the divisions between groups of people on economic, religious, cultural, and nationalistic grounds that, in many places, are growing wider. Not only are egoism and greed taking over in individuals, but nations too are increasingly egoistic, self-serving, fearful, and intolerant of other nations. In the past, people were separated in a way that modern means of communication and travel have largely pushed aside. Because we see and know the consequences of our actions and way of life, we carry a heightened responsibility for them. We all live in one world, not in many separate ones. Just at the time when it has become possible for all people to know and begin to understand one another, there emerges, alongside but counter to this, a growing inability to actually meet and show a compassionate interest in what is foreign and different from ourselves. In a similar way, although humanity has achieved the possibility of providing the physical necessities of life for all the people of the world, large parts of the world population live in dire poverty and hunger.

To begin to change all this, to turn the forces of egoism, greed, fear, and enmity aside and create a tolerant society concerned with the different needs of each and every member, one that reaches across all that separates people, will need enormous vision, courage, and commitment. It will continue to prove inadequate, even with the best of intentions, to make many small, unconnected changes and adjustments without correcting the fundamental direction in which the whole of our society continues to move. Something much more radical is needed. The restructuring of society as a whole through a recognition and understanding of its own inherent threefold nature will be the first step in solving the deeper underlying problems.

The outline of a restructured threefold society that I have presented here might appear farfetched and utopian, the changes called for too extreme and unimaginable for practical application. Certainly much of it may not be achievable other than over a long period of time, perhaps generations. But if our economic life is to be rescued from the forces of egoism and is instead to serve all people, if the legal structure of society is to be formed truly on the basis of what all members of the community feel to be fair, right, and just, and if every person is to have the possibility of fulfilling the needs of their own inner life of soul, supported and nourished by a free cultural life, then we have to have a picture, a common imagination, of the kind of society in which these things can be realized. Without that, even with the best of intentions by people of imagination, intelligence and good will, nothing lasting can be achieved. But the moment such an imagination has been grasped and the first steps taken towards achieving it, people will find healing forces already beginning to work within society.

It is not easy to imagine actually separating out the three sectors from each other. The result will be a very different society from anything existing at present. This clear separation, this decentralization, of social life will be seen as realistic only when one has observed and confirmed for oneself what I have indicated in this book, and then lived and worked with the ideas for some considerable time. When one has done this work on one's own – no one, after all, can do it for us – the need to separate the three spheres, and the consequences of this separation, will be seen as necessary and realistic, not utopian. Of course the practical application of what has been presented here cannot be achieved overnight. But first there must be the vision of what is to be striven for.

*

It will not be possible to bring money under proper control until there is a widespread recognition of the difference between a product of economic activity proper, and a "right" that belongs solely within the rights sector. Sale and purchase is something that is inherently part of the economic productive process: what is divided in division-of-labor is reunited in sale and purchase. Sale and purchase has no place in the allocation of rights. There in the rights sphere, the sale-purchase transaction will always work against social health, denying access to rights on the basis of equality, and instead delivering them up, as though they were commodities, to those able to pay.

When the economic sector is separated out and stands independently on its own ground, and likewise the rights and cultural sectors, the amount of money in circulation and held as capital will be considerably reduced. Land, or any other such "right," will not be owned as at present – it will not be subject to the market and thus will have no monetary value. The right to occupy or use land will be allocated by the democratic rights sector in a way that is just and fair to both the individual who needs it and to society as a whole. It will have no capital value and will thus not be able to generate capitalized debt, and because it will be allocated to a particular person or organization for a particular purpose, it will not be rentable and will not generate compulsory gifts.

Buildings and other such structures, after a certain time, and once the cost of construction has been fully paid, will take on, as gifts from the past, something of the nature of land as a gift of nature. As finished products they eventually pass out of the economic sector and come within the domain of the rights sector. They too will cease to be subject to the market.

Perhaps most important of all, the structure of the "limited company" or corporation will disappear. These will be transformed into something like the older mutual societies or co-operatives. The people working together on some line of economic production will be co-owners of their own business and of the products of their joint work. Their income will be a share of the profits generated when these products are sold, not the purchase price of their labor. There will be no outside owners and thus no shares that can be bought and sold.

Financial markets will more or less disappear, only those which serve the economic processes of production and distribution proper will have a function. Only enough money to facilitate the circulation and exchange of economic products will be needed at any one time. This would include money necessarily accumulated as capital for the support of new developments within the economic sector and also for what is needed for the support and development of the cultural and rights sectors. Such money may be passed on as capital, but ultimately its use can only be to purchase the products of economic activity, thus completing the cycle shown in Chapter 12.

Of course none of this can be achieved without first establishing the "economic associations" described in Chapter 13.

*

At present, society has come to rely very largely on the financial markets for the supply of money. This has brought about a very confusing situation. Clearly there are times when there has to be an increase in the money supply. As the population increases or when economic production expands and more products are produced, an increase in the money supply becomes necessary. But such an increase should be consciously brought about in line with the increase of products in circulation. It should not be a haphazard affair dependent on a market that has little to do with the productive process itself. Nor should it be a system as at present that makes a donation of new money to those who already have plenty, while those who have little or none must work for those who have been made rich. Surely it should be just those who gain from any increase in the money supply who should also carry the debt and responsibility for its eventual repayment. That is fair and just. At present this does not happen.

In Chapter 15 I showed how money was created when a bank loaned money, for example for the construction of a factory. In that situation, the person or organization borrowing and thus benefiting from the money is also the one responsible for repaying the debt. The money comes into being for a particular purpose and that "purpose" will then repay the debt – no debt is passed on to the community for others to pay. The building itself, once finished and the debt repaid, will cease to have capital value so there can be no increase in monetary value and no profit backed by capitalized debt.

A more important possibility for the creation and control of the money supply would be through the economic associations. They will have responsibility for the smooth and efficient working of the economy for the benefit of the whole. They will have the ability, working through the banking sector, to increase or decrease the money supply, as and when needed, to ensure the necessary reciprocal flow of commodities and money within the community as was shown in Chapter 12. When it becomes necessary to increase the money supply, this could, for example, be done by issuing newly created money for the construction of public works to improve the infrastructure. Such work benefits the community as a whole rather than certain individuals. Any debt would be carried by the economic associations on behalf of society as a whole, which would then be responsible for its repayment if and when there is a need to reduce the money supply.

*

There is an obvious question: if what has been shown in this book concerning capitalized debt and compulsory gift is true, why has it not been recognized before? It is, indeed, very hard to believe that others have not seen it, or at the very least have come to suspect it. Unfortunately, it is just those who are in a position to observe the true nature of the financial markets and the consequences of the present system who benefit most from them. People have to be very strong-minded and selfless to see something that denies the validity of what is in their own best interests and to actually abolish the very thing that gives them their wealth.

*

Just as more and more people have developed a revulsion at the idea that one person can be seen as humanly inferior to another, thus a similar revulsion will develop at the idea of a person's work or labor being bought or owned by another.

The concept of the equality of all people is something that has come into human consciousness only in very recent times, in fact it is still in its infancy. If we go back to the time of communities or tribes based on blood relationships, there was no concept of the equality of all members of the community. For example, right up until the first half of the last century in nearly all communities worldwide, women were regarded as inferior to men. Right into the nineteenth century in England a wife was still seen as lawfully belonging to her husband, even as one of his chattels. Women were not given the vote until after the First World War.

As a child brought up in Kenya, I remember very distinctly the pervading conviction among the white settlers that our race was superior to the black people; colonialism was therefore seen as justified. Such assumptions were widespread in western "civilized" society. Even at the time of apartheid in South Africa there was a long struggle before the idea of equality was accepted – so too in the United States of America. It was only towards the end of the twentieth century that the concept of the equality of all people became a force within western society. Once started, the change came very quickly. Now such ideas are abhorrent to an ever growing number of people. Within the United Nations and in most countries, universal human rights and the equality of all people are now enshrined in law, even if they are by no means universally adhered to.

Today, the buying of labor and the labor market are accepted as
having almost the same validity as the laws of nature. But this too is
beginning to change. It is, after all, the last remnant of slavery, which
at one time, even in countries considered to be highly cultured, was
felt to be quite acceptable and necessary. There will come a time
when such feelings will be repugnant to an increasing number of
people. Just as happened with the emerging sense of the equality of
all people, so it will happen that this last echo of slavery, the buying
of something integral to the being of another person, his or her
labor, will become more and more unacceptable in civilized society.
Thus the very basis of our corporate structure will be undermined
and change will be forced upon us.

It follows that it will be socially unacceptable for one person
to own the product of another person's work. So the legal basis of
our economic organizations and of the financial markets will no
longer be tolerated. The recognition of the right to freedom and the
inviolability of each individual human being will come with the same
inevitability, the same evolutionary force, as did the perception of
the equality of all people.

But will the necessary change come about through conscious
human intelligence and careful planning, or will it be forced on us
by a collapse of the social order? Fear brought on by a sudden loss of
confidence in our current financial system based on the marketing of
what are properly human rights might one day cause such a collapse.
When people see their savings and pensions threatened with loss of
value and the security of their future in danger, real fear can take over,
fear that can very quickly turn to panic. We saw this last during the
financial crisis of 2008. In England, a loss of confidence amongst its
depositors led to a run on the Northern Rock Bank, while something
similar happened to Bear Stearns in the United States. Such events
can be brought about by many causes. If, in a more serious situation,
what happened to those institutions spread further through a chain
reaction to the whole banking and financial system, a complete
collapse of our entire economic structure could result.

We have come to rely very heavily on money created through
the financial markets, money that, as I have shown, is a lie in that
it has nothing real behind it. The confidence that asset values will
continue to rise brings about this very rise, and it is the increased

value and profit arising that reinforces the confidence. Added into this cycle is human greed and a tendency to only see what we hope to see, that which promises more riches. With this, we have a situation that can turn, quite suddenly, in the complete opposite direction. All the unsupported values created in the market would then disappear into the realm of illusion from which they emerged in the first place.

The seriousness of what could come about should not be underestimated.

*

There is another question that will, at some time in the future, come to be asked with increasing power: Does a person, by the fact that he or she is born onto the Earth, have a right to a place on the Earth? Or is it only through money or inheritance that such a right can be acquired?

The foundations of modern economic theory were laid by such thinkers as Adam Smith (1723-1790), sometimes thought of as the founder of modern economics, and Herbert Spencer (1820-1903). Central to Adam Smith's economic philosophy is the theory that individuals serve the community best when they work to provide for themselves. The wealth of a nation, in this view, results from each of its citizens pursuing his or her own interests, thus making egoism a key ingredient to a successful economic life.

Herbert Spencer, who built on Adam Smith's work, was a contemporary of Charles Darwin (1809-1882). Spencer applied Darwin's theory of evolution by natural selection, for which he, Spencer, coined the phrase "survival of the fittest," to the sphere of economics. Spencer held that this idea of the "survival of the fittest" in nature was just as applicable, and valid, in the world of production, distribution, and consumption. In this view, the sphere of economic activity is something that follows its course through its own natural laws; human beings do not control it but are caught up into it. The wealth of a single person is accepted as the result of natural laws that lead to the survival of the fittest; the best and the brightest rise to the top while the rest go under, leaving the whole stronger. Charity, then, is in fact contrary to our wider social interests as it helps the weak survive, thus working against the overall improvement of the human race.

The kind of thinking that places the philosophy of egoism and the survival of the fittest as basic tenets of economic science continues to dominate the thinking of our time, though for how much longer remains to be seen. The super rich are still seen as people who, in following their own paths to enrichment, are assumed to have justly earned their wealth through their superior genius. They are assumed to be people who, because they have been so successful in accumulating wealth, should be regarded with a reverence similar to that bestowed upon the leaders of society in much earlier times. Such a view of the very rich is not supported by even the most cursory glance at the functioning of society. As I have shown, a substantial proportion of those with great wealth have acquired their money without making any beneficial contribution to society, while those such as nurses, firefighters, teachers, train drivers, and many others, contribute to the well-being of society each day.

What we think of as a civilization founded on Christianity has, to a large degree, descended to become one that worships money, that sees money as something that has value in itself, and sees human community as founded on the survival of the most successful in accumulating money for themselves. What has happened to compassion, and to the greater human aspirations?

*

Whatever importance we place on our physical body, it is in our soul that we are conscious and in which we have feelings, beliefs, and impulses, and where we can know happiness or suffering, courage, or fear. It is in our soul that we experience the need for life itself and thus place importance on our bodily health. And it is through our soul that we enjoy or suffer all the sensations made possible by the body.

The moral quality of a society, all that comes to expression as compassion, truthfulness, integrity, humility, sense of justice, and concern for other people, is born out of the cultural life of that community. The social and environmental quality of people's lives, the nature and tone of the laws and regulations that the community creates for itself are also, ultimately, an outcome of the quality, vitality and dynamism of the cultural life of the community. And again, the creativity, ingenuity, and imagination that go into economic life by way of invention and discovery, and the quality, design, and ultimate purpose of the products, all have their foundation in the cultural life of that community.

The poverty of soul that is apparent in so many people today is a consequence of the meager soul nourishment to be found in most of our cultural life, in just those activities which should nourish the soul. This is particularly evident in much of our education, religion, and art. This poverty of soul is also to be seen in the media, in television, on the internet, and in an extreme way in computer games, all of which have enormous influence, most particularly on the young and impressionable. Instead of a cultural sphere of activity that nourishes the human soul, that reflects back to us something of our own true nature, and which calls forth from the depths of our souls an inner moral discipline and impulses of creative will, we have one that seems incapable of rising above mere entertainment, one that is too often no more than a stimulation, or even a titillating, of the emotions and senses.

It is increasingly recognized that "junk food" is unhealthy for the body and is a cause of much of the ill health and obesity of our time. There is a growing concern that children should be given healthy, nutritious food, that is, the food that the body needs rather than just what tastes good. But the soul also needs nourishment, it also needs healthy nutritious soul food. Instead, it too is widely fed on "soul junk food." Too much of what is produced by cultural life, often at the instigation of business and financial interests, is nothing more than such soul junk food. Children or young people whose soul is nurtured on this soul junk food will not develop the moral qualities and strength to take control of their own behavior nor the resources to develop their own innate potential qualities and capacities. They will be unable to contribute to the building of a strong, healthy, and peaceful society.

The cultural sphere of society is now the weakest and least effective of the three. Where it most matters, it is largely controlled or influenced by political or economic interests. Education, an essential foundation of cultural life, is lamed by government control and the kind of thinking that comes with it, and by pressures from business and financial organizations. Nearly all popular entertainment, sports, music, computer games, fashion, and much of the sources of information in the media are controlled or influenced by businesses and the desire to make money. Until the importance and essential role of cultural life is recognized and it is freed from these controls and influences and allowed, out of its own deeper insights, to develop its work and its contribution to each and every individual soul within the community, there can be no healing of our social malaise.

It is the economic sphere of activity that makes life itself possible, and the rights life that can ensure security and human dignity within the community, but it is only through a healthy and vibrant cultural life that each person will find and live out his or her essential inner being, and so discover purpose, meaning, and fulfillment in life.

 **Michael Spence** was born in 1931 in Kenya. When he was 15, his family returned to England where he attended the Michael Hall School. After graduation and service in the army, he worked variously in a London shipping office, for the Kenya Police, as an encyclopaedia salesman (briefly), and in finance. At the age of 36 he was invited by Francis Edmunds to help develop Emerson College in Sussex, England. Mr. Spence was closely involved with Emerson College for the next twenty-seven years, carrying responsibility for its finances, administration, and campus. He is the author of *Freeing the Human Spirit* (1999) and *The Story of Emerson College* (2013).